D0866997

Cambridge Studies in Chinese History, Literature, and Institutions
General Editor, Denis Twitchett

THE SHANGHAI BADLANDS

Other books in the series

THE SHANGHAI BADLANDS

Wartime terrorism and urban crime,
1937–1941

FREDERIC WAKEMAN, JR.
University of California, Berkeley

CAMBRIDGE
UNIVERSITY PRESS

Published by the Press Syndicate of the University of Cambridge
The Pitt Building, Trumpington Street, Cambridge, CB2 1RP
40 West 20th Street, New York, NY 10011-4211, USA
10 Stamford Road, Oakleigh, Melbourne 3166, Australia

© Cambridge University Press 1996

First published 1996

Printed in the United States of America

Library of Congress Cataloging-in-Publication Data
Wakeman, Frederic E.
The Shanghai Badlands : wartime terrorism and urban crime,
1937–1941 / Frederic Wakeman, Jr.
p.   cm.
Includes bibliographical references and index.
ISBN 0-521-49744-2 (hc)
1. Crime—China—Shanghai. 2. Secret societies—China—Shanghai.
3. Sino-Japanese Conflict, 1937—1945—China—Shanghai. I. Title.
HV7120.S57W36   1996
364.951′13—dc20   95-44122
                                                      CIP

A catalog record for this book is available from the British Library.

ISBN 0-521-49744-2 hardback

Contents

TO M.

Acknowledgments

Support for the research that resulted in this book was provided by the Henry Luce Foundation in New York, the Chiang Ching-kuo Foundation in Washington, D.C., the National Humanities Center in Research, Triangle Park, North Carolina; and the Center for Chinese Studies, the Committee on Research, the Institute of East Asian Studies, and the Walter and Elise Haas Chair endowment at Berkeley.

I would like to express my gratitude to the archivists and librarians who helped me gain access to materials at the Bancroft Library (Berkeley), the Bureau of Investigation Archives (Taiwan), the Center for Chinese Studies Library (Berkeley), the East Asian Library (Columbia), the East Asiatic Library (Berkeley), the Government Documents Library (Berkeley), the Hoover Institution and Archives, the Library of Congress, the Military Reference Division of the U.S. National Archives, the Modern History Research Institute Library of the Chinese Academy of Social Sciences, the Public Record Office (London), the Second National Archives (Nanjing), the Shanghai Academy of Social Sciences, the Shanghai Municipal Archives, and the Washington Naval Yard.

Especially helpful in this regard were Cai Shaoqing, Annie K. Chang, C. P. Chen, Ch'iu Jung-hua, Suzanne Gold, Han Weizhi, Bih-jaw Lin, Shi Meiding, Wang Dehua, Wang Qingcheng, Xu Youfang, and Zhang Zhongli.

Research assistance was provided by a number of current and former Chinese history graduate students at Berkeley. These include David Fraser, Guo Qitao, Jen-ling Liu, Douglas Stiffler, Jeffrey Wasserstrom, Timothy Weston, and Yu Maochun; I owe a great debt to my professional research assistant, Elinor Levine, who literally put the book together.

Scholarly suggestions were proffered by Marie-Claire Bergère, Chang Yü-fa, Ch'en San-ching, Sherman Cochran, Thomas Gold, William Kirby, and Zhang Jishun. Members of the Berkeley Shanghai Seminar also contributed to the revision of the book, as did commentators at the Berkeley Graduate Student Conference on Chinese History. I especially appreciate the careful readings done by Timothy Brook, Elizabeth Perry, Keith Schoppa, Frederic Wakeman, Sr., and Wen-hsin Yeh.

Glossary

A

<u>Anguo qingmin</u>　安國清民
Anqing Tongmenhui　安清同盟會

B

Bao Ziying　鮑子英
baoan zuzhi　保安組織

C

Cai Xiangsheng　蔡祥生
Chang Yuqing　常玉清
Changkang　長康
Chen Deming　陳德銘
Chen Gongshu　陳恭澍
Chen Jintao　陳錦濤
Chen Junhe　陳均鶴
Chen Kaiguang　陳開光
Chen Kaiyuan　陳開元
Chen Lu　陳籙
Chen Mingchu　陳明楚
Chen Qun　陳群
Chen Yuanliang　陳元良
Cheng Zhenzhang　程振章
<u>chengli difang zhixu</u>　成立地方秩序
<u>chihua</u>　赤化
Chizhi daxue　持志大學

D

<u>Da wan bao</u>　大晚報
Dadong xin lüguan　大東新旅館
Daguang she　大光社
Dai Binyuan　戴斌元
Dai Zhiyue　戴志月
Dalu　大陸
<u>Damei wanbao</u>　大美晚報
Deng Zuyu　鄧祖禹
Ding Jiankun　丁健坤

Dong Youxian　董友賢
Dongchang　東昌
Dongjie lu　東街路
Du Zhimei　杜志梅
Duban gongshu　督辦公署

F

Feng Zongzhang　馮宗長
Fu Shaotang　傅少棠
Fu Xiao'an　傅筱庵
Fu Yewen　傅也文
Fu Zongyao　傅宗耀

G

Ganhui　甘慧
Gao Hongzao　高鴻藻
Gao Xinbao　高鑫寶
Geng Jiaji　耿嘉基
Geng Shoubao　耿壽寶
Gong Wenfang　龔文舫
gongwen　公文
Gu Qingyi　顧馨一
Gu Zhenbang　顧振邦
Gu Zhuhua　顧祝華
Guo Shaoyi　郭紹儀
Guotai　國泰

H

Han Jun　韓鈞
Hao Peng　郝鵬
Hu Anbang　胡安幫
Hu Zhenggu　胡正古
Huacaozhen　華漕鎮
Huang Yonggui　黃永貴
Huang Ziqiang　黃自強
Huangjiahua yuan　黃家花園
Huaxing　華興

Hujiang daxue 滬江大學
Huo Liangchen 霍良臣

J

Jiang Guisheng 江桂生
Jiang Haisheng 江海生
Jiang Tongyi 姜同義
Jieyan ke 戒煙科
Jin Dianyang 金殿揚
Jin Huating 金華亭
Jin Jihuan 金寄寰
Jin Yingsheng 金瑩生
Jinrong manji 金融漫記
jingcha shu 警察署
Jingchaju cunren 警察局存人
Jingchaju weiren ji renmian
    警察局委任既任免
"Jingchaju xiang zhangze" 警察局項章則
Juyili 居易里

L

Li Chunhui 李春輝
Li Guojie 李國杰
Li Jie 李傑
Li Jinbiao 李金標
Li Qiwei 李奇衛
Li Xinghe 李杏和
Liang Hongzhi 梁鴻志
Liang Tongfang 梁桐芳
Lin Zhijiang 林之江
Lin Ziren 林子仁
Liyang 栗陽
Liu Haishan 劉海山
Liu Wanqing 劉萬慶
Liu Zhan'en 劉湛恩
Liu Zhe 劉哲
Lizhishe Shanghai fenshe 勵志社上海分社
Lu Ying 盧英
Lou Bingzhang 樓秉章
Lu Bohong 陸伯鴻
Lu Jie 盧杰
Luo Zhibin 羅志斌

M

Ma Yuhang 馬育航
Ma Xiaotian 馬嘯天
Mao Liying 茅麗英
Mao Wanli 毛萬里
Mao Yiwen 毛伊文
Mao Youwen 毛有文
Mu Shiying 穆時英

N

Nakanishi (Ja.) 中西
Nanhuai 南淮

P

Pan Da 潘達
Pan Gongzhan 潘公展
Pan Hannian 潘漢年
Pan Zhijie 潘志傑
Peng Fulin 彭福林
Peng Jinyi 彭金義
Ping Fuchang 平福昌
Pu Fengming 蒲鳳鳴

Q

Qian Hua 錢華
qianfu gongzuo 潛伏工作
qingxiang 清鄉
Qinyuancun 沁園村
Quantaotuan 拳討團
Qunyi 群益

R

Ren Bao'an 任保安
Ren Yuandao 任援道

S

Satomi (Ja.) 西里見
Shao Fusheng 邵富生
Shao Xubai 邵虛白
Shen Wenyuan 沈文元
Shi Zheng 施政
Shimuzu (Ja.) 清水
Song Hailin 宋海林
Song Jianrong 宋江蓉
Su Chengde 蘇成德
Su Jinquan 蘇金全
Su min yinhang 蘇民銀行
Su Xiwen 蘇錫文
Sun Yaxing 孫亞星

T

Tan Baocheng 譚保成
Tan Baoyi 譚寶義 (山 譚寶毅)
Tanaka (Ja.) 田中
Tang Shaoyi 唐紹一
Tianxia yijia, wanfa gui yi 天下一家,
    萬法歸一
Tong Keming 佟克明
Tongshui chu 統稅處
Tu Zhengu 屠鎮鵠

W

Wang Aju 王阿菊
Wang Binnan 王彬南
Wang Delin 王德林
Wang Fangnan 王方南
Wang Guangcai 王光才
Wang Kemin 王克敏
Wang Kequan 王克全
Wang Luzhao 王魯趙
Wang Manyun 汪曼雲
Wang Qiming 王奇明
Wang Ruilian 王瑞連
Wang Tianmu 王天木
Wang Wenkui 王文奎
Wang Xianming 王憲明
Wang Yanbin 王延彬
Wang Zhigu 王志固
Wang Zihui 王子惠
Wang Zilin 王子林
Wang Ziying 王子英
Wannan shibian 皖南事變
Weng Dehui 翁德慧
Wenxian li 文賢里
Wu Naixian 吳乃憲
Wu Shibao 吳世寶
Wu Sibao 吳四寶

X

Xi Shitai 席時泰
Xi Xingshi 席行志
Xiafei 霞飛
Xiang Qiangwei 相強偉
Xie Baosheng 謝葆生
Xie Zhipan 謝志磐
Xin shenbao 新申報
Xingxiang 興祥
Xinxin Hotel 新新旅館
Xu Chuqing 許楚卿
Xu Guoqi 徐國琦
Xu Wenbin 許文彬
Xu Zhihao 徐志浩

Y

Yang Jie 楊傑
Yang Jinhai 楊進海
Yang Qiguan 楊其觀
Yao Asheng 姚阿生
Yao Zhiduan 姚志端
Yao Zidu 姚子都
Yin Zhongli 殷仲禮
Yin Zhongyu 殷仲裕
Yixin 一心

You He (Liu Geqing) 游河
You Heqing 尤何清(尤河清)
You Pinshan 尤品山
youbang 友邦
Yu Daxiong 余達雄
Yu Junqing 余均青
Yu Yaozhang 俞耀章
Yuan Dechang 袁德昌(袁得昌)
Yuguangcun 漁光村
Yun Huifang 惲惠芳
Yuqing 育青

Z

Zeng Zhongming 曾仲鳴
Zhang Fangren 張方仁
Zhang Jisheng 張繼生
Zhang Miaogen 張妙根
Zhang Shuwen 張樹穩
Zhang Songlin 張松林
Zhang Xiaoyi 張肖義
Zhang Xiaolin 張嘯林
Zhang Zhizhong 張治中
Zhao Gangyi 趙剛義
Zhao Liang 趙良
Zhao Lijun 趙理君
Zhao Songcha 趙松超
Zhao Wanyi 趙万義
Zhao Yuding 趙玉定
Zheng Yuebo 鄭月波
Zhao Zhixiang 趙志祥(Zhao Bosheng 趙伯生)
Zhongguo funü zhiye lianyihui 中國婦女職業聯誼會
Zhongmei ribao 中美日報
Zhou Fengqi 周鳳岐
Zhou Jitang 周紀棠
Zhou Shougang 周守剛
Zhou Songming 周松明
Zhou Weiying 周濰瑩
Zhou Wenshan 周文山
Zhoupu 周蒲
Zhu Ding 朱鼎
Zhu Jintao 朱錦濤
Zhu Shengyuan 朱升源
Zhu Xiaogu 朱嘯谷
Zhu Xinggong 朱惺公
Zhu Xuefan 朱學範
Zhu Yuzhen 朱玉陣
Zhu Zhonghu 朱仲虎
Zhuang Han 壯漢
zianhui 自安會

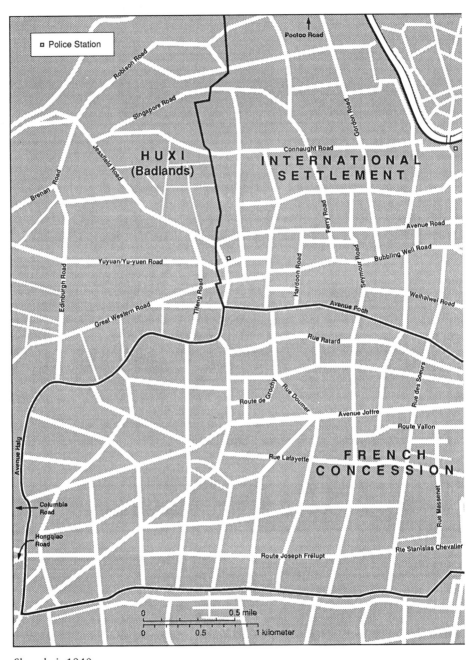

Shanghai, 1940

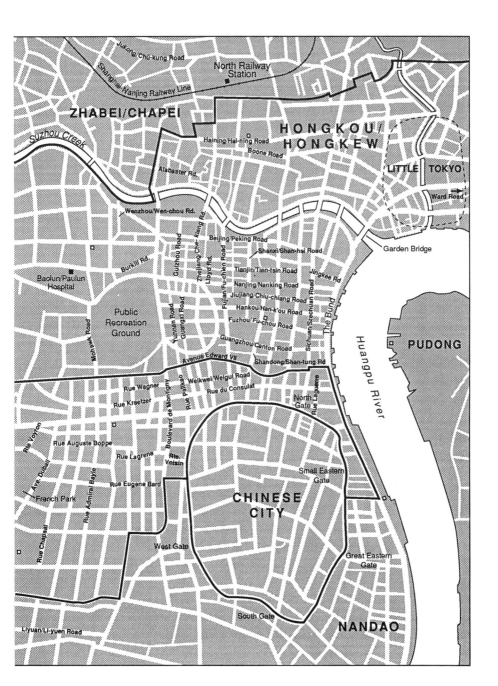

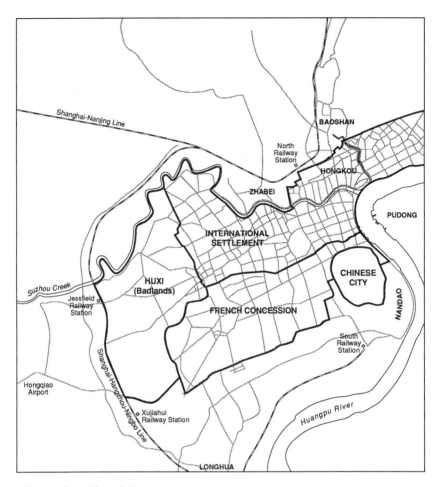

Metropolitan Shanghai

The badlands

A new institution sprang up in that extra-Settlement area which had come under semi-Japanese control, an area known as the "Badlands" where activities were mainly gambling, opium, and kindred things, with almost nightly shootings thrown in for good measure. Wang Jingwei's Shanghai residence was located about in the center of this area, an enormous grim house which had been converted into a virtual fortress with machine guns mounted on either side of the entrance and relays of Chinese and Japanese guards inside.

Vanya Oakes, *White Man's Folly,* 361

In these terrible years hundreds of people were killed and wounded. Death pounced on them in hotels, outside theaters, in crowded cafes, in the streets, in their offices, and at home as they lay peacefully in bed. This was a period of armed bodyguards, armor-plated cars, bullet-proof vests and street pillboxes. Thousands of Chinese, White Russians, and turbaned Sikhs were employed in these private armies. They were of vital importance because the situation was beyond police control. Even if no political risks were involved, the underworld was to be feared for its members protected their rackets from the invasion of Japanese thugs and hired Chinese gunmen with a brand new line of rackets spawned by the war, and blazed fresh and terrifying trails in crime under cover of the general disorder.

Percy Finch, *Shanghai and Beyond,* 310

Prologue: Consequences

It has been fifty years since the United States and the Republic of China defeated Imperial Japan in World War II. As decisive as the experience of the four-year Pacific War was for three generations of Americans, the eight-year War of Resistance from the Marco Polo Bridge incident in 1937 to VJ Day in 1945 was for the Chinese a major turning point in their history. No other event in the twentieth century has had such a profound impact on their country's subsequent course through civil war, socialist revolution, and capitalist renovation, down through the present.

Like wartime France under German domination, China experienced both resistance and collaboration—and the gray, equivocal zone many people inhabited in between—under the Japanese. Until recently, most Chinese have turned away from the troubling ambiguities of the Occupation period when individual and family survival frequently left no choice but to cooperate with the Japanese and their puppet allies. In this way, few survivors of the Occupation in China's major cities doubted that Japanese rule over China, especially in urban areas, was somewhat eased by the compliance of the civil population. At least one contemporary scholar has suggested that the Japanese were able to rule occupied Shanghai effectively because they could skillfully utilize their familiarity with "indirect structures of government" to weaken Chinese resistance and secure international cooperation.[1]

This book argues instead that Chinese resistance to collaborationist rule was savagely though ambiguously sustained; that political terrorism and violent crime became intertwined; that the triangular relationship between the foreign settlement, the Japanese military, and the puppet régime was strained and restive; and that the illicit pleasures flourishing in the no-man's-land of Western Shanghai (Huxi)—the badlands—were both a momentary escape from unbearable social tensions and a constant reminder of a cleaved city festering under foreign domination.[2] By focusing attention on Shanghai between the outbreak of the War of Resistance and the

Japanese attack on Pearl Harbor—the period when Shanghai was an "isolated island" (*gudao*)—I hope to demonstrate that resistants and collaborators fought fiercely among themselves, that choices were never easy and actions may have been uncertain, but that eventual compliance with the Occupation was the result of terrible social strains and political ruptures during unending terrorist wars across the internal boundaries of a deeply divided city supposedly "at peace" with its Japanese overlords.

In 1937 Shanghai was second in population only to Berlin, London, Moscow, New York, Paris, and Tokyo. Because of the unequal treaty system imposed upon the Qing dynasty by England, the United States, and France after the Opium War, Shanghai was three cities at once. There was, first of all, the International Settlement running along the Huangpu River front. The Settlement was a creation of Article II of the Treaty of Nanjing in 1842, sanctioned by the Land Regulations first drawn up in 1845 and endorsed by the ambassadors of the Western powers in 1869. Southwest of the Settlement, farther up the river, was the second city in the form of a special Concession assigned to French residents by the Qing authorities in 1844. The French Concession drew up its own Land Regulations (Règlement) in 1868. The third city was the Chinese Municipal Administration, which lay on both sides of the Huangpu River embracing 320 square miles of urban and suburban land surrounding the first two cities and divided into the districts of Nandao (South Market, or South City), Jiangwan, Zhabei, Pudong, and Wusong.

As we shall see, when the Japanese drove Chiang Kai-shek's armies out of Shanghai in November 1937, their portion of the International Settlement ("Little Tokyo" in Hongkou) and the occupied third Chinese city constituted a cordon around the other two: the Settlement and the French Concession, which together formed an "isolated island" offering refuge to Chinese fleeing Japanese rule, and seeking to maintain its own extraterritoriality and avoid being drawn into the Sino-Japanese conflict as Europe slipped toward war. The larger city of Shanghai thus became a contested battleground in and of itself, if only because Japan could not take the international sections over forcibly without risking war with England and the United States, not to speak of France.

The contests were six-fold: first, between the Western powers and Japan over their future claims in China, with Great Britain and the United States struggling to avoid giving the Japanese a pretext to invade the concessions as they did in Tianjin; second, between the powers and China (originally the Nationalist régime, then the puppet régime) over the extraterritoriality of the imperialists; third, between Japanese and Anglo-American residents of the International Settlement over rule of the Shanghai Municipal Council; fourth, between the Japanese army and Nationalist guerrilla units over the occupation of Shanghai's suburbs; fifth, between Shanghai's underworld and newly arrived Taiwanese and Korean gangsters over control of the city's rackets; and sixth, between Nationalist secret agents and puppet secret servicemen over the domination of banks, newspapers, and law courts.

The last of these was the most disrupting struggle because it was the most fundamental. On the one side stood supporters of Chiang Kai-shek's "Free China": the Nationalists who retreated from Nanjing to Wuhan in 1937, and then up the Yangzi River to Sichuan, which remained their bastion until the end of the war. On the opposite side were those who wanted to cooperate with the Japanese to bring the war to an end and destroy the United Front between Chiang Kai-shek's Nationalists and Mao Zedong's Communists.

On their part, the Japanese—and especially those who favored extrication from the China quagmire—needed to find a national political figure, first, with whom they could negotiate; second, who could form a reasonably legitimate Chinese government in Nanjing; and third, who could help them make the best of the economic resources Shanghai proffered to offset the cost of the expanding war in Southeast Asia. When one of China's leading Nationalist revolutionaries, Wang Jingwei, left Chiang Kai-shek's entourage in Chongqing to flee to Hanoi, and thence to Hong Kong and Shanghai, he seemed the perfect candidate. On his part, Wang Jingwei believed that he could spare his countrymen further grief by terminating the war in the occupied zones, that he could with Japanese help recover national sovereignty over Shanghai from the Western imperialists, and that he could successfully oppose and destroy the Communist movement in China's rural areas.

Although Wang Jingwei succeeded in accomplishing the first two goals, that very process paradoxically lacerated his régime—precisely because so much of the procedure centered on Shanghai. In accepting his political role as a Japanese collaborator, for example, Wang also had to countenance the existence of a puppet security service in Shanghai run by an ex-Communist turncoat who brought opprobrium and dishonor to his government from the very start. And though he eventually did get the Japanese authorities to hand over sovereign control of Shanghai to him, the transfer was both ignominious and costly because it represented a Japanese tender of legitimacy that seemingly compensated for their lack of financial support of Wang's régime. Fiscal necessity consequently forced him and his lieutenants to depend upon Shanghai's gambling, narcotics, and prostitution rackets for the income needed to fund the entire Nanjing government. This ended by utterly undermining Wang Jingwei's credibility as a national leader—a credibility already deeply compromised by his status as a *hanjian,* or traitor, who had to collaborate with the Japanese just to acquire the cloak of nationalism (recovery of Chinese sovereignty over Shanghai) in which to wrap himself.

As Wang's régime wavered, so did political loyalties vacillate. One of this book's major themes, then, is the sheer ambiguity of either resistance or collaboration. The ultimate purpose of heroic Nationalist terrorism was dubious, especially when Nationalist secret agents betrayed other patriots to the collaborationist security services in the name of political expediency. And the fact that collaborators made deals of their own with the Nationalists, promising to rise against the Japanese whenever the Americans decided to use mainland China as a staging area for a seaborne conquest of Japan, further clouded these choices. The collaborationist trials after the Japanese defeat, and the Communist purges in the early 1950s of former Shanghai Chinese Communist Party underground workers suspected of being double agents, showed how amorphous wartime allegiances sometimes were.

Of course, this reflected the social composition of the terrorist cells: petty urbanites (students, printers, shop apprentices, lens makers, jewelers, teahouse waiters, store clerks, chandlers) whose own social identities were not firmly fixed as they moved from one cheap boarding house to another, killing time, waiting for the next terrorist assignment. They drifted through a city that was deeply divided between rich and poor. Even before the War of Resistance began Shanghai was thought of as—to use Xia Yan's often quoted metaphor—"a city of forty-eight-story skyscrapers built upon twenty-four layers of hell."[3] Now, the contrast between wealthy war profiteers and homeless refugees was even more glaring.[4] The satirical novelist Qian Zhongshu captured this contradiction most aptly in *Fortress Besieged* (*Wei cheng*):

> The number of people profiting and the number going bankrupt from the national crisis increased simultaneously. Neither interfered with the other, since the poor begged only in the major thoroughfares and bustling marketplaces and stayed away from the quiet residential areas of the rich. They asked for money only from those on foot, unable to catch up with the rich in their sleek cars. Slums gradually spread like ring worm over the face of the city. Political terrorist incidents occurred nearly every day. Men of good will were so depressed that, like the transportation lines in major Western cities, they slowly began to go underground while the dark, insidious reptiles in human form which had been underground all along boosted their prestige by latching onto them. Newspapers promoting "Sino-Japanese Peace" every day published lists of new comrades who had joined their ranks, while at the same time in another newspaper these "Japanese collaborators" were often declaring themselves "apolitical."[5]

But even though the city's elites were separated in so many ways from the hoi polloi, the social impact of the terrorist wars was dispersed among them like a scattergun blast. They were doubly victims, in fact, because they were so often the targets of kidnappings and killings precisely because of who they were, and they were also unwitting witnesses to the seesaw struggle between Chongqing and the Japanese/puppet terrorist forces that culminated in the lethal crescendo of August 1941 when the sheer quantity of people shot or bombed to death numbed the population to the Occupation and shredded the fabric of a civic society only fragilely woven under recent Guomindang rule. These fierce and savage conflicts thus exhausted the populace to a point of acquiescence when the Japanese moved into the first and second cities of Shanghai on December 8, 1941, finally taking over the international zones.[6]

A final question remains: were the Nationalist assassins of puppet Foreign Minister Chen Lu or of Police Chief Secretary Xi Shitai aware of the ultimate consequences of the acts I will shortly describe? In the short run, their activities forced the civic leaders of foreign settlements to cooperate with the Japanese authorities, who were using terrorist activity in Tianjin to take over that concession and threatening to do the same in Shanghai. In the face of such a threat the British were more resistant than the Americans, being willing to conduct an embargo if the Japanese Imperial Army and Navy continued to use terrorist incidents to justify occupation of the settlements. Yet while the Americans were unwilling to back up the British, heavy-handed Japanese responses to subsequent Chinese patriotic terrorist acts led the Americans to stiffen in the direction of abrogating commercial relations. This decision by the U.S. president in turn helped lead Japan toward Pearl Harbor. Could the terrorists possibly have anticipated this dimly connected outcome, which would throw the United States into war with Japan and help ensure China's eventual victory over its conquerors?

Probably not, though Nationalist security chief General Dai Li himself certainly entertained the possibility. Inadvertently, then, the young patriots who left their mahjong games in Shanghai's downtown hotel rooms to mount a sidewalk attack on one or another high-ranking collaborator helped precipitate a war that ended with the United States deeply engaged in China's civil war, though far from sure which side—Communist or Nationalist—would emerge the ruler of the land. In that contest, Shanghai's wartime terrorists were the first to cast the die.

1

Island Shanghai

The battle for Shanghai lasted three months.[1] It was the largest and longest battle of the entire eight-year War of Resistance against Japan (1937–1945).[2] During the first few days after hostilities broke out in Shanghai on August 13, 1937, the Chinese, with extraordinary martial ardor in the face of withering artillery fire from the naval vessels anchored in the river, drove the Japanese back to the shore of the Huangpu.[3] Because of the neutrality of the International Settlement it was impossible for the Japanese to outflank the Nationalist troops until their expeditionary force opened a second front to the north between Wusong and Liuhe on September 1.[4] Even then, Chiang Kai-shek continued to pour his best troops into the duel.[5] By October the Chinese had deployed seventy-one divisions and nearly all of the Central Army's artillery units, totaling half-a-million men.[6] The Japanese forces, with six divisions and six independent brigades, only totaled 200,000 men, but their planes controlled the skies and their artillery was preponderant.[7] Zhabei received the heaviest concentration of fire ever laid on one piece of earth until then in history.[8] Yet the Chinese continued to hold their lines with a calm and incredible heroism remarked upon by all who witnessed their sacrifice.[9] On November 5, a third front was opened when General Yanagawa Heisuke landed his Tenth Army (three divisions of 30,000 men) at Hangzhou Bay and drove inland to Songjiang behind the Chinese right flank, routing the Nationalists on November 9 along the Nanjing–Shanghai Railway where the Japanese air force had already destroyed most of the bridges.[10] General Matsui Iwane's armored columns, no longer impeded by the rubble of Zhabei, turned retreat into slaughter.[11] Some 300,000 Chinese troops died in the battle for Shanghai; another 170,000 perished by the time Nanjing fell on December 12.[12]

Shanghai was the first of the world's metropolises to suffer the destruction of World War II: its industries sustained damages of over 560 million yuan.[13] Large residential areas were destroyed and hundreds of thousands made homeless.[14] Nine hundred mills, factories, and workshops had been gutted.[15] Another thousand establishments had been wrecked or seized by the Japanese. Together with the losses in the Chinese areas, 70 percent of the city's industrial potential was gone, 600,000 people in Shanghai and the adjacent industrial zone were out of work.[16] War damage was set at one billion, two billion, more than three billion Chinese dollars.[17] Nobody knew exactly how much.[18] More than U.S.$800 million in foreign investments were lost in the country. China's economic revival, which had centered in Shanghai and had appeared so promising at the beginning of 1937, was killed by the war, which set the country back decades.[19]

Refugees poured into the ten square miles of the French Concession and International Settlement, swelling the population from 1.5 to 4 million within a few weeks and increasing the size of the average household to 31 people.[20] Many left the 175 refugee camps to return to their native villages, but tens of thousands of homeless clogged the streets and hundreds of thousands more slept in office corridors, stockrooms, temples, guildhalls, amusement parks, and warehouses.[21] With winter came disease, starvation, and exposure; and by the end of the year 101,000 corpses had been picked up in the streets or ruins.[22]

Yet, incredibly enough, the "isolated island" (*gudao*) of Shanghai, surrounded by Japanese Occupation forces until the attack on Pearl Harbor four years later, began to enjoy a seemingly anomalous economic boom.[23] Cotton mills inside the International Settlement resumed operation under British and U.S. company names.[24] Profits doubled and trebled, and seven new mills were constructed.[25] Flour mills increased annual production by 10 percent. The U.S.-controlled Shanghai Power Company expanded its distribution by 10 percent and spent U.S.$2 million dollars on new equipment. Four hundred small enterprises—most of them companies moving in from Japanese-occupied territory—sprang up in the International Settlement, manufacturing industrial chemicals, medicinal oils, glassware, lamp bulbs, thermos bottles, flashlights, electric fans, candies, and cigarettes.[26] Since the raw material for these products had to be imported, shipping and insurance business enlarged as well.[27]

Part of this boom was stimulated by the increased demands of the immigrant population, including Jewish refugees fleeing European fascism.[28] Another source of growing demand was trade through Japanese lines with "Free China" in the hinterland. In 1940 that annual trade alone was estimated to be as high as U.S.$120 million, battening on the venality of Japanese military officers who were extremely susceptible to bribery by Chinese merchants.[29] The export trade also improved, primarily owing to the fifty German firms in Shanghai that shipped 60 percent of the tea, 70 percent of the sesame seeds, 75 percent of the vegetable oils, 40 percent of pig intestines, 25 percent of egg production, and all the available leather on the Shanghai market to feed, clothe, and shoe the wartime economy of the Third Reich.[30]

Puppet government

During the entire War of Resistance the Nationalists maintained a municipal government of Shanghai in exile.[31] Nonetheless, just as soon as the Nationalist Army retreated from Shanghai on November 11, the Japanese authorities approached a number of well-known figures—Du Yuesheng, Yu Xiaqing, and so forth—to take over the city administration, but their targets either left for Hong Kong or demurred, fearing attacks by Chinese loyalists.[32] Lu Bohong, the Catholic priest with huge investments in the Nandao tramway and electricity companies, as well as in the Zhabei waterworks, did agree to organize a South Market Local Self-Government Committee (Nanshi difang zizhi weiyuanhui), but he refused to become mayor.[33]

Eventually, the Japanese managed to persuade Fu Xiaoan, director of the Chinese Bank of Commerce (Shangtong yinhang) and head of the General Chamber of Commerce, to serve.[34] Fu had been one of the few to oppose lending money to Chiang Kai-shek in April 1927, and as a result was imprisoned. When he was released from jail he took refuge in Japanese-controlled Manchuria, so that it was both his closeness to the Japanese (his steel-gated residential compound was actually in "Little Tokyo") and his hatred of the Generalissimo ("I am worth fifty million dollars," he once said, "but I will spend every dollar I have to get even with Chiang") that led him to form a Shanghai municipal government of "The Great Way" (Dadao) in Pudong on December 5, 1937.[35]

Fu Xiaoan was not at first willing to accept the title of mayor. The nominal head of "The Great Way" government was Su Xiwen, a Waseda-educated collaborator who had once worked closely with Hu Hanmin and who taught Daoist–Buddhist philosophy and political thought at the private Chizhi University in Jiangwan.[36] His traditionalistic philosophy ("All under heaven one family / Myriad laws revert to one" [*Tianxia yi jia, Wanfa gui yi*]) influenced the Dadao puppet government's choice of flag, which was a *taiji* symbol on a yellow background. Su's collaborationist conservatism was reflected in the choice of a particularly stilted form of documentary Chinese for its *gongwen* (official papers), which were dated according both to the old lunar calendar and to the Showa reign, as the new administration went about the business of cleaning up South Market's streets and removing corpses from Zhabei after the Battle of Shanghai was over.[37] Along with public health work to prevent epidemics, the

Dadao régime ordered its police bureau, under Chief Zhu Yuzhen, "to establish local order" (*chengli difang zhixu*).[38] In ideological diction, this meant stressing that "All under heaven is one family, within the four seas we are all brothers: the Way of the sun and moon, myriad laws reverting to one, great harmony (*datong*) throughout the world, and using the Way to establish a state."[39] In political terms, the Dadao government promised to extirpate both the Nationalists and the Communists, eliminate the warlord scourge, and establish peace in East Asia.[40]

Although the Dadao puppet government made a number of appointments to its new police bureau—including Zhang Songlin, former chief inspector of the Jiangsu provincial police, as deputy director of general affairs—the régime was short-lived, at least in nomenclature.[41] Su Xiwen himself was not taken very seriously by the Japanese Special Services agents occupying Shanghai during and after December 1937, and they momentarily imported their own collaborator, a tough named Wang Zihui from North China, to run their local operations.[42] Meanwhile, the poet Liang Hongzhi, a former Beiyang bureaucrat with excellent connections to the Anfu clique, had been "casting romantic glances" (*song qiubo*) at the Japanese and making known his availability as a collaborator.[43] Consequently, after the puppet administrations in North China were incorporated in January 1938 into the Provisional Government (Linshi zhengfu, Rinji seifu) under Wang Kemin in Beiping, in South China the Reform Government (Weixin zhengfu, Ishin seifu) was set up in March 1938 in Nanjing headed by Liang Hongzhi.[44] The puppet régime announced that it would wipe out single-party dictatorship and establish a constitutional government, extirpate the Communists and safeguard East Asia from "red-ification" (*chihua*), consolidate peaceful cooperation between China and Japan, return refugees to their homes and establish peace-preservation organizations (*baoan zuzhi*) to exterminate bandits and "cleanse the villages" (*qingxiang*), relieve unemployment and stimulate industrial and agricultural production with the help of foreign capital and "friendly countries" (*you bang*), assist existing industries and financial institutions to increase production and enrich the country, thoroughly reform education with a combination of China's traditional moral values and international scientific learning, abolish excessive taxes and levies that had been such a heavy burden on the people before, strongly support and encourage men of talent to come forward and freely criticize the government, and severely restrict the corrupt tyranny of petty officials and clerks.[45]

The establishment of the new Reform Government in Nanjing was tepidly celebrated in Shanghai on March 28 with processions bearing the old five-bar national flag of the Beiyang warlords.[46] Meetings were held in the Wenmiao by the Self-Government Committee to celebrate the new government and to bow to the image of Confucius, and in the auditorium of Great China University to hear a speech by the editor of *Xin shenbao* (the Chinese edition of the Japanese daily *Shanghai godo*) and to shout, "Long live the new government" several times in unison to the popping of firecrackers and the music of a brass band. Members of the Special Services Department of the Japanese Central China Area Army Garrison in Nandao joined the first gathering, while a group of several hundred "loafers" (*liumang*) and coolies trucked in from Hongkou attended the second, where at meeting's end they were each given a loaf of bread, eighty cents, and a cloth badge inscribed "celebrating the inauguration of the new government of the Republic of China by the citizens of Shanghai."[47] In less than a month, on April 28, 1938, it was announced that a new Supervisory Yamen (Duban gongshu) had been commissioned by the Reform Government to take over the functions of the municipal administration formerly wielded by the Dadao puppet régime.[48] Su Xiwen—who formally recognized the superior legitimacy of the Reform Government by adopting its flag on May 3—continued as head of the Supervisory Yamen until October 16, 1938, when Fu Xiaoan finally assumed formal office as mayor (*shizhang*) of the Shanghai Special Municipality (Shanghai tebie shi).[49] Once ousted, Su was named puppet mayor of Hankou but actually repaired to Tokyo, whence he may have organized the aborted conspiracy by puppet Guard Corpsmen to assassinate Fu Xiaoan a little more than five weeks later at the civic center in Jiangwan.[50]

Japanese Special Organs

The presence of secret servicemen from the Nandao Garrison *tokumukikan* (special organ) at the inauguration ceremony fittingly exposed the close connection between various Japanese intelligence units and their Chinese collaborators.[51] During 1937–1941, "island Shanghai," momentarily neutral like wartime Casablanca or Lisbon, was a haven for spies, intelligence agents, and provocateurs. The Japanese espionage and counterintelligence apparatus was correspondingly complex.[52] By war's end, the Shanghai Tokumukikan had split into seven sections: economic, political, information, propaganda, finance, construction, and general affairs sections. Originally under the legation, this "special organ" (which included civilians attached to the army) was placed under the jurisdiction of the China Expeditionary Force (Shina haken gun) headquarters at the pentagon (*wujiao*) in Jiangwan.[53]

But it was only one of a number of Japanese intelligence units in the city. Whenever the various unit chiefs representing the consulate, the China

News Agency, the Japanese military, the Military Police (Gendarmerie), and so forth, met at the Japanese Club on Boone Road to coordinate their activities, more than twenty division heads typically showed up.[54] As far as higher-level political intelligence work went, the most vital of these secret service units was the famous Plum Organ (Ume kikan), the special services group for the Japanese army in East China.[55] As far as Shanghai counterintelligence and clandestine operations were concerned, the most important was the Special Services Corps of the Japanese Military Police, with its field operations headquartered at the New Asia Hotel on North Sichuan Road in Hongkou.[56] From there it exercised covert control over a wide network of agents, including gangsters (*yakuza*) in Hongkou who ran the protection rackets for cafés, beer halls, restaurants, and dance halls.[57]

The Western Shanghai Intelligence Section of the Military Police, for instance, was dominated by "a notorious loafer" and gambler named Ding Jiankun, who commanded a private corps of twenty gangsters armed by the Japanese.[58] Ding's headquarters at 25–27 Jessfield Road in turn spawned two other branches at 12 Jessfield Road and in an alley off of Edinburgh Road.[59] However, each of these sections, also operating under gangsters, engaged in so much private extortion and armed robbery with their Japanese-supplied Mausers that Ding himself was obliged to shut them down after shooting one of the section chiefs himself.[60] Eventually, Ding Jiankun's own office was closed, ostensibly because of inefficiency, and his men were paid off after returning their pistols to the Japanese Military Police.[61]

The Military Police's use of Ding Jiankun was a characteristic feature of the Japanese occupation of Shanghai. U.S. Treasury Agent M. R. Nicholson reported to the Narcotics Bureau on December 16, 1938:

> On the part of the Japanese, they have been wanting to secure the cooperation of the underworld influences for a long time. They believe this is the best way to secure control of the foreign areas [of Shanghai], for once they can secure these underworld forces, they will be able to create disturbances, to harass the police, to arrest anti-Japanese elements and Chinese government agents, attack Chinese government banks, law courts, and anti-Japanese newspapers, and damage the stability of the Chinese currency. This means they could control the foreign areas through these gangsters without resorting to occupying them by force. The only weapons left for the Japanese to secure the cooperation of these gangsters are opium and gambling business.[62]

The sale of drugs was also a characteristic feature of the Japanese Occupation of China at large.[63]

Although the Nationalist government reported to the League of Nations in 1939 that opium poppies were no longer grown anywhere in China, the extent of drug addiction was extraordinary.[64] In Suzhou, where opium was the main source of revenue, 500 dens were reported. Hangzhou was wide open. Beiping officially acknowledged 314 public opium establishments. Hankou had 32 wholesale stores, 340 dens, and 120 hotels that sold 4,000 ounces of opium daily to 55,000 smokers. And in some districts in Guangdong it was reported that the ratio of rice brokers to drug dealers was one to three or four.[65]

As Japanese troops took over each of these areas, the occupation authorities under the general direction of Tokyo's Asia Development Board sought to monopolize and expand the illicit traffic in narcotics.[66] Nanjing became the center of the opium trade along the lower reaches of the Yangzi River. By 1939, when pure heroin sold for about $300 per ounce, there were 2,400 dealers (many of them policemen) throughout the city, selling drugs to 60,000 adults and children alike—one-eighth of Nanjing's entire population. By 1941, poppy fields were being cultivated outside the puppet régime's capital, where an opium suppression bureau under Interior Minister Chen Qun collected about $3 million per month in taxes on opium sales in Anhui, Zhejiang, and Jiangsu.[67] Those taxes, which amounted to one-third of total revenue, were declared indispensable to the maintenance of the central government. Another $3 million of monthly profits was handed over to the Japanese Military Police and special services organs.[68]

Shanghai, with its huge refugee-swollen population, represented even greater potential gains, as well as a way of disposing of the glut of opium in Japanese hands now that their forces controlled the Turkish traffic through Suiyuan on top of the drug trade with Manchukuo.[69] There were two major aspects to the Shanghai drug trade at this time: a government or police function, assumed earlier by Chiang Kai-shek's Opium Suppression Bureau, which sold addicts licenses exempting them from arrest if they were found with drugs in their possession; and a commercial or gang function, maintained by cartels of drug producers supported by racketeers, who processed and supplied the drugs to retailers and street dealers. Both of these functions were linked in prewar Shanghai by the single person of Green Gang leader Du Yuesheng, who headed the Opium Suppression Bureau that issued the licenses as well as the drug syndicate that supplied the narcotics. After Shanghai fell to the Japanese, Du Yuesheng departed for Hong Kong, leaving behind several trusted lieutenants to try to hold the Green Gang together.[70]

Just as soon as the Japanese took over the Chinese municipality of Shanghai, one of General Doihara's Taiwanese agents was approached by

Gu Jiazhai (Ku Chia-chai), a former Green Gang subordinate who was acting on behalf of a newly formed syndicate, with a proposal to the Special Services Department for an opium monopoly license in exchange for $1 million down and $200,000 a month thereafter. The Japanese did not trust Gu and turned instead to Du Yuesheng, guaranteeing his personal safety if he would come back to Shanghai and mobilize the Green Gang on their behalf. Du somewhat ambiguously refused, preferring in the end to work out his own arrangements to smuggle Yunnan and Guizhou opium out of Hong Kong into Japanese-held territory.[71]

While these negotiations dragged on, the Chinese puppet government in Shanghai began licensing addicts.[72] Japanese military forces also shipped opium in from Dairen [Dalian] after making financial arrangements with local drug dealers to pay in advance through Japanese banks.[73] After Du Yuesheng turned the Japanese offer down, the Special Services Department separated the functions of supplying and of licensing.

On the one hand, with Minister Chen Qun's support, the Special Services Department sponsored a new coalition of Shanghai opium merchants headed by Sheng Youan, president of the People's Bank of Jiangsu (Su min yinhang) and a person quite independent of Du Yuesheng.[74] On the other hand, a conference was held in December 1938 between the Japanese military authorities and the Reform Government officials in Nanjing, which led to the opening of the Jiangsu–Zhejiang–Anhui Opium Suppression Bureau (Su Zhe Wan jinyanju) on the fifth floor of the Broadway Mansions. The new bureau's director, Yu Junqing, was "advised" by three agents of the Special Services Department: Officers Tanaka, Satomi, and Fuhama. They were empowered to control the import and distribution of opium, to enforce licensing conditions for opium hongs and smokers, and to collect revenues from opium sales. They also brought both supply and license functions back into a single organ. All fifty-eight licensed opium hongs in Shanghai and in the badlands (where there was a branch office at 94 Jessfield Road under the command of Captain Kitaoka), had to pick up their opium requisitions from the bureau on the fifth floor of the Broadway Mansions.[75]

The Opium Suppression Bureau was ostensibly an organ of the Chinese Reform Government, but the Japanese Special Services Department lurked in the wings. This quickly led to jurisdictional disputes that came to a head in June 1939 when the puppet government sequestered the licensing function for itself, forming a Shanghai District Opium Suppression Bureau (Shanghai difang jieyanju) to collect a stamp tax of $1.80 on every twelve ounces of opium sold by the city's hongs.[76] The Asia Development Board in Tokyo, meanwhile, authorized the Special Services

Department to convert the tri-provincial suppression bureau into an independent organ under the command of Officers Nakanishi and Satomi. The new opium monopoly office, which was located down the street from the Broadway Mansions at 912 North Sichuan Road, was called the Central China Hongji Benevolent Society (Huazhong hongji shantang). Its main task was daily to distribute chests of Iranian ("red") opium shipped in by the Mitsui Company on demand. The advantage of this system, according to the International Settlement police, was that "it obviate[d] the necessity of purchasing and keeping large stocks of opium" on hand, which in turn made it all the more difficult for the Shanghai Municipal Police to raid and seize. The enterprise was so successful that when the Hongji Benevolent Society held its second anniversary dance at the Lido Ballroom on June 2, 1941, more than a thousand guests came, and the affair was protectively policed by constables and detectives of the Shanghai Municipal Police in the International Settlement.[77]

Japanese pressures on the Shanghai Municipal Police

It should come as no surprise that twenty detectives and constables from the International Settlement police (Shanghai Municipal Police) protected the thousand or so Chinese drug dealers and Japanese Special Services Department officers celebrating their narcotics gains at the Lido Ballroom. By then, as we shall see, the still-British Shanghai Municipal Police and the Japanese Military Police were formally allied against Chinese terrorists, and the Shanghai Municipal Police itself was in the process of being penetrated and taken over by the Japanese.

Japanese pressure upon the Shanghai Municipal Police to act decisively against Chinese resistance fighters commenced less than a month after Nandao fell.[78] General Matsui insisted on staging a victory parade of 6,000 Japanese infantry, cavalry, artillery, and armored soldiers the length of Nanjing Road on December 3, 1937, French and British protests notwithstanding.[79] Halfway along the march, at the corner of Nanjing and Guangxi Roads, a man stepped out of the crowd and lobbed a bomb into the procession, wounding three Japanese soldiers and two native constables. The assailant, a twenty-three-year-old native of Shandong named Sun Jinghao, was shot dead by a policeman.[80]

The parade continued but the Japanese authorities were deeply perturbed, and they took the Shanghai Municipal Council to task for failing to adopt more vigorous measures against Chinese terrorists.[81] They also informed the Shanghai Municipal Council that they planned to assume policing duties in Western Shanghai.[82] Consequently, on January 1, 1938, the Shanghai Municipal Council notified the populace of the International

Settlement that anyone committing a hostile act against members of a foreign force would be handed over to that military authority. Also, on January 4, after a meeting with Japanese military and consular representatives, the Shanghai Municipal Council announced a general shakeup in the Shanghai Municipal Police (where four senior British officers, including Commissioner F. W. Gerrard himself, were retiring that year), by which ten Japanese constables were promoted to sergeants, two Japanese sergeants to sub-inspectors, two Japanese sub-inspectors to inspectors, and Inspectors Suehiro Iwashita and Tokujiro Hirai to chief inspectors. In addition, a Japanese deputy commissioner would be appointed with status equal to his British counterpart; and the Shanghai Municipal Police would sometime in the future begin to hand captured anti-Japanese terrorists over to the Japanese Military Police.[83]

The Municipal Council had readily acceded to the demand that Japanese officers be promoted into the higher echelons of the police and that a Japanese be brought in from the outside for the second highest position in the department. But the Shanghai Municipal Police dragged its collective feet, procrastinating with the encouragement of British Consul General Sir Herbert Phillips.[84] Doubting the loyalty of the newly promoted Japanese inspectors, the Special Branch formulated elaborate new security rules (stamped, of course, "secret") to prevent leakages.[85] Uncertain of the fate of suspected terrorists remanded to the Japanese Special Services Corps, the Special Branch declined to hand any of its prisoners over to the Japanese Military Police.[86]

On April 9 Consul General Hidaka Shinrokuro personally delivered a letter to Shanghai Municipal Council Chairman Cornell S. Franklin. Among other demands, the letter insisted that in addition to immediately appointing a special deputy commissioner with authority over the entire Japanese staff of the Shanghai Municipal Police, the Council also put a Japanese officer with the rank of assistant commissioner in charge of "C" Division (Hongkou, or "Little Tokyo"). Chairman Franklin complied, and within six weeks the Shanghai Municipal Police had a new special deputy commissioner: Akagi Chikayuki, the very epitome of an enlightened Japanese imperial police official. Akagi, who was forty-four years old, was born in Hiroshima prefecture and educated at Kyôto University. After graduation, he entered the Ministry of Home Affairs and became police superintendent of Shizuoka prefecture at the age of twenty-six. In April 1925 he was commissioned a sub-lieutenant in the Imperial Japanese Army, and two years later appointed chief of external police affairs for Hyogo prefecture (Kôbe). From there he went to Shanghai to serve as head of the Japanese consular police for six years (1928–1933), returned to Japan to be chief of police of Kochi prefecture, and in 1935 became head of the police section in the Ministry of Overseas Affairs. On May 20, 1938, after the initial reorganization of the Shanghai Municipal Police, he was formally appointed special deputy commissioner of the International Settlement police. Akagi would do much to dovetail the Shanghai Municipal Police's antiterrorist activities with the aims of the Japanese consular police and Military Police until 1941, when he himself fell victim to Blue Shirt bullets during the apex of the assassination wave.[87] As we shall see, political assassination soon became a way of life and death in Shanghai, where killing was in the air.

2

Blue Shirts

Foreign observers detected a strong wave of "patriotic sentiment" in Shanghai during June 1938. Chinese Nationalist flags were flown on all anniversaries. The "mosquito press" published jingoistic editorials. Regular newspaper articles urged young people to join or organize guerrilla bands. On June 10 the first of seven terrorist attacks on collaborators occurred. You Yaosun, a cotton broker who belonged to the Japanese-sponsored Shanghai Citizens Association, was wounded and one of his Russian bodyguards was killed. The next day a minor Reform Government official was wounded. On June 18, the land commissioner of the puppet government, Ren Bao'an, was killed at a party of Chinese collaborators and Japanese friends. Six days later one man was killed in a lawyer's office, and four of You Yaosun's friends were shot in a hotel room. The day after that, Gu Qingyi, a cereal merchant who was also a member of the Shanghai Citizens Association, was assassinated. On June 29 assassins disguised as beggars shot and killed Chen Deming, chief of the puppets' boat inspection office.[1]

The public had a number of theories to account for the terrorist wave. There were some indications of a falling out between rival groups of collaborators, each trying to win Japanese political favor and monetary support. People speculated that these patriotically disguised deeds were actually struggles over the spoils of Japanese victory. Others thought that they were revenge killings by disgruntled rice dealers or boatmen enraged by the onerous taxes collected by the boat inspectors. "The consensus of opinion was, however, that there was a Chinese Nationalist organization functioning in Shanghai and that these killings were all patriotic in motive."[2] Most believed, moreover, that this organization was identical with the Blue Shirts (Lanyishe), a fascist brotherhood fanatically loyal to Chiang Kai-shek, and devoted to extirpating "traitors" (*hanjian*).[3]

The Blue Shirts did exist, of course, as part of an integument that included the Restoration Society (Fuxingshe), although their "fascist" character has been repeatedly questioned.[4] The original Blue Shirts Society was founded in 1932 as a satellite (or what we would call a "front") group for the Vigorous Revival Society (Lixingshe), which was a group of right-wing Whampoa graduates fanatically dedicated to supporting their "Leader" (Lingxiu), Chiang Kai-shek. By 1934, their partisan activities in North China, including the dramatic assassination of the collaborator Zhang Jingyao, led the Japanese military to believe that the Blue Shirts were the "masterminds behind comprehensive anti-Japanese activity in north China and Manchukuo."[5] Indeed, they were also believed to be the chief organizers of anti-Japanese terrorism in central China, which was yet one more reason for the Japanese to insist, in the Ho–Umezu agreement of 1935, that the Blue Shirts be disbanded.[6]

The Nationalists complied—up to a point.[7] As Chen Lifu later remarked, "Although Mr. Chiang [Kai-shek] ordered dissolution of the [Fuxingshe], it was dissolved only on the surface."[8] In Shanghai, Wu Xingya, chief of the Bureau of Social Affairs and the local branch of the Guomindang, sponsored three organizations to continue the work of the Fuxingshe under the supervision of former Blue Shirts: the Youth Strength Society (Qingnian lishe) for university students, the Middle Vanguard Society (Zhongfeng she) for middle school students, and the Shanghai Municipal Aid Society (Shanghai shi huzhu she) for unattached youth.[9] Once Wu Xingya passed away on August 4, 1936, however, all three organizations ceased to function actively.[10]

Nonetheless, both official and unofficial organs continued throughout 1937 and 1938 to attribute anti-Japanese terrorism to the notorious Blue Shirts, whom they took to be coordinated by former police chief General Cai Jiangjun in his guise as head of the Shanghai branch of the Moral Endeavor Society (Lizhishe), secretly headquartered in the Paris Mansions (Bali gongyu) at the corner of rue Lafayette and rue Chapsal in the French Concession:[11]

> When the Shanghai Battle ended in 1937, although the Chiang forces retreated, they left behind them a hideous heritage—the Terrorist and the Blueshirt. At that time, both the police of the Settlement and the Concession could easily have stamped out the monster that subsequently was allowed to grow into a stalking Frankenstein bent on having its fill of victims at regular intervals.[12]

The truth of the matter was simply that the term "Blue Shirts" had become common usage for two different sorts of anti-Japanese activities in the Shanghai area after the Occupation began: suburban guerrilla resistance movements and urban political terrorism. Both were, to a degree, organized by Chiang Kai-shek's military secret police chief, Dai Li.[13]

After war broke out on August 13, Dai Li had driven down to Shanghai to meet with Green Gang leader Du Yuesheng at 10 rue Doumer in the French Concession. From this meeting stemmed the formation of the Pudong Guerrilla Brigade (Youji dui), the Lake Tai Special Action Command (Biedong du), the Loyal and Patriotic National Salvation Army (Zhongyi jiuguo jun) and eventually the Jiangsu–Zhejiang Operations Committee (Su–Zhe xingdong weiyuanhui).[14] According to intelligence reports gathered by the Shanghai Municipal Police, Chiang Kai-shek's Military Affairs Commission decided at the beginning of September to organize an "emergency period service group" (*feichang shiqi fuwutuan*) to deal with traitors and spies in Shanghai. Shanghai already had a Peace Preservation Corps (Baoandui), but its purpose had been mainly to serve as a surrogate police force for the Chinese municipality after the Japanese withdrew in July 1932.[15] In order to fight the Japanese now, both before and behind enemy lines, Chiang decided to create an urban guerrilla force. The Military Affairs Commission accordingly set aside $500,000 for this group, which was put under the orders of General Wang Jingjiu, commander of the 87th Nationalist Division. His headquarters at Jiangyin had already been training cadets for intelligence work in a *junguan xunlianban* (officers training depot) that was also a "preliminary training" (*rumen xunlian*) course for the Special Services Department; and three days after hostilities broke out in Shanghai, 240 of these cadets were sent to Longhua Primary School to serve as special forces.[16] General Wang's deputy commanders of the "emergency period service group" were General Cai Jingjun, chief of the Shanghai Public Security Bureau, and Du Yuesheng, who immediately tried to turn the new organization to his own use:

> On receiving their appointments and instructions, General Wang Jingjiu and General Cai Jingjun found it inconvenient in their present positions and the work they entailed to actively participate, so left the matter of organizing this new unit in the hands of Mr. Du Yuesheng, deputy commander. In carrying out the organizing of this unit, Mr. Du saw a chance to use his own followers as heads of sections and appointed Mr. Lu Jingshi, Chief Judge of the Military Court at Longhua, and Mr. Zhu Xuefan [Chairman of the Shanghai General Labor Union], to those positions.[17]

However, when Du Yuesheng submitted the names of his lieutenants to the Military Affairs Commission, they were rejected, greatly annoying him and insulting Lu Jingshi and Zhu Xuefan.[18]

As a result of Du Yuesheng's momentary indifference, the Shanghai chief of police, General Cai Jingjun, decided to step in and establish a headquarters for the special group within the Public Security Bureau with the help of the Loyal and Patriotic Association (Zhongyihui), a group described by Shanghai Municipal Police informants as being "composed of Whampoa cadets" and which was led by Pu Fengming. He and General Cai subsequently set up two squads or regiments (*tuan*): the Defense and Protection Squad (Fanghutuan) and the Special Services Squad (Tewutuan).[19]

The Defense and Protection Squad performed different functions north and south of Suzhou Creek. In the northern parts of the city, and especially in Hongkou (Hongkew), they formed a so-called Shanghai Snipers Corps, which was composed mainly of "loafers" and unemployed workers given Mauser rifles or pistols to snipe at the Japanese behind enemy lines.[20] South of the creek, in Nandao, the Fanghutuan consisted mainly of residents conscripted to dig bomb shelters. The principal tenant in every house in South Market was supposed to supply one member of the household daily for work with the squad, which was commanded by one of General Cai's lieutenants out of an office in the Wu'an Primary School at Luxiangyuan Road.[21] By September more than 300 persons were serving as conscripts and 57 dugouts had been finished.[22]

The Special Services Squad had its headquarters in a private school that was part of the Shaoxing guildhall off of Liyuan Road in Nandao.[23] It was commanded by General Cai's former Criminal Investigation Department superintendent, Liu Huai. His two deputies in turn were Public Security Bureau Inspector Chen Bannong and a former bus conductor named Zhang Guoquan.[24] Regular members of the Tewutuan were recruited mainly from among the ranks of unemployed workers. They were promised a wage of $9 a month, plus room and board on the premises of the school, which was built to house 1,000 people. By late September 1937, about 400 men had enlisted.[25]

The Special Services Squad also had an investigation section, which consisted of thirty members under a man named Yang Fulin. These men were billeted in the Jingqin Primary School on Xilin Road outside the West Gate. One of them, a primary school principal named Fu Duoma, reported that he had been assigned by Liu Huai to report on the activities of Japanese plainclothesmen in the International Settlement. He had also been instructed to investigate Chinese "traitors," and if sufficient evidence could be found, to get the Chinese police to arrest the collaborators and remand them to the custody of the Special Services Squad headquarters for further questioning.[26]

Dai Li undoubtedly had his men among the two groups serving under General Cai, and especially within the investigation section of the Special Services Squad. But the secret police chief concentrated most of his attention on Du Yuesheng's networks of disciples among the labor unions, in mercantile circles, and within the underworld. It was apparently Dai Li who brought the insulted racketeer and his Green Gang followers back into the orbit of the Military Affairs Commission in late September and early October by persuading Chiang Kai-shek to establish the Military Affairs Commission Jiangsu and Zhejiang Operations Committee (Junshi weiyuanhui Su–Zhe xingdong weiyuanhui) in order to transform "gang-land" (*banghui*) members into paramilitary cadres.[27]

The Su–Zhe Operations Committee was chaired by Chiang Kai-shek himself, and its members included Du Yuesheng, Huang Jinrong, Wang Xiaolai, Yu Xiaqing, Zhang Xiaolin, Yang Hu, Mei Guangpei, Xiang Songpo, and Lu Jingshi. The secretary general (*shujizhang*) was Dai Li, who set up offices off of Shanzhong Road in the French Concession. The committee's activities were divided by departments (*chu*) for planning (*canmou*), political indoctrination (*zhengxun*), intelligence (*qingbao*), training (*xunlian*), and general affairs (*zongwu*); and the department chiefs were Special Services Department officers such as Chen Xudong, Wang Zuhua, Xie Ligong, and Yu Lexing.[28]

The main task at hand was to train cadres and enroll militiamen. Special classes were opened in Songjiang and Qingpu to train people to join and lead action teams (*zhidui*). Then, in early October, Dai Li used the authority of the committee to organize a General Command headquarters for the Special Action Army (Biedongjun zongzhihui bu). The headquarters of what would become known as the Song–Hu biedong zongdui (Song–Hu Chief Special Action Corps) was located at Number 1 Shenjiazhai near Fenglinqiao opposite Route Ghisi in South Market. Although it was nominally directed by Du Yuesheng, the organization's real chief—according to one of the corps' members—was Dai Li, "who is known to be [the] leader of the Blue Shirt Society."[29] Du Yuesheng's "foreign affairs" assistant, the old Green Gang warlord from Shandong, Liu Zhilu, was titular deputy-head of the Special Action Corps.[30] But the key department personnel were all Dai Li's men: Chen Xudong as chief of staff, Fang Chao as staff executive, Zhou Weilong in charge of indoctrination, Zhou Jiali and later Tan Liangfu as chief managers, Zhou Jiwen responsible for general affairs, and Yu Lexing looking after technical matters. Yu was also responsible for the Songjiang and Qingpu training camps, along with Xie Ligong.[31]

The Song–Hu Chief Special Action Corps was divided into five branch brigades (*zhidui*) of 500 to 3,000 men each, totaling 8,000 militiamen in all. Branch brigades in turn were broken down into three large brigades (*dui*), subdivided yet further into medium (*zhong*), small (*xiao*), and district (*qu*) brigades. All officers from district brigade commanders on up were either agents of Dai Li's Special Services Department or "backbone cadres" (*gugan*) from the Hengshe.[32]

The rank and file were drawn from various social sectors: retail clerks (*dianyuan*) from the Shanghai Shopkeepers Association, local ruffians (*dipi* and *liumang*) from the gangs, routed Guomindang soldiers, laborers thrown out of work by the closing of the factories and shops during the Japanese attack, and organized labor union members.[33] A Shanghai "merchants militia" (*shangtuan*) had been formed as early as February 1937, when the Chinese Chamber of Commerce had taken out advertisements in the Shanghai press offering free courses in civic training to shop assistants. One of the young men who answered the ad was a twenty-one-year-old named Tao Minzhou from Shaoxing. He was put through a four-month course (March–June) in Zhabei. Tao went back to his civilian job in a dyeing shop after the course was over, but when hostilities broke out in August 1937 he joined the Peace Preservation Corps (Baoandui) in Nandao, and in early September this corps was reorganized as the fifth section of the Shanghai Special Action Corps under Colonel Tao Yishan, who had been named by Nanjing head of all the Shanghai civic training centers and whose headquarters was in the Wusong–Shanghai Garrison Command.[34]

Tao Minzhou was subsequently provided by Colonel Tao with a Mauser pistol, ten rounds of ammunition, and four hand grenades. Quartered in an unnumbered house across from the Sun Sing Cotton Mill, his assignment was to examine pedestrian and vehicular traffic at the Branan Road barrier to make sure that no "traitors" entered Chinese territory. Tao Minzhou's official brevet consisted of two cloth badges. One identified him as "Number 06595" of the "Shanghai Special Service Corps," and enjoined him to "obey instructions, maintain strict discipline; be loyal to your duties; resist to the bitter end." Another identified its bearer as being attached to the Special Service Corps of the "Jiangsu and Zhejiang Movement Committee." On October 24, 1937, Tao Minzhou and a comrade tried to search a truck and were impeded by Constable F. P. S. Smith. When they pulled out their Mauser pistols, Smith grabbed Tao, who was arrested. The other man escaped. Eventually Tao Minzhou was handed over to the Shanghai Garrison Command.[35]

Colonel Tao Yishan's merchant and worker unit was one of several groups provided with khaki uniforms and armed with old Mauser rifles.[36] Section Two was barracked at the East Asia Athletic School on Luban Road in Nandao, where it was ordered to help the police preserve law and order.[37] However, according to the testimony of one Yun Huifang, who was a member of the Special Action Corps well known to the International Settlement police "for his terrorist activities in 1932," when he was charged with an attempted murder in the French Concession, the purpose of his section of the corps (which was armed with Mauser pistols) was "solely to locate traitors (*hanjian*)," whom they supposedly turned over to the nearest Chinese police bureau.[38]

Section Three was assigned to Zhu Xuefan, the chairman of the Shanghai General Labor Union whose nomination had originally been turned down by the Military Affairs Commission.[39] It was supposed to maintain labor control.[40] Other working-class units included branch teams of postal workers and seamen, under Lu Jingshi, and a longshoremens' brigade.[41]

Many of the recruits were simply unemployed youths. Lin Defu, an eighteen-year-old hawker from Ningbo, was arrested near Race Course Road by the International Settlement police for trying to recruit "plainclothes boy scouts." Under interrogation, Lin said that he himself had been brought into the Special Action Corps by a thirty-year-old newspaper vendor named Li who had harangued a group of young males on Jiujiang Road into enlisting in the militia. Moved by his appeal to their patriotism, or just plain curious about the opportunities he seemed to offer, Lin and about forty other young men had followed the vendor, surnamed Li, to the Special Action Corps depot at the Shaoxing Fellow Countrymen's Association on Liyuan Road in Nandao. Once there they were told that if they were willing to receive military training, they would get $9 a month plus two meals a day and a place to sleep. If they refused they could return home. About 600 men remained, "young and strong fellows" all between eighteen and thirty-six years of age.[42]

Naysayers later described the Special Action Corps as "a motley rabble" (*wu he zhi zhong*), which had very little military effectiveness against the Japanese.[43] Du Yuesheng's lieutenants, Lu Jingshi and Shui Xiangyun, suddenly threw off their regular underworld roles as "rats in dark corners," and adorned themselves in bright uniforms, becoming heroes of the hour.[44] They were initially supposed to defend the zone from the south bank of Suzhou Creek along Fanwangdu and Caojiadu across to Rihuigang. But once the Japanese launched an attack across Suzhou Creek, the Special Action Corps retreated.[45]

Before the Chinese parts of the city fell, Dai Li fled to quarters on Avenue Haig in the French Concession. He still hoped to rally his own men in a heroic defense of the Nandao, striving to emulate the feats of regimental commander Xie Jinyuan, whose defense of the Four Banks Depository (Sihang cangku) in 1932 had already become patriotic lore.[46] But many of his cadres simply abandoned their commands and sought refuge in the foreign concessions. As the Japanese troops fought their way into the Chinese portions of Shanghai, the most prominent leaders of the resistance left the city. In November 1937 Mayor Yu Hongjun,

T. V. Soong, Qian Xinzhi, and Wang Xiaolai all secretly went to Hong Kong.[47] Du Yuesheng joined them there, and was soon organizing a clandestine intelligence operation for Chiang Kai-shek, financed in part through a narcotics enterprise that he and Dai Li set up, called the "Gangji Company."[48]

Meanwhile, the Shanghai Special Action Corps scattered. Most armed units made a dash for the Anhui–Jiangsu border area, and especially for Tunxi and Shexian counties, where they either fell in with warlords like the former Hunanese bandit Chen Shihu and became guerrillas (*youjidui*) who "wandered but never attacked" (*you er bu ji*), or else they were later organized by Dai Li into units of the Loyal and Patriotic National Salvation Army (Zhongyi jiuguo jun) that was eventually armed by the Americans.[49] The last batch of Special Action Corps withdrew from Shanghai on February 1, 1938, issuing a farewell letter to the Chinese press that stated that they were leaving the concessions "for the safety of the residents of the foreign settlements."[50] By then Dai Li had escaped from Shanghai to Changsha via Hong Kong, and the Su–Zhe Operations Committee was completely dissolved.[51] Of those units remaining in the suburbs, several to the west of Shanghai defected to the Japanese and became puppet troops.[52] Although one detachment of Pudong guerrillas did remain active resistants, launching a coordinated attack on September 11, 1938, against a Japanese military outpost and the puppet offices at Dongchang Road before being driven off by heavy machine guns, the guerrilla forces remained outside of the city.[53] The war in Shanghai had become an underground operation, and for the next thirty-four months, until Pearl Harbor, terrorism would be conducted in secrecy from the concessions.

During his August 1937 visit to Shanghai, Dai Li also looked after his own urban intelligence and counterintelligence operations, putting the Shanghai Zone (Shanghai qu) Station of the Military Statistics Bureau (Juntong) on a wartime footing. Until then, the five "field personnel" (*waiqin*) groups of the Shanghai Station, which was under the command of Zhou Weilong, had mainly devoted their attention to anti-Communist surveillance and communications interception. Zhou promised Dai Li that he would stay behind in the French Concession and set up a sabotage unit in the "underground zone" (*qianfuqu*) to harass the enemy.[54] For reasons of security, these spy organizations were supposed to remain completely apart from the Special Action Corps, responding directly to Dai Li through Gong Xianfang, who had been head of the Shanghai Special Services Department personnel office and was now designated as the liaison and principal courier for the Shanghai net. However, these underground intelligence cells were either compromised by the foreign concession police, smashed by Japanese counterespionage, or absorbed by collaborationist secret service organs working for the puppet government.[55]

The new head of intelligence, Wang Fangnan, blew his own cover within a year and had to be transferred by Juntong to Hong Kong.[56] In early 1939 Zhou Weilong was arrested by the French Concession police, and then transferred to Chongqing after Juntong secured his release. One of his successors,[57] Wang Tianmu, was betrayed by the station's personnel chief to the puppet secret police at 76 Jessfield Road, and in turn defected early in 1940. And Wang's own successor, Chen Gongshu, ostensibly defected when he was tumbled by the secret police and offered the choice of collaboration or death.[58]

Although the Shanghai Station of Juntong was quickly disabled, two special operations units (*xingdong zu*) were much more efficacious through the period of "island Shanghai." Because of Chiang Kai-shek's fury over the "treacherous activities" (*hanjian huodong*) of collaborators in Shanghai, Dai Li organized two secret action units under Zhao Lijun and Lin Zhijiang.[59] These *xingdong zu,* and especially Zhao Lijun's squad, were responsible for many of the major assassinations of the time, including the deaths of Zhou Fengqi, Lu Bohong, and Zhang Xiaolin.[60] According to one estimate, Dai Li's men carried out over 150 assassinations in Shanghai between August 1937 and October 1941, when even the operations units were penetrated by the puppet secret service at 76 Jessfield Road.[61]

The Special Branch of the Shanghai Municipal Police was certainly aware that the Blue Shirts as such were no longer active in Shanghai.[62] Like the Japanese-owned *Xin shenbao,* Special Branch knew that some of the assassination squads were Nationalist secret service agents.[63] It even knew that these squads were under the command of Dai Li:

> Following the withdrawal of the Chinese armed forces from the Shanghai area, neither the Blue Shirt Society nor the newly formed Sanminzhuyi Youth Group was responsible for the assassination of Chinese pro-Japanese elements in the International Settlement and the French Concession. Information on hand indicates that one Tai Lieh [Dai Li], a staff officer of the Military Affairs Commission, Chongqing, and ex-member of the Blue Shirt Society who is now in command of the Special Service Corps of the Jiangsu–Zhejiang Operations Committee, a guerrilla unit operating in the suburbs of the city, is taking charge of the assassination work in this city.[64]

Yet both the press and the International Settlement police continued to refer to the terrorists as Blue Shirts throughout the entire period.[65]

One reason the term endured was its striking symbolic significance, especially in light of the Brown and Black Shirts then dominating Europe.

Another reason was simply that the phenomenal terrorism of "island Shanghai" was more than just the work of one or two organizational headquarters. Political assassination grew naturally out of the national salvation movements of the early 1930s, which created a raft of partly coordinated, partly spontaneous, groups and organizations among the "petty urbanites" (*xiao shimin*) of Shanghai, who acted for both patriotic and self-interested reasons. Sometimes these individuals linked up with Nationalist military special service units, sometimes not. As we shall see in the next chapter, the role of Sun Yaxing and his men in the bombings of July 7, 1938, the first anniversary of the Marco Polo Bridge incident, makes this ambiguity perfectly clear.

3

National salvation

Sun Yaxing, the twenty-seven-year-old bachelor who organized the bombings of July 7, 1938, was the son of a traveling salesman from Jinjiang. He had five years of primary school and three years of private tutoring before coming to Shanghai at the age of fourteen to live with an aunt at the corner of Bubbling Well and Hardoon Roads. After another six months of primary school, he studied for a year at a Hankou middle school and then came back to Shanghai to learn the watch trade in the shop of one of his father's friends. During his four years of apprenticeship as a jeweler he also took evening classes in a private night school. By the time his training was completed early in 1931, he was ready to open his own jewelry store, the Xingxiang (Prosperity and Good Fortune), on rue Palikao in the French Concession.[1] A few months later the Manchurian Railway incident occurred, and Sun promptly closed his shop doors and joined the Shanghai Citizens Volunteer Corps "with a view to serving my country in a more beneficial manner."[2]

The Shanghai Citizens Volunteer Corps, run out of an office over a Fuzhou Road silk shop by a lawyer named Wang Bingnan, had 500 members when Sun Yaxing joined up. On January 28, 1932, after some military drills on the public recreation ground of Nandao, 300 of these young men agreed to participate in the conflict. Sun was named a section chief by Wang Binnan, who led the group to Baoshan where they were drafted into the Chinese military and attached to the 19th Route Army. After action against the Japanese with light casualties, the Shanghai Citizens Volunteer Corps withdrew to Songjiang for further military training. Before they could be sent back to the front, however, Chiang Kai-shek transferred the 19th Route Army to Fujian, the Shanghai Citizens Volunteer Corps was disbanded, and Sun Yaxing returned to Shanghai.[3]

During the winter of 1932–1933 Sun organized a mutual benefit group, the Qunyi (Profit the Many) society, whose fifty-odd members from various walks of life met at his shop on rue Palikao to "advance their political knowledge." The "profit," however, did not materialize, and early in 1933 Sun had to disband the group because of financial difficulties. Using $2,000 of his mother's money, who then lived in Hankou, Sun opened an exchange shop optimistically called China Revives (Huaxing) at the corner of rue Ratard and rue des Soeurs.[4] He was barely able to eke out a living, but he refused to join some of his Citizens Volunteer Corps comrades—including Yun Huifang, wanted for terrorism by the French police—who had formed "anti-traitors societies" to extort money from merchants dealing in Japanese goods. Instead, as funds ran out when the effects of the world depression finally reached Shanghai, he closed down his shop and moved in with a student friend living in a boarding house on rue Auguste Boppe. He returned to Hankou in November of that year when he learned that his father was ill, but by the time he got home, the old man had died.[5]

Back in Shanghai in January 1934, Sun Yaxing got the help of two friends—an editor at the Zhonghua Book Company and a student at Nanyang College whose Beiping parents were quite wealthy—to open the Yamei Watch and Clock Shop at the corner of rue du Consulat and rue Palikao. The watch business did well; Sun opened a branch on Bubbling Well Road, moved his main store to Weikwei Road, and took classes in night school to improve his education.[6]

Moving again from self-help to mutual aid, always with a patriotic motive, Sun Yaxing, together with another student and a cigarette factory manager, formed in September 1936 the One Heart (Yixin) League in Zhabei. The ostensible purpose of the One Heart League, composed of thirty members who were mostly laborers, was "promoting the political knowledge of the people" and "furthering national salvation activities." The latter led to reunion with Wang Bingnan and the Shanghai Citizens Volunteer Corps, which the Yixin group joined as a special action corps (*biedong dui*) in October 1936.[7] In January 1937 corps members were given military training and promised weapons to attack the Japanese from the rear if war should break out, but when the guns and hand grenades never materialized, members dropped out and the corps was disbanded.[8]

On July 8, the day after the Marco Polo Bridge incident, Sun Yaxing and Zhao Gangyi—later his link to the Dai Li organization—resolved to form the Chinese Youths National Salvation Association.[9] Sun sold his two watch shops for $1,000 and opened a preparatory office in the Guili Temple at the Old West Gate in Nandao.[10] On July 15, 1937, after posting advertisements, the Chinese Youths National Salvation Association was formally inaugurated at the Guandi Temple, where a depot had been established. More than a thousand people showed up to hear speeches by the head of the association, Zhao Gangyi, and by the chief of its execution department, Sun Yaxing.[11] A number of those who came then or later in answer to advertisements in *Zhongyang ribao* (Central Daily News) were taken aside and interviewed by Sun Yaxing, who asked them to write about their reasons for joining. Three of these young men later became members of Sun Yaxing's assassination group: Wang Zhigu, a twenty-three-year-old factory apprentice;[12] Jiang Haisheng, a nineteen-year-old student;[13] and Zhou Shougang, a twenty-five-year-old printer.[14] A fourth, Sun Jinghao, was to throw the bomb on December 3 at the Japanese victory parade on Nanjing Road.[15]

For the next few days, these new members—all students, apprentices, or shop assistants—attended lectures on the current political situation. On July 21, after being addressed by an officer representing General Zhang Jizhong, they were asked to volunteer to help dig fortifications outside Shanghai. About 200 men, mostly between eighteen and twenty years old, volunteered, and under Sun Yaxing's command they proceeded to Nanxiang, where they were attached to the 87th Nationalist Division. For the next month, supplied with food but not pay, they dug trenches. After hostilities broke out on August 13, they worked mostly at night to avoid Japanese bombers. Conditions were rugged, and 50 of the original 200 got sick and dropped out.[16]

Toward the end of August Sun Yaxing told them that they had been reorganized into a Special Services Corps and that they would have to undergo military training. On September 2, 1937, they were transferred to Longhua and reorganized as the Third Company, Seventh Battalion, Second Regiment of the Jiangsu–Zhejiang Special Services Corps. Their regiment commander was Zhu Xuefan (head of the Shanghai General Labor Union and a disciple of Du Yuesheng).[17] After a month of arduous military training they were provided grenades, pistols, and rifles, and taught how to use them. More dropped out due to ill health.[18]

The Special Services Corps

In late September the company was transferred to the Dongya Physical Culture School in Nandao and assigned to patrol the area surrounding the martial law commander's headquarters at West Gate. They were authorized to take whatever measures they deemed necessary "to suppress traitors": if they arrested persons "for perpetrating traitorous acts," the suspects were tried by a military court within the headquarters and summarily executed when found guilty.[19]

At the end of October 1937, the company was despatched to the police station on the Nandao Bund to help the police reserve unit defend the area from attack by the Japanese from the Huangpu River. This was where the last stand of the Chinese Nationalist forces took place on November 11, the final day of the Battle of Shanghai. Edgar Snow witnessed the door-to-door fighting from the neutrality of the French Concession, just across the creek:

> We saw the Japanese moving up cautiously, from cover to cover, behind their tanks which only ran a few feet and then stopped, filled the air with a stuttering fire, and retreated. Opposite us, close enough to hit with a ball, a Chinese machine gun spout[ed] out of a square mouth in a concrete pillbox built on the left bank of a narrow canal branching off from Siccawei [Xujiahui], directly ahead. A long line of stilted huts leaning over the canal was filled with Chinese snipers. . . . Bombers appeared and set a string of huts afire. . . . I watched Japanese infantry sidling up behind broken walls just across the Creek, getting ready for an assault over the canal. Several tanks came up and poured their fire into a pillbox sunk at the intersection. . . . A trench mortar finally made a direct hit and I saw some helmeted Chinese crouch and make off to the rear. Fires were burning brightly now all over Nantao [Nandao]. . . . The Chinese were retreating.[20]

Sun Yaxing's unit fought alongside the police reserves until nightfall, when the Chinese police quailed and fled into the French Concession. The special services company followed close behind, escaping through a small iron gate at the south end of boulevard de Montigny. Awaiting them were French police, who rounded them up, forced them to throw down their weapons, and conveyed them to an internment camp on the Shanghai Law College campus.[21] With typical initiative, Sun Yaxing managed to slip away enroute with five other members of his section.[22]

For the next week, Sun moved from hotel to hotel until he found a room in a boarding house on Yuyaqing Road. Still grimly determined to continue his "anti-traitor activities," in the course of the next month he began to accumulate a small arsenal of bombs, Mauser machine pistols, a revolver, and several Browning automatics, which he got from former members of the Third Company or purchased from Special Services Corps men who had served in the Eighth Battalion. He cached the arms, along with Mills hand grenades, in the attic of his former business, the Yamei Watch and Clock Shop on rue de Weikwei. Early on the morning of December 3, Sun Yaxing and his terrorist group learned of General Matsui's plan to lead a victory parade down Nanjing Road. Sun Yaxing and three others, including Sun Jinghao, retrieved some of the grenades and joined the crowds lining Shanghai's main thoroughfare. As the troops approached, the police forced the onlookers back out of the street so that Sun Yaxing and two of his comrades were a good thirty meters down an alley away from the parade route. Sun Jinghao, however, was close enough to push through the crowd and reach the street in time to throw his bomb, wounding the soldiers and constables and being shot in turn on the spot. The other three men, terrified, made good their escape. A few days later, on December 16, when Sun Yaxing heard rumors that the Japanese were going to arrest anyone who had been a member of the Chinese Special Services Corps, he decided to leave Shanghai for Ningbo by steamer, and went on from there by train to Hangzhou.[23]

In his deposition to the Shanghai Municipal Police, Sun claimed that after an interview in Hangzhou with the chairman of the provincial government, he was assigned to serve as a police officer in Shaoxing county until the end of February 1938, when he returned to Shanghai "with a view to bring[ing] all the ex-members of the Third Company of Special Services Corps, who were in Shanghai, to Hankou to further [the] National Salvation Movement in the latter city."[24] However, two of the future members of his assassination team, Jiang Haisheng and Zhao Liang, remember his coming to their respective refugee camps in middle or late January. In Jiang's case, he and a group of former Special Services Corps "plainclothesmen" were told by Sun, in a camp on Alabaster Road, that they should join the national salvation movement in Hankou, and that he would arrange for repatriation through local native-place associations; Jiang remembered leaving for Hong Kong on February 9, and reaching Hankou by train from Canton on February 15.[25] Zhao Liang, on the other hand, recalled being told that Sun Yaxing himself would provide transportation for the ex-corpsman who left Shanghai on a British steamer for Hong Kong on February 23, 1938, and took the same route to Hankou two days later.[26]

By then Sun was already in Hankou, having precipitately left Shanghai when he saw a report in one of the newspapers that the leader of the Chinese Youths National Salvation Association—that is, Sun himself—was in the city. Sun Yaxing fled to Ningbo, and when he reached Hankou he discovered that some of his former colleagues in the Chinese Youths National Salvation Association had already opened up an office and were receiving a monthly government subsidy of several hundred thousand dollars. The money, which no doubt came partly from secret service funds, was mainly used to support the association's thousand or so members, some of whom were ex-Special Services Corps members who had gotten to Hankou on their own.[27] One of them, Wang Zhigu, had come to Hankou to visit his uncle, Wang Shihe, who just happened to be Chiang Kai-shek's chief bodyguard, infamous for having carried out the execution of Deng Yanda, leader of the Guomindang's left wing, in December 1931.[28] Wang Zhigu accidentally bumped into Sun Yaxing on the streets of the Japanese

Concession in Hankou, and learned of the anti-Japanese work of the Chinese Youths National Salvation Association directly from his former commander.[29]

The others, recruited by Sun in the refugee camps of Shanghai, were divided into two groups: twenty for military service, and twenty-five to tend wounded soldiers in the First Military Hospital. Of the latter, ten were detailed for "special duty" in Changsha, and a couple more dropped out. The remaining thirteen were told on April 25, 1938, that they had been chosen for urban guerrilla work in Shanghai "to suppress traitors."[30] This was the assassination group's one point of contact with General Dai Li, according to Zhao Liang's confession to the Shanghai Municipal Police:

> Zung Yah Shing [Sun Yaxing], the twelve others, and myself were then spoken to by Dan Lih [Dai Li], Chief of the Secret Service Department in Hankow [Hankou], and he informed us that we were proceeding to Shanghai on a secret mission and that we had to take all our orders from Zung Yah Shing [Sun Yaxing], whom we were to obey implicitly.[31]

Joined by Wang Zhigu, the group was divided into three- or four-man teams, which proceeded via Jiujiang, Nanchang, and Jinhua to Ningbo. On May 1 two of the teams left by boat for Shanghai followed by two more teams on May 2, accompanied by Sun.[32]

Sun Yaxing's assassination squad

At first, the assassination squad observed good security. Individual teams moved every couple of weeks from one lodging house to another, struggling to make ends meet on the $30 monthly expense fund each man received. Sun Yaxing would meet periodically with the team leader in a park or other public place to discuss plans.[33] Guns and grenades were stored in a single place—the attic of Sun Yaxing's former Yamei jewelry store—and then distributed by messenger the day before an operation was mounted. Altogether, between June 10 and July 22 the squad carried out four assassination attempts, two of which succeeded, plus public bombings on the anniversary of the Marco Polo Bridge incident that caused a tremendous public uproar. But as events unrolled, the squad of patriots grew overly confident, security grew lax, and one mistake led to another until half of the original group, including Sun Yaxing himself, was in police custody.[34]

The moment they arrived in Shanghai the four teams went their separate ways within the French Concession, used by them as a sanctuary from which to enter the International Settlement and Chinese sector of the city. Team One—Wang Zhigu, Zhou Weiying, and Gu Zhenbang—rented a room in a lodging house on Fujian Road, and then moved five days later, on May 8, to another rooming house on route Voisin. Gu Zhenbang slipped away during the move, never to reappear, and Sun replaced him on the team with Dai Zhiyue from Team Two. By then Sun's former comrade in the Chinese Youths National Salvation Association and now his superior officer, Zhao Gangyi, had arrived from Hankou, and the two leaders moved into the ground floor of a foreign-style house at the corner of rue Lafayette and Avenue Dubail. Zhao was "running" two squads in Shanghai: an intelligence squad whose personnel remained unknown to Sun and his men, and the execution or assassination squad headed by Sun Yaxing. Zhao, who had by now probably been through one of Dai Li's special agent training depots (*xunlian ban*), was very much the person who decided on individual targets, and he selectively passed on information to Sun on a need-to-know basis.[35]

On June 6, 1938, Sun Yaxing received orders from Zhao Gangyi to kill Yue Chueh-sun (Yu Chueh Ueh-sen) [Yue Juesun], a member of the executive committee of the Shanghai Citizens Society. During the next three days Sun brought a revolver and a Browning automatic to the three members of Team One in the route Voisin lodging house, provided them with a photograph of their target and the license number of his car, and reconnoitered the Sassoon House on the Bund where Yue paid a daily morning call. The assassination was set for June 10. At 8:00 that morning, Sun, who had stationed himself in front of the Palace Hotel on the southeast corner of the Bund and Nanking Road, heard gunfire. He quickly left the scene. Later that afternoon he met Wang Zhigu, who had been posted as a lookout for the two shooters, Dai Zhiyue and Zhou Weiying. From Wang he learned that his agents had wounded Yue and killed his Russian bodyguard, but that Dai Zhiyue had been killed and Zhou Weiying arrested. Team One was now defunct, and Wang Zhigu was transferred to Team Two.[36]

Team Two—now composed of Jiang Haisheng, Zhao Liang, and Wang Zhigu—had stayed at three different rooming houses in the French Concession. On June 11, spooked by the arrest of Zhou Weiying, the group moved yet again, taking lodgings at the Dahua rooming house at 17 rue Auguste Boppe. Wang Zhigu, who did not have a great deal of faith in his new companions, moved to another room in the Dahua hotel at 47 rue Auguste Boppe. He shared the room with his girlfriend, Wang Aju, who had been introduced to him by her mother, a charwoman in the hostel.[37]

Team Three and Team Four were shadowier groups, if only because they evaded arrest or were sent out of Shanghai. Their membership has been reconstructed by comparing depositions given by members of the other two teams along with Sun Yaxing's confession.[38] Team Three was composed of Jin Yingsheng (alias Du Zhimei), Li Chunhui, and Wang Guangcai; Team Four of Zhao Songchao, Dai Binyuan, Zhou Songming, and Li Qiwei.

Team Three was assigned in early June to check on the movements of Green Gang leader Zhang Xiaolin after Zhao Gangyi told Sun Yaxing that he was suspected of being a traitor. The three members of the team moved into an attic in an alleyway across from the residence of Zhang Xiaolin off of rue Wagner. Their presence was quickly discovered, however, by the sons of the alley watchmen, and they had to scratch the mission.[39] Team Four members were never taken into custody and they seem not to have played a major role in the Sun Yaxing assassination squad's activities.[40]

On June 17, Zhao Gangyi passed on information to Sun Yaxing about the treacherous activities of a lawyer named Wu Zung-yu [Wu Zongyu], who had offices in the Taiwu Building on Lloyd Road. Sun ordered Team Two to reconnoiter the building to see if a mission was possible. After Jiang Haisheng, Zhao Liang, and Wang Zhigu had made their investigation, they told Sun that they felt capable of executing the assassination. Sun subsequently had his courier, a Miss Zhou, take two Mauser pistols in a stocking box from the Yamei Watch and Clock Shop and hand them over to one of the Team Two members (identified by a white handkerchief tied around his wrist) at the corner of rue du Consulat and boulevard de Montigny on the evening of June 21. The next day Sun told the three men that they had to complete their mission within three days. They struck on June 24, but they shot the wrong men—two law clerks, one killed and one wounded—while the collaborationist lawyer remained unhurt. Sun Yaxing was furious. Not only had they completely missed their target; they had also discarded their precious pistols. Sun angrily told the members of Team Two that they were not fit for assassination work, and instead would be demoted to bombing missions.[41]

Double seven

Sometime during the next few days, Zhao Gangyi instructed Sun Yaxing to arrange for a patriotic demonstration on July 7, the first anniversary of the Marco Polo Bridge incident, by setting off the six bombs being kept at the Yamei shop plus two potato-masher grenades that Zhao would provide.[42] This proved, in retrospect, to be a fatal decision for the ring.

Mindful of the need for at least a couple of more bomb throwers plus a new courier (Miss Zhou had gone to Hangzhou after handing over the Mausers to Team Two), Sun Yaxing dropped his guard and began to accept walk-ins, which is foolhardy in underground work. The first was a

man known to him from Chinese Youths National Salvation Association
and Special Services Corps days at Nanxiang and Longhua. In February
1938, Zhou Shougang, the printer from Chongming who went home ill,
had returned to Shanghai where he was completely dependent on relatives
for bed and board. One day in late June, Zhou bumped into Wang Zhigu
and recounted his economic woes, saying that he was "practically
destitute." Wang pondered this briefly, and then said that "he might be
able to find [Zhou] work, should [he] care to participate in the assassination of 'traitors.'" Zhou said that he would be willing to do so, and he
repeated this vow when Wang Zhigu brought Sun Yaxing to his residence
at 13 rue du Weikwei and asked him again if he wished to participate in
the assassination of traitors. On July 3, Sun Yaxing told him to move his
residence to 62 route Vallon, where his job would be to function as Sun's
courier and point of contact with other members of the squad. Zhou
Shougang thereby became the only person who knew of Sun Yaxing's
whereabouts, and it was he who would pass messages on to team members
to meet Sun—usually in the French Park just off route Vallon between
7:00 and 8:00 in the evening—whenever the need arose.[43]

The second new member of the squad, Zhu Zhonghu, was also a former
Special Services Corps man who had worked as a clerk at the Changkang
refugee camp on Alabaster Road before getting sick and losing his job.[44]
After Zhu was introduced to Sun Yaxing by Jin Yingsheng, he was immediately drafted as a messenger. It was he who actually picked up four of the
grenades from the boarding house on rue Auguste Boppe and conve-
niently delivered them to Jin on the eve of the July 7 bombings. This
service had its price, however: Zhu later identified five of the execution
squad members for the police.[45]

The third new member was a seventeen-year-old named Chen Kaiguang, who had been unable to find work since graduating from primary
school the year before.[46] He was approached by Zhao Liang who at one
time had lived in the same alleyway off of rue Wagner. Zhao invited him to
join the Chinese Youths National Salvation Association, and out of patriotism Chen Kaiguang agreed, expressing his "willingness to help in the
extermination of traitors." Zhao then told him that, "in order to prove
[his] loyalty to the cause," Chen would be given "a duty to perform on
July 7, 1938." Chen agreed to serve.[47]

At 7:00 p.m. on July 6, Chen Kaiguang met together with Wang Zhigu
and Zhao Liang in a corner of the French Park on route Vallon. The squad
had begun to assemble for the next day's bombing mission, and already
basic security rules were being broken as members from one team gathered with men from another. That morning a twelve-year-old boy named
Wang Qiming had brought six bombs from the Yamei store to Wang

Zhigu's room at 47 rue Auguste Boppe. Two of these were taken by Zhou Shougang to Li Qiwei of Team Four. The remaining four were, as we have seen, picked up by Zhu Zhonghu for Jin Yingsheng of Team Three. Later that afternoon Wang Zhigu had gotten another two bombs from the boy-messenger, and he was carrying both grenades now as they met in the park. One of them he handed to the just-recruited Chen Kaiguang, who was taken over to a park bench and introduced to Sun Yaxing, who had evidently decided to ignore basic tradecraft and accept this new team member on sight. Sun asked Chen whether or not he "could throw a bomb properly," and when the seventeen-year-old said no, Sun showed him how to undo the screw cap and put his small finger into the loop of a piece of cord that would pull the pin when the grenade was thrown. As Chen Kaiguang later told the police, "I listened carefully and finally agreed that I could accomplish this job."[48]

In the meantime, Jiang Haisheng (Team Two) and Li Chunhui (Team Three) also joined them in the park. Sun Yaxing explained their assignments to them, handing over a Mauser pistol to Zhao Liang who was told to cover Li Chunhui when he threw his bomb the next morning between the lifting of the curfew at 5:00 and the setting up of daytime security measures at 6:00 a.m. Sun said that he expected them to report in afterwards at the Deyi Teahouse on rue Kraetzer. At 8:00 p.m. the six men left the park.[49]

Although they went their separate ways to cache their weapons and bombs, the five bombers, joined by Wang Guangcai (Team Three), ended up an hour later in the lodging at 17 rue Auguste Boppe. Restless, and afraid that they might disturb the other guests in the small rooming house, the six terrorists decided to rent a room at the Zhongnan Hotel on Avenue Edward VII, where they sat up all night playing mahjong. At 4:30 a.m. they packed up their tiles and set out for their arms caches and the various points around the city assigned to them: Li Chunhui and Zhao Liang on foot to the Settlement boundary on Xining Road, Chen Kaiguang by ricksha to Sichuan Road, Wang Zhigu by rented bike to the Peking Road floating restaurant at the Bund, and so on.[50]

The bombs went off on schedule. At 6:00 sharp Li Chunhui threw his missile at a Japanese sentry on Xining Road and rushed off with Zhao Liang. A few moments later, Wang Zhigu hurled his grenade down the gangway of the floating restaurant, and then tore off on his bike. As he pedaled furiously past Chen Kaiguang on Jingkee Road, the teenager panicked and tossed his bomb into an alleyway. He heard the explosion go off behind him as he ran toward Sichuan Road. All four men escaped.[51] Chen Kaiguang took two rickshas and a tram to get back to the lodging house on rue Auguste Boppe where he packed up his and Wang Zhigu's belongings. On rue Admiral Bayle he chanced into Jin Yingsheng, and the two walked to a lodging house on rue Kettner where they took a room.[52] En route, Li Chunhui joined them. Once in their room, Jin Yingsheng told them that he had seen Jiang Haisheng's ricksha being stopped by French police on rue du Consulat, where he was searched and taken into custody. The exhausted men pondered Jiang's fate for a few moments, and felt relieved that they had changed to new addresses. Then they lay down and slept till noon.[53]

During that hour between curfew and daytime security, eighteen hand grenades were thrown (two did not explode), two Japanese mill employees were assassinated, two Chinese were dead (killed by Wang Zhigu's attack on the floating restaurant), and eight more Chinese were wounded.[54] The American consul general, Frank P. Lockhart, reported to the secretary of state that it had been necessary to employ "practically all military and police protection together with a part of the Shanghai volunteer forces, including the Russian company, to prevent disorder"; July 7, 1938, was "one of the tensest days spent in Shanghai for some time."[55] Two Japanese civilians were shot dead in the U.S. sector, where marine patrols were doubled. The Japanese military authorities requested permission to send their own forces in to back up the Americans, but the U.S. commander, Colonel Price, refused to admit them, saying that he would provide every possible protection for Japanese nationals.[56]

Close patrols were maintained throughout the day and night. Within twenty-four hours the Shanghai Municipal Police arrested nearly a thousand suspects, and the French Concession Police hundreds more.[57] Among the latter was Jiang Haisheng, the nineteen-year-old middle school student of Team Two found with grenade in hand on rue du Consulat. Under interrogation, Jiang "confessed to being one of a group of Chinese terrorists sent to Shanghai from Hankow [Hankou] with the necessary equipment to create terrorism in the Settlement and French Concession."[58] Because the crimes committed by that group occurred in the International Settlement, Jiang Haisheng was handed over to the Criminal Investigation Department of the Shanghai Municipal Police on July 10, 1938.[59]

Jiang's confession confirmed common belief in the Settlement that the terrorism was instigated by the Nationalist authorities in Hankou. As a result, Cornell Franklin, chairman of the Shanghai Municipal Council, asked that the U.S. and British ambassadors be instructed to bring the matter to the attention of the Chinese government, which should cooperate with the Settlement in preventing future acts of terrorism.[60] On July 11 the British ambassador in Hankou received such a message from Shanghai just as he was about to keep an appointment with the Generalissimo. He put the message in his pocket and later read it to Chiang, who assured the ambassador "that while he disclaimed any connection with these crimes . . . he would use all of his influence to prevent their occurrence."[61]

Countermeasures

On the day after the July 7 bombings and killings, the chiefs of the intelligence sections of the Japanese Consulate General, the China News Agency, the Japanese Military Police, and the Japanese military held a conference in the Japanese Club. Seven resolutions were passed:

> First, that the Consulate General presents a time limit to the foreign concessions' authorities for apprehending the terrorists.
> Second, that the concessions' authorities be requested to allow the establishment of Japanese special services organs and the admission of Chinese [puppet] military special services agents within their jurisdictions in order to facilitate the investigation of anti-Japanese elements.
> Third, that the Japanese authorities be allowed to exercise free police rights, including the power to investigate and make arrests.
> Fourth, that the police authorities of the two settlements be asked to suppress Chinese anti-Japanese associations.
> Fifth, that officers of the Shanghai [puppet] police be despatched to the two concessions to conduct investigations.
> Sixth, that Japanese and Chinese [puppet] intelligence agents redouble their efforts.
> Seventh, that capital punishment be meted out to members of anti-Japanese associations.[62]

Similar resolutions, plus a request that the Shanghai Municipal Police increase the strength of Japanese and Chinese police units in Huxi, were passed by members of the Special Services Squad organized by ex-servicemen among the Japanese employees of the N.W.K. Cotton Mills mainly living in Shanghai's Western District badlands.[63]

The Shanghai Municipal Police responded to the fiat by taking three measures. The first was to organize a task force to investigate terrorist outbreaks. This new section began operating out of Louza police station on Friday morning, the day after the July 7 outbreak:

> The new section's goal is to stamp out terrorism in the Settlement or at least to make an effort in that direction. Some of the best detectives on the force have been taken from their jobs at police stations and assigned to the new unit. Actually the section will function more or less as a "homicide squad." Its creation will centralize the handling of investigations into assassinations and other acts of terrorism, and because of this it is hoped that quick and definite results can be obtained.[64]

Second, the Shanghai Municipal Police tried to restrict the use of the French Concession as a sanctuary for Chinese terrorists. The French police were anxious to curb terrorism, but such cases were tried before the Chinese branch, Second Special District Court, and the Third Branch High Court of Jiangsu, located in the French Concession. The judges were appointed by the Nationalist government in Hankou, and (at least according to the *North China Daily News,* a mouthpiece for the Shanghai Municipal Council) tended to regard these political activists as patriots rather than terrorists, treating them with leniency and indulgence. The Shanghai Municipal Police wished, therefore, that the French not permit the terrorists to be tried in Chinese courts, but handed over to the Japanese instead.[65]

This policy of handing terrorists over to the Japanese constituted the third countermeasure proposed by the Shanghai Municipal Police. On January 1, 1938, the Shanghai Municipal Council had proclaimed that "any persons committing an offense against armed forces in the International Settlement will be liable to be handed over to the armed forces concerned." On July 19, this provision was amended to read: "Any person found in the International Settlement in possession of arms or explosives without a permit from the Settlement authorities or engaged in or connected with terroristic activities will be liable to be expelled from the Settlement." The measure was opposed by the U.S. consul general on the grounds that in such cases there was no public trial and the accused was likely to be maltreated by the Japanese in order to get information about the terrorist organization, but it was promulgated nonetheless in order to appease the Japanese by precluding terrorists from using the International Settlement as a base of operations.[66] The *China Weekly Review* noted bitterly that "by its unprecedented action, undoubtedly caused by the Council's anxiety to placate the belligerent Japanese Army, the Council has arbitrarily appointed Gendarmes [Military Police] as the Supreme Court and the Chief Executioner and, simultaneously, made the possession of arms—a simple felony—a crime punishable by death."[67]

The next day, July 20, Criminal Investigation Department detectives took young Jiang Haisheng to the Garden Bridge, thereafter known as the "Bridge of Sighs," and handed him over to the Japanese Military Police.[68] When news of this was released to the public on July 26, after the Zheng Yuebo killing, there was an instant public outcry:

> By this immature move, the foreign "City Fathers" have in effect given a pledge to cooperate with the invading military forces in hunting down Chinese patriots and groups resisting the rape of their country. . . . There is . . . practically one hundred percent disapproval of the police action in handing the prisoners over *without public trial,* to the Japanese executioners. . . .

The action of the Council in handing the Chinese young man over to the Japanese Army probably has done more to foster Bolshevist sentiment here than anything which has happened since the Nationalist Revolution in 1927.[69]

The *Hankow Herald* editorially castigated the Shanghai Municipal Council, arguing that it had no legal right, even during the emergency, to surrender criminal jurisdiction to Japanese authorities. Yet even though the Chinese government on July 27, 1938, filed a formal protest with the British and U.S. governments, arguing that the handing over of Jiang Haisheng was a violation of the Shanghai Provisional Court Agreement, the Shanghai Municipal Police continued to convey suspected terrorists across the Bridge of Sighs, pushing them through Japanese lines into the arms of the Military Police.[70]

The assassination of Zheng Yuebo

The arrest of Jiang Haisheng by the French Police had no discernible effect on the terrorist activity of the Sun Yaxing squad, which regrouped after the July 7 bombings. By then, the seventeen-year-old Chen Kaiguang had brought his younger brother, Chen Kaiyuan, into the group.[71] Zhao Liang put both of them up in his room at a lodging house at 276 rue Eugene Bard.[72] While the more experienced members of the squad, with Special Services Corps backgrounds, were busy bringing about the assassination of Van Chi-sen on July 21, the two Cantonese adolescents were being prepared for a strike against Zheng Yuebao, a sixty-three-year-old Chinese who had become a Japanese subject several years earlier.[73]

On July 16, after Zhao Gangyi had informed Sun Yaxing that Zheng Yuebao was a traitor and supplied Sun with intelligence as to his whereabouts, Zhou Shougang gave Chen Kaiguang a written description of the target and instructions to reconnoiter.[74] Three nights later, Chen was ordered to report to Sun Yaxing in the French Park. They met at the southwest corner about 8 o'clock. Sun told him that he and his brother had been "elected" to assassinate Zheng, and he gave him two pistols taken from the cache at the Yamei Watch and Clock Shop. Chen Kaiguang took the pistols and returned to his room at rue Eugene Bard.[75]

The next two mornings Chen Kaiguang and Chen Kaiyuan waited near the bus stop at Jessfield and Tifeng Roads, but their victim did not appear. On the morning of July 22nd, at 9:10 a.m., Zheng Yuebao came down the street toward the bus stop. Chen Kaiguang waited, while his brother stood on the other side of the street. When Zheng Yuebao walked past Chen Kaiguang, the seventeen-year-old took out his pistol, wheeled, and shot Zheng twice in the back. Zheng Yuebao staggered toward a wall for cover but collapsed before he could reach it.[76] Just then a mounted policeman—Sergeant H. Edgar—came upon the scene and chased Kaiguang down the street, exchanging shots with the assassin. Chen's gun jammed, and he threw it down just before the policeman jumped off his horse and arrested him. Unnoticed, his younger brother slipped away.[77]

The police were surprised by Chen Kaiguang's youth ("A youngster of about eighteen years of age, Chen looks like anything but a killer. He is a tall youth, slender and round-shouldered"), which made him all the more vulnerable to interrogation.[78] This was when Sun Yaxing's foolhardy mixing of teams and careless recruitment of last-minute agents proved fatal to the ring. Not only did Chen Kaiguang confess everything, including the fact that Sun Yaxing was the leader of the terrorist group; he was able to reveal the names and addresses of other team members.[79]

The raids began immediately, starting with the planting of a squad of detectives at 276 rue Eugene Bard. An hour after Chen's arrest, Wang Zhigu's mistress, Wang Aju, was seized. Zhao Liang and Zhou Shougang were picked up shortly afterwards, and by evening the police had Sun Yaxing's name and address. Sun was arrested at 11:00 p.m. while he was waiting for his courier; and the Yamei Watch and Clock Store was raided at 11:30, its remaining arsenal seized. All in all, ten suspects were in custody by midnight, and the raids went on into the next morning when Wang Zhigu and Zhu Zhonghu walked into a police stakeout at Sun Yaxing's apartment.[80] Forty-eight hours after the Zheng killing, twenty-four terrorist suspects were in custody. Of these, the ten who had confessed complicity in the Zheng Yuebao affair were going to be turned over to the Japanese Military Police, following the recent agreement between the Shanghai Municipal Council and the Japanese authorities.[81]

This was hardly the end of it. Though Chen Kaiguang had given the French and Settlement police the address of Jin Yingsheng and Zhao Gangyi's lodgings on route de Siours, the detectives' raid of the premises yielded only the information that the suspects were "of the student type."[82] Thus, the main leader, Zhao Gangyi, got away, and may well have continued to lead other Special Services Corps operations in months to come. Sun Yaxing told the police, after all: "From the fact that there were a number of anti-traitor assassinations other than those committed by the squad under my control, I concluded there must in Shanghai be more than one assassination group working on a line similar to that adopted by my squad. I do not know them because we have been working independently from each other."[83]

The Shanghai Municipal Police could not but concur. There had to be other Chinese Nationalist squads working underground in Shanghai, waiting for the chance to emerge and strike again. Try as they might to prepare for various wartime anniversaries, creating the appearance in Shanghai of an "armed camp," the four sectors' authorities could only watch and wait as terrorists from both sides mustered for a much more intense struggle to come.[84]

4

Retaliation: Pro-Japanese terrorism

There were two major pro-Japanese societies active in Shanghai at this time, both founded around January 1938. The more respectable of the two was the China Rehabilitation and Public Welfare Society (Zhongguo fuxing gongyi hui), the stated aims of which were to accelerate the movement to restore peace between China and Japan, to establish a new order in the Orient, and to bring about the rehabilitation and public welfare of the Chinese.[1] Whereas the Rehabilitation Society was generally directed toward propaganda work, especially in newspaper circles, the second major pro-Japanese group, the Chinese Imperial/Yellow Way Society (Zhonghua huang/huang daohui), was devoted to "special work" and terrorism.[2]

The Rehabilitation and Yellow Way Societies

The Rehabilitation Society was subsidized by the Japanese military headquarters and controlled by a Japanese agent named Kimura. The society's puppet chairman, Liu Song, and puppet vice-chairman were each paid $500 per month; and the chiefs of its five departments (secretariat, special services, general affairs, social affairs, economic rehabilitation) were each paid $360. Since members were given up to $180 apiece, and there were additional expenses for servants, rent, gasoline, and so forth, the total monthly subsidy was $23,000.[3]

The regulations for the society were drafted by a somewhat shady character named Yang Kya-chu [Yang Jiachu]. Yang, who was known to everyone as "Colonel Walter Yang," had gone to work for a U.S. law firm after graduating from St. John's University. Accused of embezzlement, he was caught trying to set fire to the office and its records, and had served a term in the Ward Road jail before becoming Manchurian warlord Zhang Zuolin's English interpreter. Colonel Yang had also served as an intelligence officer in the Shandong army of the infamous Zhang Zongchang, and from there he had gone on to head the Japanese intelligence department in the Nationalist Chinese espionage service. Dismissed for obscure reasons, Yang then went to work for a foreign detective bureau in Shanghai, but once again there were charges of embezzlement and he found himself jobless when the war with Japan began. Because of his background as a legal clerk, the Japanese hired him to draft the constitution for the Rehabilitation Society, and he quickly rose to become chief of the General Affairs Department.[4]

If Colonel Walter Yang seemed shady, the head of the Chinese Imperial/ Yellow Way Society (Zhonghua huang/huang daohui), a "notorious Kompo [Jiangbei] loafer" named Chang Yuqing, was downright sinister. A monstrous 315-pound gangster, "Two-Ton Chang" was a former butcher and wharf coolie who, like many Subei racketeers, owned bathhouses and theaters around the Chinese sectors of Shanghai. A close friend of Gu Zhuxuan, the leader of the Subei faction within the Green Gang, Chang Yuqing was serving as chairman of the North Jiangsu Residents Guild when the Japanese took over Zhabei in January 1932. During that four-month occupation of northern Shanghai six years earlier, Two-Ton Chang was the Japanese Military Police's choice for native chief of police; and when the Japanese finally left Zhabei in May 1932, Chang Yuqing was forced to depart with them, fleeing to Dalian (Dairen) in Manchuria.[5]

When the Japanese military came back to Shanghai in 1937, he returned in its van, setting up the Yellow Way Society to recruit Green Gang hoodlums for special operations under the aegis of the Japanese Special Services Corps represented by Special Agent Konomi.[6] The Yellow Way Society and the Rehabilitation Society cooperated closely out of the rented rooms at the New Asia Hotel (Xinya jiulou), where Mayor Fu Xiaoan also stayed under Japanese Military Police protection.[7] The Yellow Way Society had affiliates as well in the Shanghai Seamen's Labor Union under Dong Youxian (an agent of the Japanese Special Services Corps), and in the Shanghai Wharf General Labor Union under Shen Wenyuan.[8]

Shortly after the Rehabilitation Society was founded, the publisher of *Shehui wanbao* (Social Evening News), Cai Zaodu (Tsai Tsao-tu), approached Colonel Walter Yang through a mutual friend. Cai's newspaper had been shut down by the Shanghai Municipal Council, allegedly because of a protest by the Japanese, and he hoped to foster a friendship with the now powerful Colonel Yang, whose Japanese backers might be persuaded to withdraw their opposition. The two men became sworn brothers, often seen in restaurants and teahouses together. Special Agent Kimura, however, told Yang that Cai was actually a spy for the Hankou government. Cai tried to clear himself by showing Liu Song, the head of the Rehabilitation Society, a document from General Yang Hu (former Wusong Garrison Commander) ordering the suspension of *Shehui wanbao*. This backfired, as language in the document seemed to implicate Cai Zaodu even more. On February 5, 1938, Walter Yang invited Cai to a dinner party at the New Asia Hotel given by Liu Song and Konomi, the special agent in charge of the Yellow Way Society.[9] Near the end of dinner he was asked by Walter Yang and Konomi to report to a room on the sixth floor where Chang Yuqing's Yellow Way gangsters lay in wait.[10] Two days later Cai Zaodu's freshly washed head was found on the pavement near the French police station on route Stanislaus Chevalier.[11]

The Yellow Way Society conducted other terrorist activities as well, including the bombing of the China Travel Service and two radio stations on June 12.[12] But it was the Cai Zaodu decapitation and Japanese-led agitation on August 13 that made the society notorious and that led to its dissolution.

On August 13 there was very little by way of anti-Japanese activity. Rather, in all sectors of the city anti-Nationalist incidents were instigated by members of the Special Services Corps of the Japanese army or by members of the Yellow Way Society. Antiforeign and anti–Chiang Kai-shek leaflets were distributed from cars bearing Japanese "Shanghai Defense Force" license plates or dropped from airplanes, shopkeepers displaying Chinese flags were threatened with pistols or assaulted, and the Chinese superintendent in the Shanghai Municipal Police in charge of antiterrorist activities was murdered by gunmen connected with the Huangdao hui.[13] Altogether sixteen Japanese were arrested in the Western District (Huxi), most of them dressed as Chinese and carrying arms.[14]

In the Huxi sector patrolled by U.S. forces, three plainclothes members of the Western Shanghai Squad (Caojiadu station) of the Japanese Special Services Corps were forcing a Chinese store owner to haul down a Guomindang flag when U.S. Marines approached. The Japanese ran to their car and tried to escape. Sergeant "Slug" Marvin, an ex–prize fighter, jumped on the running board and, when one of the Japanese agents put a gun to his throat, drew his own automatic and aimed it at the driver's head. The driver stopped the car and drove to the Pudu (Pootoo) police station, but refused to leave the car. When the Marines removed them, one of the agents, Hiroshi Yoshizaki, suffered a badly banged head. This, and similar incidents elsewhere in the city, led to an exchange of protests between the Japanese military authorities and the Shanghai Municipal Council.[15] In the end, the Japanese consul general admitted only to responsibility for the incidents perpetrated by Japanese Army Special Services Corps personnel seized in foreign defense force sectors of the city, and denied any connection with other acts of terrorism, which seemed most unlikely given the confessions of several members of the Yellow Way Society.[16]

The assassination of a Criminal Investigation Division superintendent, Cai Zaodu, by members of the Yellow Way Society precipitated an indictment. The trial was held September 17, 1938. Colonel Walter Yang was convicted of the slaying and given a life sentence in jail. Zong Bing (Zung Bing), who implicated the the Japanese agent Konomi, and Zong Sihkong, who placed the severed head in the French Concession, both got three-year sentences. All three of these men were also associated with the Rehabilitation Society. The fourth person, Xu Duling (Hsu Tuh-ling), claimed to know of neither the Yellow Way Society nor the Rehabilitation Society. Rather, he testified that he was only a janitor at the New Asia Hotel who was forced against his will to wash Cai's bloody head. Nonetheless he was given a four-year jail sentence.[17]

The corpulent Chang Yuqing, meanwhile, had left Shanghai, more or less dissolving the Yellow Way Society.[18] His plan was, with Japanese backing and under the guidance of Special Agent Shimizu (former chief of the consular police of Nanjing), to organize a region-wide association of Green Gang members in Anhui, Jiangzu, and Zhejiang under the banner of the Anqing League (Anqing tongmenghui), which invoked the name of the eighteenth-century predecessor of the Green Gang, the Anqing bang (Pacify the Qing Fleet), organized by Grand Canal boatmen transporting tribute grain.[19] Instead of setting up branches along the imperial canal system, Chang set up chapters of the Anqing League along the Nanjing–Shanghai and Shanghai–Hangzhou railway lines, with headquarters in the former office of the Mongolian and Tibetan Affairs Commissioner in Nanjing.[20]

On December 6, 1938, Chang Yuqing inaugurated the Anqing League in Nanjing.[21] Three hundred Green Gang members met before an incense-shrouded altar containing the spirit tablet of Weng Dehui, a late Ming cult leader said to be one of the ancestral founders of the Qing bang. Over the altar hung the Japanese and five-barred flags. The new members took an oath in front of the altar. Speeches about the history of the league, the meaning of its full title (*Anguo qingmin*—Bring Peace to the Country and Brightness to the People), and the purpose of its founding were given by Chang Yuqing and several others.[22] "The function ended with cheering for peace in the Orient, the Imperial Government of Japan, the Republic of China, the Reform Government, and the Anqing League."[23]

That same day, Shanghai branch members held a meeting of their own at 31 Lane 1136 Yuyuan (Yu Yuen) Road, a house ostensibly occupied by a Japanese named K. Hanano. The participants were described in police reports as being former members of the Yellow Way Society, and their leaders were identified as Fu Shaotang and Zhao Wanyi, "both being well-known loafers in the Gordon and Pootoo Road districts."[24] These same reports estimated that, in February 1939, the Anqing League had 700 members in Shanghai. Their chief task was "combatting the Kuomintang [Guomindang] and Communist influence in Shanghai," mainly through terroristic activities, which were under the general direction of Chang Yuqing in Nanjing. At this they were quite ineffective. All of the assassinations and bombings between December 1938 and February 1939 were the work of pro-Chongqing loyalists, and Chang himself felt obliged to come secretly to Hongkou on February 10 to shake up the Shanghai branch of the Anqing League in person. He dismissed Fu Shaotang and Zhao Wanyi, and brought in five new leaders he could trust to be effective: one being a relative, and two being former lieutenants in the Yellow Way Society. The League's new religious "master" (*shifu*) was Feng Zongzhang. Zhang Jisheng (Chang's relative) was made director of the General Affairs Office, which managed finances; Dong Youxian was appointed chief of the Central Branch, Shen Wenyuan chief of the Southern Division (French Concession), and Sun Shuzong chief of the Western Division (Huxi). Sun, formerly a detective in the Shanghai Public Security Bureau, owned three gambling dens on Jessfield Road in the heart of the badlands.[25]

Chang Yuqing had to flee from Shanghai the moment this shakeup was accomplished because a warrant for his arrest as "the director of the terroristic activities within the Settlement" had been issued by the First Special District Court at the request of the Shanghai Municipal Police. But Chang left instructions to redouble efforts against the Guomindang and Communist Party, and promised monetary rewards should Anqing League members "succeed in locating and apprehending active members of the two parties, chiefly members of the assassination gangs and propagandists in Shanghai."[26] By June, the first of several pro-Nanjing terrorist incidents occurred, which is perhaps what prompted a Nationalist retaliation, probably organized by Dai Li on August 13, 1939 (the second anniversary of the beginning of the war in Shanghai). While walking along a street in Nanjing, surrounded by his bodyguards, Chang Yuqing was gunned down by seven assailants. Chang's bodyguards wounded or killed the assassins, but they failed to save the huge gangster, who died of his wounds.[27]

Terrorist waves, August 1938–January 1939

Although both sides engaged in bombings and assassinations, the Chinese loyalists, or Nationalist resistants, predominated during the fall and early winter, when there was a relative abatement of activity. Chen Yun, the thirty-two-year-old lawyer who was chairman of the Shanghai–Nandao District Administration and who was being considered for the presidency of the puppet Nandao District Court, was shot on August 30, 1938, as a kind of finale to what had been a month of high tension and frayed nerves.[28]

September, on the other hand, turned out be relatively less fretful. On September 13, two bombs were tossed through the front door of the Chinese Import and Export Company on rue du Consulat; two employees were injured.[29] Three days later two hand grenades were thrown into a crowd at the south end of the Sichuan Road Bridge, wounding a dozen people.[30] All of the authorities took special precautions on September 18, the seventh anniversary of the Mukden incident, but precisely because of the extra armed patrols, the street barricades and searches for concealed weapons, and the careful vetting of hotel clients, "the day passed off without any incident whatsoever." Altogether, during the entire month of September, there were only five incidents resulting in fifteen injuries and two deaths.[31] One of the latter, however, was the assassination on September 30, 1938, of the prominent political figure Tang Shaoyi, whom General Doihara was hoping would become president of the Nanjing puppet government.[32]

In 1938 the main endeavor of Prime Minister Konoye's strategy vis-à-vis China was to persuade a notable Chinese politician to form a central government under Tokyo's control in order to make a peace settlement. The three most likely choices then were Cao Kun, Wu Peifu, and Tang Shaoyi. Cao Kun passed away. Wu Peifu had no intention of assuming responsibility unless Japan withdrew its troops. That left Tang Shaoyi, who indicated his willingness to become head of a new national government.[33]

When Zhou Weilong, Juntong's Shanghai station chief, received word that Tang Shaoyi was negotiating with the Japanese, he decided to recommend his assassination. Dai Li concurred. As was often the case, the Juntong "action group" (*xingdong zu*) got to Tang Shaoyi through a relative, Xie Zhipan, who also worked for the Military Statistics Bureau. From Xie, Juntong action group chief Zhao Lijun learned that Tang Shaoyi was an avid antiques collector. He and the other members of the assassination squad, Xiang Qingwei and Lin Zhijiang, took a rare antique vase and placed it in a box with a false bottom, within which was a small, keenly honed hatchet.[34] Introduced by Xie Zhipan, they brought it into Tang Shaoyi's living room, and while he was admiring the vase, one of the men reached into the box, pulled out the hatchet and chopped Tang's head, killing him on the sofa.[35] The death of so famous a personage led to extensive police raids, but Xiang Qingwei and Xie Zhipan managed to escape to Chongqing via Hong Kong and the case was never solved.[36]

The second terrorist wave, also greatly diminished, ran from October to late November 1938, culminating in an attempt to assassinate the puppet mayor of Shanghai, Fu Xiaoan. During October, there were eight attempted assassinations, three resulting in death.[37] There were several murders and attempted assassinations in November, but many of these were not politically motivated.[38] On November 25, however, Mayor Fu Xiaoan was nearly killed—not by Hankou-despatched assassins, but by an assailant within the ranks of the puppet government.

That morning, Mayor Fu left his residence in the New Asia Hotel by car, with a Japanese military policeman at his side and two Chinese bodyguards following in a motorcycle with a sidecar. The automobile reached the Special Municipality building in Jiangwan at 9:50 a.m. As the mayor got out of his car, a uniformed policeman stepped forward and fired at him, missing. Fu fell to the ground in fear. The Japanese bodyguard started to draw his weapon and the policeman turned and felled him with three shots. Then he ran until he was cornered, and turned his gun upon himself. The Japanese soldiers cut out his heart and liver and placed them before the killed Japanese gendarme as a sacrifice.[39]

The assailant was Zhou Wenshan, a twenty-year-old graduate of the pre-Occupation police academy from Hubei. He had joined the puppet Guard Corps under former Dadao mayor Su Xiwen on the recommendation of Jiang Tongyi, an inspector in the police academy of the puppet government.[40] The Japanese Military Police immediately sent a squad to arrest Jiang, but three days earlier he had left his home with family in tow. The next day the Japanese military arrested Chen Jintao, the chief of the Guard Corps, and thirty of his subordinates, all of whom were taken to the ominous headquarters of the Military Police in Hongkou.[41] Other recommenders, or guarantors, of Zhou Wenshan among the officers of the puppet police and police training depot were also arrested by the Japanese Military Police.[42] It would have been natural to suspect the Nationalist Juntong, with its still-strong connections among the Shanghai police, of inciting this daring assassination attempt. But the Japanese Military Police appears to have concluded, after extensive interrogations, that the officers and men of the Guard Corps were acting on behalf of their ousted Dadao chief, Su Xiwen, in an internal puppet struggle against Fu Xiaoan.[43] That was scant consolation to Fu, who went into such a shock over the shooting that he was hospitalized in the Fuming Hospital for the following ten days.[44]

There was no third terrorist wave. Shanghai quieted down during

December and January, and the next major incident was not a bombing or dramatic public assassination but rather the quiet, professionally managed murder of a major Japanese intelligence agent by Nationalist secret servicemen.

The death of Ma Yuhang

At 7:00 p.m. on January 29, 1939, the room boys at the Sun Sun [Xinxin] Hotel heard pistol shots from the direction of Room 605, occupied by a man whom they knew as Ma Yuhang. When they let themselves into Room 605 they found Mr. Ma lying on his back in a large pool of blood with a bullet wound in his right temple. He seemed to have been shot while sitting at his table reading a biography of Mussolini. The staff of the hotel, which was over the Sun Sun [Xinxin] Department Store on Guizhou Road, called the Louza police station at 7:06, and Ma was conveyed immediately to the Chinese Lester Hospital, where he died at 9:45 without ever regaining consciousness.[45]

When the police searched his remains, they found a special pass with his photograph, and the name Ma Yuhang, identified as a native of Fujian, forty-two years old, who served as an advisor to the executive yuan of the Reform Government. The pass, which was issued by the Japanese and signed by the president of the legislative yuan of the Reform Government, entitled the bearer to enter Nanjing, Hongkou, and Jiangwan. Back in Room 605, the Criminal Investigation Division also found an empty cartridge case. Ballistic analysis of the case and its fired bullet proved that the assassin had used a Demon .32 caliber automatic, number 1306, found by the Shanghai Municipal Police at the scene of an armed robbery in 1930 and confiscated by the Shanghai Special District Court. Because court records showed that the gun had been turned over in March 1934 to the Shanghai–Wusong Garrison Command, the Division had good reason to believe that Ma had been murdered at Dai Li's orders by one of Juntong's special operations squads.[46]

The curious circumstances of the assassination were already inspiring melodramatic headlines in the press—"Mystery Man Murdered in Local Hotel," "Mystery Shrouds Shooting"—but in this case the confidential investigation was yielding even more sensational evidence than journalists might have supposed.[47] The newspapers reported correctly that Ma Yuhang had worked for the Japanese occupation forces in Canton, serving as chief of the Finance Bureau of the Guangdong Provincial Government, but they fell short of the truth when they identified him as likely being the secretary of the Japanese-sponsored Nanjing municipal government.[48]

Shortly after the shooting, the police had learned from the room boys that during his stay at the hotel, Ma Yuhang was visited daily by five or six men, all well dressed and speaking Mandarin.[49] When they actually examined Ma's effects, the inspectors found his address book, which contained hundreds of names, ranging from policemen and compradores to businessmen and politicians.[50] They also found three extremely interesting documents:[51]

"Matters to Be Carried Out in South China"—A schedule and arrangements for subverting the "men in power" in Guangdong and for establishing intelligence services in Shanghai and Nanjing. A budget of $150,000 was included for press propaganda.[52]

"Organization of a News Agency"—An outline for organizing a press agency to influence the press in Hong Kong and conduct propaganda work among Chinese residents in America and the South Sea Islands, pursuant to the instructions of the new special services department that was to be organized.[53]

"Organization of a Boxing Expedition Group (*Quantaotuan*)"—A proposal to form a special action group for Wang Jingwei supporters in Guangdong. The group would act under the orders of the special services department and "enforce the 'iron and blood' policy which is to deal with reactionaries by means of force." There would be district units around Hong Kong and Kowloon, and a mobile unit to collect intelligence and conduct special operations including assassination.[54]

Ma Yuhang was evidently engaged in considerably more than serving as a political counselor to the Reform Government.

This was secretly confirmed the morning of January 30 just before an inquest was to be held at the public mortuary. Special Branch received a telephone call from the Shanghai Telephone Company saying that one of their Chinese staff members wished to provide anonymous information about the Ma Yuhang case. During a convincing face-to-face conversation with a detective sergeant, this person—"a male Chinese from Formosa"—identified Ma as a friend since 1918, when the informant worked for the Guangdong Provincial Government and Ma Yuhang was chief of the provincial Ministry of Finance, serving directly under General Chen Jiongming. Ma was then on very good terms with Cai Xiangsheng—a Nikkajin (lit. Japanese–Chinese person) who spoke impeccable Japanese—who was a close associate of Wang Jingwei. After Chen Jiongming was overthrown, Ma and Cai evaded arrest by fleeing to Japan. Cai entered Tokyo University and remained in Japan when Ma Yuhang returned to China to join Wang Jingwei's faction and serve as a counselor for the Military Affairs Commission of the Nanjing government.[55]

When hostilities broke out in July–August 1937, Cai Xiangsheng succeeded in obtaining positions in several puppet organizations, and a year later became chief of the Japanese special services political section under General Tanaka. In December, after Wang Jingwei broke with Chiang Kai-shek, Cai went to Hong Kong and recruited Ma, who returned with him to Shanghai on January 1, 1939, to become assistant chief of the Japanese Special Services Corps political section at 483 Bund Road, Apartment 4. He had since then been living in Shanghai at Cai's expense, moving from one hotel to another until he met his death in Room 605 at the Sun Sun.[56]

If there were any doubts about the basic veracity of the Formosan's account, they were dispelled for the Criminal Investigation Division when Ma Yuhang's son, together with Cai Xiangsheng and representatives of the Japanese Special Services Corps, showed up at the mortuary to claim Ma's remains. Ma Yuhang's assassin was never found.[57] His death, along with the imprisonment of Colonel Yang and the death of Two-Ton Chang, thus marked a setback for the Japanese Special Services agents and their Chinese collaborators. As daily survival in *gudao* Shanghai grew more and more difficult, the terrorist initiative was seized by the Nationalist agents bent upon spectacular assassinations of senior puppet officials designed to discourage collaboration across the board.

5

Provocation: The Chen Lu assassination

The prosperity of the refugee-driven economy of 1937–1938 began to wane by the fall of 1939, when it became clear that the Japanese were going to keep the Yangzi River closed to commercial and passenger traffic and thus cut Shanghai off from much of its hinterland:[1]

> In Shanghai commodity prices, like a kite with its string broken in the wind, soared high above the ground as though they had achieved Nirvana and immortality. Public workers struck again and again. Trams and buses wished they could have hung out "Full House" signs like movie theaters and hotels. Copper and nickel coins were all confiscated. Stamps were temporarily put to a new use as supplementary currency. If only people could have been sent like mail, then the painfully crowded conditions on public buses could have been avoided. The struggle for survival was gradually stripped of mask and ornament to reveal a primitive brutality. A reasonable sense of shame was not cheap at all; many could not afford it.[2]

During 1940 the Shanghai stock market went out of control. Speculators quoted "war baby" shares at outlandishly high values, and the exchange "dashed up and down with every rumor."[3]

In May 1940 hoarders purchased huge stocks of cotton at $1,000 per bale and stored them in warehouses, holding up both the domestic market and foreign trading companies waiting to ship cotton goods to Europe via French Indochina. By the end of the month they had run the price up to $2,000. On June 25, France signed an armistice with Germany and Italy, and Japan promptly pressured the Vichy authorities at Haiphong to close the port to vessels from China. The artificially inflated cotton market collapsed. Over fifty import–export companies went bankrupt; requests for margin could not be met with money so tight, and quotations on the stock market fell sharply as well.[4] "Rackets! Large rackets, small rackets, mammoth rackets like the cotton yarn affair, depriving people of necessities and endangering the life of the whole city."[5]

By early 1941 there was a peculiar prosperity about Shanghai, different from the highly stratified prosperity of 1937–1938 just after the war with Japan began. It was next to impossible to get a room reservation (except for the vastly overpriced Cathay Hotel), and even to take in a weekend movie required advance booking. Nightclubs were packed:

> Life among the Americans and British seemed to follow pretty much the pre-'37 pattern, though with rather more dining and dancing than before and certainly more drinking. Most of these people were in the employ of the large firms, so their salaries were in American dollars or pounds sterling, and, with the Chinese dollar falling, it was easy to imagine the halcyon days were back—at least for the moment. But underneath, Shanghai was already suffering from a creeping miasmic fever, and there was the ominous gathering confusion of a household where someone is falling very sick indeed.[6]

This fever was the symptom of inflation, which struck white-collar and blue-collar labor alike.[7]

If the cost of living of Shanghai workers in 1936 is indexed at 100, then in March 1941 the price of foodstuffs was 774; of rent, 385; of clothing, 503; of fuel, 636; and of miscellaneous goods, 599.[8] Nandao, which boomed after the Japanese military occupied Southern Shanghai in November 1937, stagnated.[9] The busy market where one could buy jade, goldfish, and tropical birds in 1937 was deserted in 1941 except for a few poor persons bargaining for noodles and rice. In the once-crowded Temple of the City God, beggars slept on the floor below the dusty idols.[10]

When the journalist Vanya Oakes left Shanghai in 1940, just as Japanese puppets were being picked off right and left, she reported a do-or-die determination to resist the aggressor. When she returned in 1941, she could feel the collapse of Chinese spirit. Why, she asked her Chinese friends, had they become so passive and accepting of the Japanese occupation? Their answer was simply "rice."[11] According to Oakes, the Japanese used rice as a weapon to dominate Shanghai much as Hitler used the control of food supplies to subjugate Europe. The ominous, steady deterioration of morale in occupied China was intimately connected to the seizure of rice in Indochina by the Japanese. That is, Chinese rice grown in the provinces was used to feed the Japanese army or the civilian population in Japan. Cities such as Tianjin and Shanghai, therefore, had been living on rice imported from Indochina, so that "when Japan secured control of Indochina's entire output of nearly six million tons, she naturally came into possession of a weapon with which to force 'cooperation' upon Occupied China."[12]

This weapon was also used very concretely as a means of social control.

For example, there were five cases of Japanese being shot between September 29 and October 18, 1940. In retaliation, the Japanese Military Police sealed off the lanes of suspected areas, and "subjected [them] to a vigorous blockade, which in some sections was sustained long enough, according to current reports, to cause several deaths through starvation."[13]

Rice shortages and inflated prices shortened tempers and inflamed public opinion.[14] On August 23, 1939, the price of rice had risen from $40 to $45 a *picul*. As usual, profiteers were blamed for the hike. That evening "loafers" twice tried to sack a rice store on Ferry Road, and a mob smashed down the doors and windows of a pharmacy on Ward Road where grain was reputedly stored. The following day five more rice shops were stoned and looted in Huxi.[15] Although the government tried to formulate food distribution systems, by January 1941 long lines of customers, mainly women and children who had the time to wait, stretched in front of most rice stores, requiring the presence of police to maintain order and prevent riots.[16] On March 15, 1941, the Shanghai Municipal Police and a Chinese team had a soccer match at the Canidrome in the French Concession. After a foul, a Chinese player was ordered off the field. His fellow teammates marched off with him, causing the 20,000 Chinese spectators to stream onto the field, tear up the goal posts, and throw stones and bricks at the policemen who tried to break up the riot. Police reinforcements and the fire brigade, which turned its hoses on the crowd, managed to force the rioters out into the street. More than thirty people were injured.[17] This riot was taken as a sign of worse to come should rice prices continue to rise, and both the Wang Jingwei puppet and the two foreign settlements' régimes bought what rice they could to distribute or sell at a considerable discount in order to keep the lid on at a time when political relations with the Japanese and the puppet government were increasingly strained.[18]

Police sovereignty

One major source of strain was long-standing: the question of police jurisdiction over the extra-boundary roads outside the International Settlement and French Concession. For over fifteen years, the Chinese police and the foreign settlements' police had struggled over these roads and the properties built along them.[19] The contest, which was partly resolved by 1931, flared anew when Japan and China went to war. And it intensified throughout 1938 and 1939 as crime and vice thrived in the badlands of Western Shanghai.[20]

On January 22, 1939, copies of a notice from the Western Branch of the Shanghai Police Bureau were posted outside the various stations (*suo*) and substations of the puppet police throughout Huxi. They read:

> It is a custom that the residents in the extra-Settlement road area in the Western District report all cases relating to peace and order to the Settlement Police. Such procedure is wrong, for the Shanghai Municipal Police have jurisdiction over the roads only and not the areas between these roads, which are Chinese-controlled territories. The people in the Western District are hereby warned that hereafter they should report all cases to the Western Branch Police Bureau instead of to the Shanghai Municipal Police.[21]

The notices were signed by Wang Delin, head of the Western Branch Bureau.

At that time—January 1939—the Western Branch Bureau of the puppet police did not have the manpower to bring law and order to Huxi, especially since the number of opium and gambling establishments was growing daily.[22] But police chief Lu Ying was also steadily increasing the size of his force in the Western District: from 64 constables in January to 230 in early February, approximately half of whom carried pistols or rifles while on patrol.[23] The puppet constables were also backed up by the Kaneya Military Police Detachment at 94 Jessfield Road, adjoining the Western Branch Bureau at Number 92; the Japanese Military Police supplied eight machine guns to the Chinese police, but withheld ammunition until the need arose.[24]

As its ranks in Huxi swelled, the Chinese police grew more assertive toward the Shanghai Municipal Police, having been instructed by the Shanghai city government "to stiffen its attitude toward the Settlement authorities regarding matters concerning jurisdiction over the extra-Settlement [area] in the Western District."[25] The Western Bureau was also able to reduce the number of men on patrol to six groups of five fully armed constables by dint of issuing five rounds of ammunition per weapon instead of just one bullet. This meant that fewer constables were issued weapons, reducing the risk of mutiny, while also meeting Wang Delin's request for more ammunition because armed gangsters proliferated in Huxi and the areas around the gambling and drug dens required better-equipped patrols.[26]

By April 1939, the regular police roster of the Shanghai puppet government had grown to 5,155 members, an increase of nearly 60 percent since February.[27] On April 10, the Japanese Special Services Section also established a Military Armed Police (Wuzhuang jingcha) force consisting of 400 Chinese guerrillas who had surrendered, along with their weapons, in return for a one-time payment of $10 and the promise of $20 a month thereafter. The Military Armed Police was headquartered at Huangjiahua yuan in the Western District under the command of Han Jun, a former brigadier general in Wu Peifu's service.[28] The Japanese Special Services Section advisor was one Colonel Nishimura, and the intelligence office or detective squad was headed by Gu Zhuhua and Hu Anbang, "a follower of the Green Gang" who formerly was "a trafficker in narcotics."[29] The Japanese planned eventually to enroll 15,000 paramilitary policemen in the Military Armed Police, arming each with a rifle and fifty rounds of ammunition. Two hundred of these puppet gendarmes, who were paid $30 a month to combat guerrillas, were stationed at police headquarters; the remainder were distributed equally among branch bureaus (*fenju*) in the Western District and Pudong, where loyalist guerrillas had been ousted in March by regular Japanese forces.[30] In May 1939, a former magistrate who had once served as a detective sub-inspector in the Shanghai Municipal Police was appointed chief of staff of the Military Armed Police, which was given legal jurisdiction in Pudong over criminal cases involving anti-Japanese elements.[31]

Some measure of the appearance of these hastily recruited rowdies can be gleaned from the following incident. On May 21, 1939, four of these new plainclothes constables attached to the Military Armed Police headquarters entered a gambling den on Connaught Road. After they took their seats, each "policeman" took out a Mauser pistol and placed it on his chair. Regular puppet police inspectors in the casino mistook them for armed robbers and called for assistance.[32] It was only when a larger party of police descended on the scene that it was discovered that these toughs were formally appointed plainclothes constables belonging to the Military Armed Police.[33]

For the Shanghai Municipal Police, these new puppet police were no better than bandits, and the situation in the badlands was simply out of control. Ballistic reports showed that 90 percent of the armed crimes in which pistols were seized or bullets recovered were committed with "hot" weapons stolen from Chinese and Sikh constables while they were on duty in the badlands.[34] On January 4, 1939, eight gangsters engaged in a running gun battle with Shanghai Municipal Police officers there. That same night, twelve Britons and Americans returning to their homes from the Columbia Country Club were robbed by armed gangsters right in front of the Columbia and Great Western Roads substation. The puppet police made no effort to intervene.[35]

In the International Settlement and French Concession, longtime foreign residents believed that the "carnival of crime" flourishing in Huxi's badlands was almost entirely owing to the protection that criminals received from the puppet Reform Government's regular police and from the

secret police force at 76 Jessfield Road, to which miscreants routinely fled
for asylum:[36]

> "No. 76" . . . is the center not only of local political gangsterdom, but is
> known to harbor murderers, thieves, thugs, holdup men, and all other man-
> ner of fugitives from the Settlement and Concession police. "No. 76" also
> has held kidnapped Chinese awaiting ransom and other Chinese who disap-
> peared through its gates to be heard of no more.[37]

In 1946, after the Japanese were defeated and some of the most notorious
collaborators were being put on trial, S. B. Wong, general manager of the
China General Machinery Corporation (which in 1939 and 1940 minted
215 million aluminum coins on behalf of the Nationalist Ministry of
Finance for use in the foreign settlements), recounted the circumstances of
his own imprisonment by the "puppet gestapo" in the "black hole of
Shanghai." Although he himself was not tortured, he was handcuffed,
chained, and forced to sleep on two cold tombstone blocks in a hole
beneath a straw hut before he managed to buy his way out of "76" with
the help of tycoon Yu Xiaqing.[38]

The Special Services Corps of "76" had eight or more different squads
of backbone cadres, located in police suboffices around the badlands on
extra-Settlement roads (Jessfield, Singapore, Edinburgh, Connaught,
Brenan, and so forth).[39] Each suboffice had five members armed with
pistols. Four of the five conducted three-month training classes for groups
of twenty members each, who eventually constituted assassination squads
such as the Qingnian tuan (Youth League), located in House 119, Lane
37, Brenan Road.[40] The Youth League itself was really only a front for the
pro-Japanese Rehabilitation and Yellow Way Societies.[41]

Given the obvious overlap between elements of the underworld and the
sleazy pro-Japanese activities of "76" agents, the International Settlement's population of Westerners applauded enthusiastically when on January 13, 1939, British soldiers led by Major B. H. Ashmore forcibly closed
a puppet subpolice station at Great Western and Columbia Roads, eject-
ing a group of Chinese plainclothesmen and studding the locked entrance
with barbed wire.[42]

During February 1939, after a relative lull, Shanghai experienced a
"serious wave of terrorism," which foreign authorities believed was conducted by Nationalist military agents under the control of Chongqing.[43]
On February 1, Geng Shoubin, the chief of detectives of the puppet police
force, was assassinated by Nationalist secret agents.[44] This was followed
by a series of attacks on puppet police stations and diverse assassinations
of pro-Japanese collaborators, including Zhu Jintao, in charge of provisions for the puppet Bureau of Social Affairs, on February 5; Qian Hua,

former star reporter for *Shen bao* and since December 1937 adviser to the Japanese-controlled press censorship bureau, on February 6; Zhou Jitang, director of the Jiangsu–Zhejiang Tax Bureau and counselor to the Nanjing Ministry of Finance, on February 7; He Shushuang, commissioner of education, and Zhang Zhaoqi, president of the Shandong High Court, on February 10; Tu Zhengu, chief justice of the Nanshi Local Court (Difang fayuan), and Gao Hongzao, secretary of the puppet River Police Bureau, on February 16.[45] These exterminations culminated on Sunday, February 19, with the daring murder of Chen Lu, minister for foreign affairs of the Reform Government, plus an attack on two Japanese and their women companions, two Japanese taxi dancers.[46]

The assassination of puppet foreign minister Chen Lu

Newspapers described the murder of Chen Lu as "by far the most important assassination on patriotic grounds effected in Shanghai since 1937."[47] Chen Lu, who was sixty-one at the time of his death, had attended the Arsenal School in Fuzhou, obtained a law degree from the University of Paris, served as a Hanlin Compiler for the Qing, and under the Beiyang warlords been appointed ambassador to Mexico (1914–1918) and to France (1920–1927). After the Guomindang took power, Chen Lu became vice-chairman of the Treaty Commission of the Ministry of Foreign Affairs. He remained in Shanghai when the Japanese took over, and agreed to serve as minister of foreign affairs for Liang Hongzhi's Reform Government. His son, Chen Youtao (Victor L. Chen), who was married to Zhang Xueliang's sister, also worked in the puppet Ministry of Foreign Affairs as chief of intelligence.[48]

The assassination of Chen Lu was engineered by Wang Tianmu, the head of Juntong's Shanghai Station, in an effort to impress Dai Li.[49] The leader of Wang's action unit, Liu Geqing, had already carried out eleven major assignments in Shanghai and was on the Japanese Military Police's list of most wanted men.[50] Beginning in the fall of 1938, Liu started to assemble two teams of agents, including two Military Statistics Bureau training school graduates, Ping Fuchang and Tan Baoyi.[51]

Ping Fuchang (age twenty-four), whose family was from Funing, was born in Zhabei. He had attended primary school in Nandao and the Yuqing Middle School in Jiangwan before dropping out at the age of eighteen to work in his father's optical shop in South Market. He must have found lens grinding for his sixty-three-year-old father a tedious trade. Living in such close quarters with his father's young wife, at nineteen only a year older than himself, Ping Fuchang decided in 1935—when he was twenty—to join Dai Li's Juntong. Ostensibly serving as a detective on the Hubei Police Force in Hankou, Ping was actually attached to the second section of the Central Statistics Bureau of the Central Military Affairs Committee, "engaged in supervision and inquiries into the movements and thoughts of actors" working in the Yongxing Garden Cinema Studio.[52]

In June 1937, Ping Fuchang was detailed to Shanghai by the cinema studio. Within a month the Sino-Japanese War erupted, and Ping joined a special plainclothes unit, becoming chief of a squad of the Jiangsu–Zhejiang Action Corps under Zhu Xuefan. He remained behind in the French Concession when the Japanese took over the Chinese sectors of Shanghai, doing underground work until he was ordered to report to the Military Statistics Bureau's Linli Training Depot in Hunan. The training depot was divided into three sections: military, action, and intelligence. Ping graduated from the military section, but he was nonetheless assigned to the action group and ordered in September 1938 to go back to Shanghai and report to an operational director whom he called You Heqing, but who is better known to us as Liu Geqing.[53]

Traveling via Hong Kong, Ping and three other Bureau agents—Jiang Su, Shi Zheng, and Lin Ziren—arrived in Shanghai shortly after Double Ten (October 10, the anniversary of the Xinhai Revolution). This first team was soon contacted by Wang Luzhao, who said he represented Wang Tianmu, "the head of the Shanghai branch of the Military Committee." As Ping Fuchang revealed much later to the Japanese counterespionage agents interrogating him:

> The ringleader of my party was Wong Loo Jao [Wang Luzhao], but Mao Van Li [Mao Wanli] took command of the party in Shanghai, and the leader of the party when the assassination of Ching Loh [Chen Lu] was carried out was Yue Woo Ching [Liu Geqing] . . . I do not know whether the leaders of the party were in communication with Chungking [Chongqing] government organs or guerrillas in Shanghai.[54]

Mao Wanli was, of course, the cousin of Mao Renfeng, one of Dai Li's most trusted associates and relatives.[55] Wang Luzhao, his assistant, was the head of the Bureau's hit team that attempted to assassinate Wang Jingwei on March 21 in Hanoi and ended up killing Wang's confidential secretary, Zeng Zongming, instead.[56]

According to Ping Fuchang, Wang Luzhao told the three men that they were going to be ordered "to engage in assassination activities as few people have been engaging in assassination activities at present in Shanghai," and issued them salaries of $48 per month. Ping and Shi Zheng, meanwhile, moved from one cheap rooming house to another in the

French Concession to avoid surveillance. They of course stayed in frequent touch with Wang Luzhao.[57]

The second team, which arrived in Shanghai a little less than four months later, included Tan Baoyi, age twenty-three. Somewhat less experienced than Ping, Tan was the son of farmers from Songjiang. His brother was a corn chandler in Shanghai, and his cousin worked as a clerk in a drygoods store. Tan had attended primary and middle school in Songjiang, and he had graduated from the Shanghai Zhonghua Business School in Nandao. Until the Sino-Japanese War broke out, Tan worked as a surveyor for the Hanyeping Steel Company in Hengyang. Then he signed up with Juntong and in July 1938 took the training course at the Linli Depot, After three months of the half-year course, he was transferred by the Bureau to Changsha, and ordered to proceed to Shanghai to conduct anti-Japanese activities there. Accompanied by two others, Zhu Shanyuan and a commanding officer named Xu Guoqi, Tan arrived in Shanghai via Ningbo around February 1, 1939. While Xu reported directly to Liu Geqing, who told him to have the others stand by for further orders, Tan Baoyi moved in with a cousin living and working in a piece goods shop on rue Frélupt in the French Concession.[58] Superficially, then, he resembled yet one more local *shimin* (urbanite), like many of the petty clerks and apprentices who were less formally recruited subagents for Nationalist assassination squads. But Tan, both as a Linli Depot graduate and in his own eyes, was a full-time secret agent, a "direct member" of Juntong sent out from central Bureau headquarters without any personal knowledge of the "local organ" of Dai Li's Shanghai Station.[59]

One week before Chinese New Year, Tan Baoyi went to see Xu Guoqi and Zhu Shanyuan in their rooms in the Guotai Hotel adjacent to the Great World (Da shijie) amusement hall. Xu told Tan to be ready for an urgent call and instructed him to move to the Dongchang Hotel on Avenue Joffre. Ping Fuchang was also alerted about an imminent operation.[60]

The alert was issued by Liu Geqing because he had learned—probably on February 16 or 17—that Foreign Minister Chen Lu was planning to come secretly to Shanghai to spend Chinese New Year with family and friends in their mansion at 668/25 Yu Yuen [Yuyuan] Road. The sources of his information were two of Chen Lu's bodyguards, He Peng and Zhao Yuding, who were Manchurians from Fengtian recommended to the foreign minister by one of his own bureau chiefs. Only they would have known on February 16, while they were all together in Nanjing, that Chen Lu intended to make this dangerous trip.[61]

Liu Geqing had been able to cultivate these sources in the first place because Chen Lu had surrounded himself with Manchurian guards who joined his entourage when the sister of Zhang Xueliang, the "Young Marshal" who had dominated the Northeast, became his daughter-in-law.[62] Reliance on a single group of co-provincials, especially if not of your own province, was a risky business, because once one was subverted, others might quickly follow. In this case, Liu Geqing chose to approach the former head of the Young Marshal's Manchurian body-guards, Liu Haishan, who agreed to serve Chinese Military Intelligence and participate in the assassination attempt. It was through Liu Haishan's contacts with former brethren among the Manchurian bodyguards in the Chen household service that Liu Geqing obtained Chen Lu's travel schedule as well as a blueprint of the mansion.[63]

On February 17, Victor Chen arrived in Shanghai with the bodyguard He Peng in order to make advance arrangements for his father's arrival. At 10:00 the following morning Chen Lu telephoned from Nanjing to say that he would be arriving at North Station at 3:00 that afternoon. Promptly at 2:30 Victor Chen left for the railway station with two automobiles. Chen Lu's personal car, driven by his chauffeur Huang Yonggui, carried bodyguard Zhang Shuwen and Miss Chen Ganhui, a relative who also worked as a clerk in the Reform Government. This party was waiting on the platform at 3:00 when Chen Lu's railway car pulled into North Station exactly on time, and Chen Lu descended with bodyguard Zhao Yuding. The second car, driven by Victor Chen and carrying bodyguard He Peng, was waiting at the corner of North Sichuan and Julong Roads. Both cars proceeded together to the Broadway Mansions, where the Reform Government had its Foreign Affairs Bureau on the fourth floor and which Chen Lu sometimes used as his living quarters when he came to Shanghai. After a brief ten-minute visit, the Chens and their bodyguards—wearing identical camel hair coats and felt hats "so that should any attempt be made to assassinate [Chen Lu] while the car was in motion, it would be hard to distinguish one from the other"—got back into the two cars and drove to the Chen mansion on Yuyuan Road.[64]

By 4:00 p.m. that same Saturday afternoon, the day before New Year, Liu Geqing knew of Chen Lu's whereabouts in Shanghai.[65] He had already asked Ping Fuchang if he "had the courage to do some active work for the Nationalist government." Now he told Ping about Chen Lu's presence in Shanghai, and instructed Ping to meet him at the Burlington Hotel early the following day.[66] The next morning, Chinese Lunar New Year, Ping Fuchang came to the hotel and was sent by Liu (who was, of course, only known to Ping as You) to go to the house of "someone named Liu" just off rue Legrene and collect the weapons for the operation. Ping duly went off to rue Legrene and came back to the Burlington Hotel with a wooden picnic box containing what he later stated to be four Browning pistols with four rounds each and a Japanese pistol with fifteen rounds.[67]

Meanwhile, the other members of the action group were also being contacted, and by the time Tan Baoyi was picked up by Xu Guoqi and taken to the Burlington Hotel at 4:00 p.m. on New Year's Day, six other agents were already present: Ping Fuchang, Zhu Shanyuan, Xu Zhihao, You Pinshan, Liu Haishan, and Liu Geqing.[68] Liu, who may have just been in touch with the two Manchurian bodyguards, took four of the pistols out of the picnic hamper and gave one each to Xu Guoqi, You Pinshan, and Ping Fuchang, keeping one for himself.[69] According to Tan Baoyi (who probably was given the fifth weapon a little later), "He then informed us that we were going to assassinate one Cheng who was the high official of the Reform Government and who had just arrived at Shanghai from Nanking."[70] Liu told the men to split up into groups of two or three and regroup outside Yuguangcun on Yuyuan Road.[71]

Ping Fuchang and Xu Zhihao took a double-decker No. 1 bus to Yuyuan Road, while You Pinshan, Liu Haishan, and Liu Geqing rented a car for the rendezvous. All five were waiting when Tan Baoyi, Xu Guoqi, and Zhu Shanyuan arrived on foot at 6:00 p.m. After reconnaissance determined that there were still too many guests for them to attack the Chen compound at once, they killed time in a neighborhood bar until a heavy rain began to fall shortly after seven o'clock. Under cover of the rain the eight men, dressed in long gowns, moved silently through the dense network of lanes north of Yuyuan Road surrounding the mansion.[72]

There were normally two watchmen at the front gate. The principal guard, Shao Fusheng, was away from his post.[73] That left a single watchman, Song Hailin, armed with a small unlicensed revolver, on duty alone. He saw the Nationalist agents approaching from both sides. One of them—probably Liu Haishan—asked him in northern Mandarin if he was armed. Before he could answer the others set upon him and took away his pistol. Leaving Liu Haishan and Xu Zhihao outside in the alley to guard the gate, Zhu Shanyuan and Ping Fuchang took the watchman into the courtyard. The assassination team—Liu Geqing, Xu Guoqi, Tan Baoyi, and You Pinshan—drew their weapons and silently tried the kitchen door, which was unlocked.[74]

Inside the house, where the table was laid for New Year's dinner, Chen Lu and his wife were entertaining Mr. and Mrs. Luo Wen'gan in the drawing room. Chen Lu and Luo Wen'gan, the former minister to Denmark, reclined on a couch, while the two women sat in armchairs on either side. Suddenly a man walked in from the door at the back of the room, drew a pistol and fired three shots point-blank at Chen Lu.[75] Mrs.

Lu threw herself between the gunman and her husband, and the Luos rushed to the other door. They fumbled with the lock and threw it open, only to have Liu Geqing, who had been standing in the hall, slip by them and empty his pistol at the foreign minister, who was fatally struck with a shot to the temple.[76]

As Chen Lu slid from the settee to the floor, Liu Geqing drew out a scroll he had prepared earlier in the hotel room and threw it over the traitor's body. It read in large black characters: "Death to the Collaborators. Long Live Generalissimo Chiang Kai-shek!" Another sheet, strewn on the sofa, read: "Resistance Will Result in Victory. Construction of the Country Will Succeed. Keep China's Property Forever!" Both were signed by the "Chinese Iron and Blood Army." Moments later the four action squad members came out of the house, accompanied by the two Manchurian bodyguards He Peng and Zhao Yuding. Saying, "The job's done" (Shijian chenggong), Tan Baoyi and Liu Geqing drove off in the hired car.[77] The others released the night watchman and melted back into the alleys, throwing away their pistols along the way. By the time the Shanghai Municipal Police had answered the hysterical phone call from one of the seven frightened women they found beside the corpse at 7:30 p.m., the Nationalist agents were on buses or in rickshas riding back to their respective lodgings.[78]

The Chen Lu assassination was a triumph for Dai Li's Juntong. Perhaps no other murder during this period set collaborators' teeth on edge so gratingly. At the same time, however, the incident intensified the conflict between the Western powers and Japan over the status of the international concessions, ultimately taking both sides a few more fateful steps down the road to Pearl Harbor.

6

Capitulation: The Xi Shitai assassination

The assassination of Chen Lu thrilled Chinese patriots, who read about the incident in one newspaper account as a paired literary couplet: "A valiant man descended from the heavens last night. / The collaborator instantly entered his name in the roster of ghosts."[1] The Japanese, who had difficulty finding a successor to Chen Lu as puppet foreign minister, were predictably outraged.[2] Yet they could not blame the British for failing to guard Chen Lu from harm, because even though Settlement policemen from the Bubbling Well Road station had rushed to the murder scene, the Shanghai Municipal Police quickly discovered that 668/25 Yuyuan Road was an address under the jurisdiction of the Japanese Military Police.[3] Once this was pointed out to the Japanese, all the latter could do was to grumble that the Shanghai Municipal Police had not informed them of the puppet foreign minister's arrival in Shanghai in the first place.[4]

Chinese loyalist attacks and the threat of Japanese intervention

The assault on the same day as Chen Lu's assassination of four Japanese civilians, one of whom was severely wounded, was consequently treated with extraordinary gravity by the Japanese authorities—almost as though it were a surrogate case. The four persons—an official Japanese army photographer (Koyanagi Jiichi), a taxi dancer (Morioka Masako), a man named Sato Rokuo, and another Japanese prostitute—had just lunched at a Chinese restaurant in the Settlement and were about to set off in an antiquated taxicab when a man dressed in Chinese clothes stepped forward and began firing randomly through the car window. Miss Morioka narrowly missed death, the bullet glancing off a rib on the right side of her chest. Mr. Sato suffered a flesh wound in his right wrist. Police opened fire on the terrorist, wounding a nearby Chinese beggar, but the assailant outran the two Chinese constables and the Sikh policeman who chased him down an adjacent alley in close pursuit.[5]

Although some bystanders claimed the man was Japanese or Korean, suggesting that he may have been a jealous admirer of the taxi dancer, the Japanese military authorities described the attack as a "preliminary and deliberate assault upon persons concerned with the army."[6] While *Tairiku shimpo* invoked the January 3, 1938, agreement between the Shanghai Municipal Police and the Japanese Army Special Services Section that "entitled the Japanese military authorities to resort to 'independent action in case of a recurrence of similar incidents,'" other Japanese newspapers urged "a final and effective solution of terrorism in Shanghai" by seizing the French Concession and the International Settlement.[7]

The U.S. State Department, with the situation in Tianjin in mind, commented:

> On the one hand, the Chinese, by means of organized terrorism, apparently sought not only to intimidate Chinese serving the Japanese, but also to embroil the foreign powers with the Japanese. On the other hand, the Japanese appeared to be seeking still further to undermine the [Shanghai Municipal] Council in pursuance of a policy which seemingly envisaged the ultimate seizure of the International Settlement and perhaps the French Concession; in acts of terrorism they found a convenient pretext.[8]

Asahi shimbun quoted a Japanese military spokesman as saying ominously: "The terroristic acts are symptoms of the decadence of the General Chiang Kai-shek régime. The recent occurrence of the crimes, especially the fate that befell Mr. Chen Lu, are matters which are causing grave concern among the authorities of the Japanese Expeditionary Force to Central China."[9]

Such saber rattling aroused a flurry of diplomatic activity among the Americans and British, and considerable anxiety among members of the Shanghai Municipal Council. On February 22 Consul General Miura Yoshiaki, accompanied by the commanders of the Japanese Naval Landing Party and the Japanese Army Garrison, called on Shanghai Municipal Council Chairman C. S. Franklin to hand over a letter that accused the Shanghai Municipal Council of failing to take adequate precautions during the Chinese New Year's holiday.[10] The letter also demanded the strict enforcement of the Shanghai Municipal Council's July 19, 1938, proclamation concerning the arrest and expulsion of criminals; permission for Japanese police organs to take necessary measures in the International Settlement to protect Japanese subjects; and a guarantee that the Japanese branch of the Shanghai Municipal Police would be strengthened.[11]

The Shanghai Municipal Council immediately began to enforce stringent measures in the International Settlement by barricading alleyways, conducting frequent raids and searches, and constantly patrolling city streets.[12] It also sought to curb Chinese loyalist terrorism through two different avenues: Chinese personal connections and diplomatic channels.

Chinese members of the Council were urged to convey to the Nationalist authorities in Chongqing their conviction that continued terrorism would place Chinese interests in the Settlement in grave danger.[13] At the same time, Ambassador Sir Archibald Clark Kerr instructed the first secretary in the British mission in Chongqing to write to Chiang Kai-shek urging the Chinese government to cease sending terrorist missions to Shanghai. Chiang Kai-shek replied orally, saying that strict orders would be telegraphed to the persons concerned.[14] The U.S. chargé d'affaires, Peck, also called upon the minister of foreign affairs with an identical request, but that answer was, if more honest, also more equivocal:

> He asserted that where the victims were "puppet" Chinese officials, the assassinations were probably perpetrated by persons acting spontaneously from patriotic motives or in revenge for wrongs suffered at the hands of the Japanese. He said that the Japanese themselves had instigated murders of political opponents, and he did not exclude the possibility of their killing their own partisans as well in order to discredit the Municipal Council.[15]

The minister asked Peck to inform the U.S. State Department that the Chinese government "did not approve of political assassination," that he would convey the U.S. request to "the appropriate authorities"; but he specifically asked that Peck inform his superiors of the "complexity of the problem."[16]

Some of that complexity—or at least the difficulty of trying to rein in terrorists aroused by the hedonistic escapism of Shanghai's moneyed classes—was underscored on Wednesday, March 1, when a group calling itself "the blood and soul traitors-extermination corps" set off bombs simultaneously outside four Chinese dancing establishments: the Oriental Hotel, Ciro's, the Café and Paradise Ballroom, and the Great Eastern Ballroom. Fortunately, only one person was wounded, but the terrorists left behind "A Warning to Our Dancing Friends" in the form of leaflets that read:

> Dancing friends: some of you can dance the foxtrot, others the waltz. Why don't you go up to the front to kill? Some of you spend lavishly on brandy and whiskey. Why don't you give the money to our troops so that they can buy more munitions to kill the enemy?
> Dancing friends: why spend your money for cosmetics when your bodies smell the odor of a conquered people? The only way to remove that smell is to give our warm blood to the nation. You have been amusing yourselves

over the Lunar New Year. Our meager gift tonight—bombs—will help to
give you added pleasure.
Dancing friends: if you like them, we shall meet each other in the
ballrooms![17]

The Shanghai Municipal Police stepped up their patrols and raids, especially after three decapitated heads were found on a fence along Brenan
Road in puppet territory and an attempt was made to assassinate Zhu
Ganting, the head of the puppet tax bureau in Pudong.[18] But that did
nothing to forestall the formation by the local Guomindang branch on
March 23, 1939, of a Shanghai People's Mobilization Society "to develop
a wide-spread mass movement in Shanghai to carry on military, political,
[and] all anti-Japanese and National Salvation work provided they are not
contrary to the laws and ordinances of the Government." The society's
manifesto read:

> We swear hereafter we will not live with the enemy robbers under the same
> sky, and will demonstrate the strength of the various classes of the people.
> Not only will the obstinate enemy in the suburbs be caused to shrink and to
> conceal themselves and to return Chinese territory to us, but also in the
> foreign concessions we should make known the heroic and unyielding spirit
> of descendants of our Chinese ancestors. . . . Some may assume responsibil-
> ity for detection and secret service work; some may undertake the work of
> assaulting and killing the traitors.[19]

The Shanghai Municipal Council, meanwhile, had sent a conciliatory
note over Chairman Franklin's signature in response to the Japanese demands. The note, dated February 25, 1939, consisted of four points: (1)
the Shanghai Municipal Police, in accordance with the July 1938 emergency decree, would continue to maintain vigilance against anti-Japanese
terrorism; (2) the Shanghai Municipal Council welcomed the cooperation
of Japanese police organs against terrorists (which meant, in effect, continuing to allow Japanese plainclothesmen to operate alongside Shanghai
Municipal Police officers); (3) Chinese leaving and entering the Settlement
would continue to be searched with additional rigor (in the presence, of
course, of Japanese plainclothesmen); (4) Japanese vacancies in the
Shanghai Municipal Police would be filled as soon as suitable men could
be found.[20]

While Rear Admiral Kanazawa, chief spokesman for the Navy Ministry
in Tokyo, said that appointing a Japanese to head the Shanghai Municipal
Police would be "one good way" of dealing with Shanghai terrorists, the
Japanese Consulate prepared a formal response to Franklin's February
25th note. Consul General Miura acknowledged the Shanghai Municipal
Police's state of preparedness, declared that Japan regarded the note as

consent on the part of the Shanghai Municipal Council to cooperate in the future, and announced the intention of Japanese police organs to collaborate thereafter.[21]

And cooperate they did.[22] In March 1939 acts of terrorism decreased markedly, thanks to "the extraordinary precautions taken by the police of both the Settlement and the French Concession, who searched thousands of Chinese and made a large number of raids."[23] During the first ten days of April, when Consul General Miura gained the help of the Shanghai Municipal Police in suppressing Chinese publications carrying anti-Japanese propaganda, there was only one minor terrorist incident.[24] The lull was shattered, however, on April 11 when the chief secretary (*mishu zhuren*) of the puppet police bureau, Xi Shitai, was assassinated at 9:15 a.m. as he left his home on Lloyd Road in the International Settlement.[25]

The Xi Shitai assassination

Xi Shitai, forty-nine years old at the time of his death, had studied medicine in Japan before returning to Shanghai to practice as a registered Shanghai Municipal Council physician in his own Shitai Hospital.[26] After the Nationalist forces withdrew from the city, Dr. Xi became Shanghai Police Commissioner Lu Ying's principal secretary, as well as chief of the Department of Health and a special member of the Japanese military press section.[27] As "a brave worker for the construction of a new order in the Orient in cooperation with the [Japanese] authorities," Xi Shitai was a prime target for assassination by agents under the command of the Chongqing-sponsored guerrillas operating in Pudong.[28]

The leader of the assassination squad was a twenty-two- or twenty-three-year-old Songjiang native named Yuan Dechang.[29] Because Yuan was never captured, we can best see the conspiracy through the eyes of Zhao Zhixiang, who failed to get away and who was eventually handed over to the Japanese for execution.[30]

Zhao Zhixiang, a typical Shanghai *xiao shimin* (petty urbanite), was also about twenty-three years old and a native of Pudong. At the age of thirteen he had been apprenticed to a tailor's shop catering to foreign women in the French Concession, and after his apprenticeship was over five years later he worked as a sales clerk in two other "foreign dress shops." He earned enough money as a clerk to marry the daughter of a villager east of his home in Pudong, but at the height of the depression in the summer of 1937, before they were able to have children, Zhao lost his job in the dress store and had to go back to live with his brother, a boatman. His wife returned to her mother's home, and even though Zhao Zhixiang got a job as a coolie in a Japanese shipyard in Pudong, they remained apart because he was soon laid off and had to live from hand to mouth, doing casual tailoring work for some of his friends while war raged across the river in South Market.[31]

On March 5, 1939, Zhao Zhixiang decided to cross the river once again to find a job in the unoccupied International Settlement, where he located temporary shelter in his brother-in-law's cramped attic room over a rice shop on Ferry Road. Zhao searched in vain for three days, and then he recalled once meeting Yuan Dechang, a man with Pudong guerrilla connections, who often used to book rooms in the Great Shanghai and Nanjing Hotels.[32] There was no trace of Yuan at the Great Shanghai, but when Zhao Zhixiang approached the telephone operator (who was probably a Juntong agent himself) at the Nanjing Hotel on Shanxi Road, Yuan Dechang was immediately contacted and emerged from a back room.[33]

Yuan Dechang recognized Zhao and instantly led him out of the hotel.[34] On the street, standing in front of the hotel, Zhao Zhixiang said he needed a job. Yuan must have made a telephone call at this point, because when he took Zhao to the tram stop near the Great World amusement hall, another agent appeared to vet him and was apparently satisfied by Zhao's story.[35] Yuan then told Zhao to meet him at 2:00 in the afternoon on March 14 in front of the Great World, and they parted.[36]

Zhao Zhixiang duly made the rendezvous on March 14, and Yuan Dechang took him from the Great World to a house at 11 Wenxian li, rue Lafayette, where Yuan paid $22 to rent an attic room for one month.[37] That same day, the third member of the team, Peng Fulin—a slim twenty-year-old waiter who habitually wore a nondescript beige gown and grey felt hat—moved in with them.[38] Thereafter the three of them lived together as "bosom friends," with Yuan supplying food each day. The attic was even large enough for Zhao Zhixiang to bring his wife into the city to stay for a week before returning to her hometown.[39]

On the afternoon of April 4, 1939, Yuan Dechang sent Zhao Zhixiang out with 20¢ to buy food. When Zhao returned with provisions shortly after three o'clock, he found Yuan and Peng cleaning a couple of pistols. Nothing was said—or had been said—about their eventual target.[40] Five days later, the three men moved to Room 411 at the Nanjing Hotel, where they spent the next two nights. Zhao mainly stayed in the room, while Yuan and Peng came and went. Returning late on the night of April 10th, the two agents told Zhao that he must prepare himself for the next morning when they were going to go to an address on Lloyd Road to "assassinate a traitor."[41]

At this point Yuan Dechang produced a letter supposedly sent to Zhao Zhixiang at a Ningbo address.[42] Dated March 29, the letter was addressed to all three men and signed by one Zhou Jianhua, surely a patriotic nom de guerre.[43] The letter—which Yuan had to read aloud to the other two semiliterate men—spoke about their carrying out the duties entrusted to them by the "four hundred million citizens" of China, and enjoined them to be "brave, steady, enthusiastic, [and] clever," and to "take exercises to make [their] bodies strong." It urged them to lead their lives "in accordance with the principles of the New Life Movement laid down by General Chiang," namely:

> *Piety*—As comrades they should love each other.
>
> *Righteousness*—As citizens they should be dutiful toward the nation so that "our country will be prosperous and the present enemy exterminated" by crushing "the traitors who are breaking this principle and betraying their mother country."
>
> *Integrity*—As heroes they should punish corrupt officials and traitors who defraud and sell out the nation.
>
> *Conscientiousness*—As patriots they should not only take steps against those traitors who "pay no attention to the fate of the nation and the family but aim at securing high positions for themselves and obtaining money for their own pockets," but also deal with the large number of people who ignore the war of resistance by "enjoying themselves in dancing, gambling, and other amusements."

The letter concluded: "I hope that the 'rules' will always lie before you and you will love your mother country and support the 'organization' so that we will not go beyond the expectations of our leader, General Chiang. Kill the enemy and annihilate the traitor!"[44]

At 7:00 a.m. the next morning, April 11, Yuan Dechang gave Peng Fulin one of the two revolvers and told him that his assignment was to take care of the watchman inside Lane 139 (Juyili alley), Lloyd Road.[45] To Zhao Zhixiang, Yuan gave 10¢ with instructions to rent some books from the stall at the north side of the entrance to Juyili alley and keep an eye out for police patrolmen.[46] The three men left the Nanjing Hotel singly and reassembled at the head of Lane 139 at 8:45. They took their positions as planned: Yuan inside the lane, watching the back entrance to Xi Shitai's house; Zhao sitting at the stall outside, pretending to read the four novels he had just rented; and Peng surveying the guard's post, unaware that the watchman had already invited the beat patrolman (Chinese Police Constable 730) inside for a cup of tea.[47]

At 9:15 Dr. Xi stepped out of his backdoor and started down the alley toward Lloyd Road, where his chauffeur was waiting for him in an Oldsmobile sedan. Although licensed to carry a .765 Union automatic, Xi was unarmed. About twenty-five yards from the entrance to the lane Yuan Dechang waited in the shadows. As the doctor approached, Yuan stepped in front of him and started firing .38 caliber dumdum bullets. One shot tore high through the right breast, another in the left breast, and two more up through the abdomen into the lungs. The revolver's last two bullets caught in Xi's clothing as he staggered back toward the house.[48]

As the shots rang out, Peng Fulin rushed toward the guard post, drawing his pistol. "Don't move," he shouted confidently, but when he saw the police constable at the watchman's side he panicked and pulled the trigger, striking the policeman in the right arm.[49] The watchman swiftly drew his own gun and fired back, hitting Peng in the chest. Peng turned and ran back out the alley, bumping into the chauffeur before fleeing through the rear door of a teashop at 564 Yuyaqing Road. Behind him the mortally wounded Xi Shitai fell into the arms of family members who helped him back into the house where he died on the living room floor.[50]

Meanwhile, Yuan Dechang and Zhao Zhixiang escaped by separate ways—the more experienced assassin for good, the freshly recruited lookout only temporarily. Zhao Zhixiang made the mistake of returning to the Nanjing Hotel on Shanxi Road, where he stood helplessly by the entrance to the telephone operator's room waiting for Yuan to come to his rescue. Instead of Yuan, however, it was the badly wounded Peng Fulin who stumbled into the hotel lobby supported by a man whom he identified as his brother, but who was actually a fellow waiter Peng had appealed to for help.[51] Zhao had no choice but to lead the two men back through the lobby—he was afraid it would look too suspicious for him to help support Peng Fulin—and out onto the street, where they hailed three rickshas and asked to be taken to nearby Paulun [Baolun] Hospital.[52]

The hospital staff promptly admitted Peng Fulin, and just as quickly phoned a report of the gunshot wound to Louza Station. By 11:00 a.m. Shanghai Municipal Police detectives were at Paulun Hospital. Peng Fulin had too deep a chest wound to be interrogated formally, but he did tell the investigators that he and Zhao Zhixiang had been walking along Lloyd Road, minding their own business, when a stray shot somehow rang out and struck him down. Zhao Zhixiang corroborated this tale at Peng's bedside, and was instantly detained and taken to Louza Station for questioning. Members of the Japanese Military Police, including Sergeant Major Katoda, attended the interrogation.[53]

While Zhao Zhixiang was being questioned, other Shanghai Municipal Police detectives quickly exposed the terrorists' flimsy story. First the rickshaw coolies reported that they had picked the wounded man up at the Nanjing Hotel, not Lloyd Road. Then the injured beat patrolman tentatively identified the clothing of Peng Fulin as being that of the man who shot him. Finally, when Shanghai Municipal Police detectives enlisted the help of the French police to search Peng and Zhao's room at 11 Wenxian li, they found the letter from Zhou Jianhua that incriminated them as members of a Nationalist secret service assassination squad. Confronted with this evidence, Zhao Zhixiang broke down and confessed. At 2:30 that same afternoon the officers took him in handcuffs to Peng Fulin's hospital room, and when Peng—who was in "a very weakened condition"—heard Zhao's confession, he too admitted his complicity. For Peng, it was too late anyway; at 3:00 the next morning he gave up the struggle and died. For Zhao Zhixiang, a greater ordeal lay ahead.[54]

The Shanghai Municipal Police could hardly be faulted for delay in solving the murder, but the Japanese and pro-Japanese press in Shanghai was nonetheless determined to use the case to bludgeon the International Settlement authorities yet again. On April 12, 1939, the very morning of Peng Fulin's demise, the lead article in *Tairiku shimpo* called for a minute of silent prayer for the martyred Dr. Xi Shitai and accused the Shanghai Municipal Council of abusing its extraterritoriality by tolerating Chongqing terrorists:

> So long as the agents of the Chongqing government are to be found in Shanghai, this in itself constitutes the principal cause of the disturbances of peace and order in Shanghai. . . . Japan and China are now engaged in rebuilding the Orient at the cost of many lives. The new régimes and the reborn Chinese people are in complete union with Japan in the rebuilding of China. There is no reason to permit a power which is obstructing this great work of rebuilding to exist. Out of consideration for the military operations and the maintenance of peace and order, a definite and final measure should be resorted to.[55]

In urging the Japanese military authorities to "adopt a strong attitude to cope with the situation," the editors of *Tairiku shimpo* also charged the Shanghai Municipal Council with "insincerity"—a theme that was echoed by the collaborationist *Xin shenbao*.[56] Noting that the assassination of Xi Shitai was the first serious incident since Franklin's February 25th note, *Xin shenbao* faulted the Settlement authorities for poor police work and attributed the recurrence of Nationalist terrorism to the Shanghai Municipal Council's feeble, half-hearted measures. "In other words, they have failed to accept with sincerity the requests of the Japanese authorities for the rigorous suppression of the activities of the secret organs of the Guomindang."[57]

Puppet Mayor Fu Xiaoan also called into question the "sincerity" of the Shanghai Municipal Council (which by now was insisting that press releases never again refer to "a member of the reform government [being] shot"), and insisted that the regular Chinese police be permitted to search for terrorists within the International Settlement.[58] The Shanghai Municipal Council paid scant attention to Mayor Fu's demand, but Chairman C. S. Franklin could hardly afford to be cavalier about Consul General Miura

Yoshiaki's appearance in his office on April 16, protesting the assassination of Dr. Xi Shitai and requesting strict enforcement in the future of the understanding reached between the Japanese authorities and the Shanghai Municipal Council on the prevention of terroristic activities in the Settlement.[59] Three days later, on April 19, 1939, the Shanghai Municipal Police escorted Zhao Zhixiang across the boundary line at Suzhou Creek and up to the headquarters of the Japanese Military Police. At 4:00 that afternoon, as a token of their "sincerity," the Shanghai Municipal Police detectives handed Zhao over to the Japanese gendarmes, and the former tailor's apprentice slipped into the maw of the enemy, never to be seen again.[60]

Appeasement

Terrorism abated in May, but the policy of cooperation was further tested over the issue of Chinese Nationalist flag raising.[61] In order to appease the Japanese, the Shanghai Municipal Council had issued orders on March 12, 1939, that the Chinese Nationalist "blue sky and white sun" flag be hoisted on no more than eight days throughout the year. Instead, loyalist Chinese shopkeepers tried to display the national flag on every patriotic occasion, despite threats of assault by Japanese Special Services Section agents dressed in Chinese clothes and backed up by Chinese collaborationist gangsters.[62] The puppet press complained bitterly about the hoisting of the Nationalist flag on March 27, the anniversary of the execution of the seventy-two revolutionary martyrs, and accused the International Settlement authorities of failing to enforce its prohibition strictly enough. Accusing the Guomindang branch in the Settlement of using the recently formed Shanghai People's Mobilization Society to arouse the public in this fashion, puppet mayor Fu Xiaoan declared:

> The "blue sky and white sun" flag signifies the sovietization of China; the flag is also [of] anti-foreign significance. This surmise is not at all groundless, for the Kuomintang [Guomindang] anthem contains the following sentence: "Down with the powers, down with the powers." Is this not sufficient to show that the flag has a strong anti-foreign significance? The authorities of the foreign settlements are certainly aware of all this. Therefore it will be better to suppress the hoisting of the flag.[63]

On May 1, International Labor Day, Chinese Nationalist banners were displayed all over the International Settlement, while the Chinese-language press harshly criticized the Japanese consul general for requesting the Shanghai Municipal Council to suppress such flag waving in the first place. Once again the puppet *Xin shenbao* attacked the Shanghai Municipal Council, complaining that "the action of the Shanghai Municipal Council in appointing Chinese and foreign policemen, and not Japanese members of the police force, for patrol duty on the streets on May 1 constitutes sufficient proof of the council's insincerity and disregard of the demands made by the Japanese authorities," and warning that "should anti-Japanese elements become active, the Japanese authorities will find it necessary to take new measures."[64]

Consequently, on May 10, 1939, the French consul general, in his capacity as head of the French Concession, and the chairman of the Shanghai Municipal Council met with their respective police authorities. The U.S. and British consuls general attended by invitation. Together, they all shared the feeling that

> the continued secret but active functioning of the Guomindang is directly responsible for much of the terrorism, political agitation, and anti-Japanese propaganda which are to be found here. The local Guomindang is not only largely responsible for such organizations as the [Shanghai People's] Mobilization Society but is also believed to be connected with terrorist societies such as the so-called "Chinese Youths Iron and Blood Corps for National Salvation."[65]

The municipal authorities agreed "that firm measures must be taken to impress upon the Chinese that continued political activities must cease," and they proceeded to issue a proclamation cautioning the public to respect the neutrality of the foreign areas. At the first indication of opposition to police measures a strict and drastic curfew would be imposed, and consideration would be given to prohibiting the display of the Chinese national flag entirely.[66]

That same day, the Chinese Ministry of Foreign Affairs protested to the British and U.S. embassies about the Settlement's flag restrictions, and requested them to remind the Shanghai Municipal Council of "the responsibility of respecting the freedom of Chinese residents of the Settlement to hoist flags."[67] Consul General Gauss subsequently complained to the secretary of state that when prominent Chinese leaders such as T. V. Soong were warned that continued loyalist political activity might result in the Japanese occupation of the foreign concessions, they countered with the opinion that Japan would not dare to antagonize the foreign powers:

> The Chinese government apparently does not understand that there is not sufficient strength and no intention on the part of the foreign garrison forces here to prevent a Japanese occupation of the Settlement and Concession if the Japanese determine to undertake it. The Chinese terrorism and anti-Japanese activities have given abundant pretext for such action.[68]

There was also no intention on the part of the U.S. State Department to exert pressure, however slight, on the Japanese government. Craigie, the British ambassador to Tokyo, recommended to London on May 19 that the U.S. government be consulted about some kind of allied ad hoc action, such as an embargo on specified imports and exports, in the event of the Japanese military moving against the International Settlement. He also suggested that this might have a deterrent effect if the U.S. and British governments were to inform the Japanese minister of foreign affairs of their joint intention. But Joseph Grew, the U.S. ambassador in Tokyo, refused to recommend this course of action to his government, given the failure of the Roosevelt administration to get Congress to repeal the arms embargo (the Bloom and Pittman bills about to be debated in both houses would soon be defeated by the isolationists led by Senator William E. Borah).[69]

With very little choice in the matter, Secretary of State Cordell Hull duly prepared an aide-mémoire to be delivered on May 22, 1939, to the Chinese minister of foreign affairs by the U.S. chargé d'affaires in Chongqing, Willys R. Peck. The memoir patronizingly noted:

> Shanghai has been developed as a great cosmopolitan center in which are concentrated large interests of Chinese and foreign nationals alike. In times of strife the Settlement affords protection to both sets of interests. However, the international character of the Settlement means avoiding disputes originating elsewhere, lest the protection afforded by that international character be jeopardized.

Hull went on to note the existence of the Shanghai People's Mobilization Society, and to remark that however patriotic its goals might appear from the Chinese national point of view, those activities could impair the position of the International Settlement. Hence, the U.S. government was convinced that Chinese insistence upon legal rights to hoist their flag or to pursue Chinese national political activity in the International Settlement was not in the best interests of China.[70]

The secretary of state's effort to appease the Japanese, whose army's activities in China and along the Soviet border remained bellicose, and whose civilian members of Baron Hiranuma's cabinet lived in constant terror of assassination by Young Turks in the military, failed to forestall an arrogant and provocative announcement by the Japanese Foreign Office on May 24 with respect to the foreign concessions in Shanghai:[71]

> As the object of Japanese action in China is to control Chinese sovereignty, this sovereignty may be controlled in the settlements as in parts of China under Japanese occupation. There is no room for admission of foreign interference in the elimination of anti-Japanese activities in the occupied areas.

Japan has rights in the administration of the international settlements and she may, therefore, resort to force to safeguard these rights, which should be legally recognized.[72]

Japanese diplomats in Shanghai amended the statement slightly, but this was by way of strengthening Japan's military claims:

In the areas under Japanese occupation, Japan aims, so long as hostilities are being carried out, at expelling China's sovereignty from the areas and placing it under Japan's military control. Since the anti-Japanese terrorism in the Settlement is a disturbance under the direct order from the Chungking [Chongqing] government, it is to be regarded as a part or extension of China's military operations. Therefore, Japan is justified in the attempt to clean anti-Japanese elements out of the Settlements.[73]

If Japan needed any further justification for intervention, it did not have to look very far. On June 10, five days after the Shanghai declaration on the cleaning up of anti-Japanese elements, terrorists struck again, this time within the Japanese Consulate.

On that night the Japanese consul general was giving a dinner in honor of Vice-Minister Shimizu, visiting Shanghai on behalf of the Foreign Office. The head of the Reform Government, Liang Hongzhi, and his ministers of education and finance attended along with the two Japanese naval attachés (Funayama and Miyashita), Shanghai Garrison commander Lieutenant General Yamada, and Nanjing Mayor Gao. Somehow, Chinese loyalists had managed to plant an agent in the consulate's cooking staff, and the sous-chef in turn was able to poison the wine Consul General Miura's guests consumed before and during dinner. According to diplomatic reports, General Yamada and the two attachés died, and Mayor Gao was hospitalized. However, instead of using this incident to renew their demands, the Japanese authorities withheld information about the poisoning from the public, perhaps out of fear of seeming too vulnerable.[74]

On June 12, the Chinese Foreign Office finally responded to Secretary Hull's May 22 aide-mémoire. Declaring that "on no account should the legal relations between the Chinese government and the Settlement be allowed to be altered without the former's consent," the Ministry of Foreign Affairs insisted "on the maintenance of the status quo ante Japanese invasion," and refused to recognize any restrictions on hoisting the Chinese national flag in the Settlement. The note went on to say that the activities decried by the Settlement's authorities were engaged in by private individuals prompted by patriotism. Their activities, moreover, paled beside the truly "terrorist" behavior of the Japanese and their puppets. Needless to say, the Chinese could not recognize any restrictions on hoisting their national flag in the Settlement. Having reiterated this position, however, Chongqing's aide-mémoire ended on a conciliatory note, expressing the gratitude of the Chinese government for "the friendly and sympathetic spirit in which the government of the United States . . . presented views upon the entire subject of American protection, which it has along with other governments striven to accord to Chinese lives and interests found within the confines of the Settlement."[75]

The Chinese government's sympathy notwithstanding, the Americans found themselves in the summer of 1939 unable to respond to British requests for support in the discussions being conducted in Tokyo over the fate of the settlements in Tianjin. In their classic study published more than forty years ago, Langer and Gleason described the situation well:

> During July, 1939, the British attempted to reach agreement with the Japanese with respect to Tientsin [Tianjin], only to find that the Japanese insisted on treating the issue solely within the larger framework of their Chinese claims. Though fully aware that such a larger settlement might involve a "Far Eastern Munich," the British felt helpless without American support, which was denied them. They therefore felt obliged to yield. On July 24, 1939, the British Ambassador in Tokyo accepted the so-called Craigie–Arita formula, by which the British recognized "that hostilities on a large scale were proceeding in China; that the Japanese Army was responsible for security and the maintenance of law and order in the areas occupied by its troops; and that British consular officers would not impede the measures considered necessary by the Japanese military authorities for this purpose."[76]

However, news of the Craigie–Arita formula did lead the U.S. Congress, just after defeating revision of the Pan-American Neutrality Act, to question once again the termination of the commercial treaty of 1911 with Japan.[77] Even isolationist Senator Vandenberg was in favor of abrogation. On July 26, 1939, President Roosevelt announced his decision to give Japan the required six-months' notice to repeal the treaty.[78] The Chinese were momentarily cheered. The Japanese, and especially the militarists in Tokyo, took this as a sign of critical changes in U.S. policy in East Asia, beginning with the imposition of economic sanctions—sanctions that in a matter of months would eventuate in the surprise attack on Pearl Harbor.[79]

After the Tokyo talks further undermined the autonomy of the concessions, the Americans may have paradoxically—some would say perversely—stiffened their backs, but the Craigie–Arita formula did, after all, hold for the British authorities in the Shanghai International Settlement. Through the summer and early fall of 1939, Shanghai Municipal Police officers and the Japanese security organs continued to collaborate. On September 13, for example, at the behest of the Japanese, the Shanghai

Municipal Police arrested three clerks of the National Commercial Bank and two Chinese engineers. (The French police followed suit by arresting a Chinese vaudeville actor with Nationalist political connections.) The next day, September 14, Shanghai Municipal Police detectives arrested a Chinese stockbroker, again at the request of the Japanese. "In each case the Shanghai Municipal Police minions brought their captives into the street to receive the approval of Japanese plainclothesmen who were waiting."[80] Collaboration with the Japanese police was rapidly reaching the point of abject capitulation to the Japanese military. That pill was made all the more bitter to swallow, however, by the unpalatable behavior of the Japanese puppets who ruled over the badlands, arousing revulsion in those who might otherwise have been less resistant to cooperating with the New Order in East Asia.

7

The puppet police and 76 Jessfield Road

If communications between the Shanghai Municipal Police and the Japanese Military Police were much more expeditious after the Craigie–Arita formula went into effect, International Settlement police and Chinese puppet police relations were increasingly strained.[1] This was partly owing to the expansive growth of the Chinese police, which in turn reflected a widening of its jurisdiction outside of Shanghai proper.[2] The extension occurred as a result of regular Japanese forces' defeat or cooptation of Chinese loyalist guerrillas operating in the Shanghai suburbs.[3]

Before March 1939 Fengxian district in Pudong, for example, was completely under the control of guerrillas. But after military forces under General Nakajima launched a one-month mopping-up operation, the district was cleared of resistance.[4] The Japanese continued to station 120 troops from the Songjiang Garrison in Fengxian, but in May 1939 Mayor Fu Xiaoan ordered Shanghai police chief Colonel Lu Ying to establish a new branch bureau there at Nanqiao. The bureau had 220 constables armed with about 100 rifles of miscellaneous types, all under the command of Yin Zhongli, advised by a Special Services Section agent named Yamashita.[5]

Meanwhile Shanghai city law enforcement personnel grew. By June 1939 the police bureau of the Shanghai city government comprised eleven branch bureaus, five police stations, and eight other police units (detective corps, garrison, reserve unit, river corps, training depot, police van, detention house, and police hospital) with a total roster of 5,662 men and women, an increase of 507 persons since April.[6]

In July, the Shanghai police bureau enjoyed another increase in strength after Interior Minister Chen Qun ordered Chief Lu Ying to assume jurisdiction over Jiading prefecture and Chongming Island.[7] Lu Ying promptly appointed his secretary, Jin Dianyang, chief of the Jiading police force of 230 men; and named the Fengxian bureau chief Yin Zhongli head of Chongming Island's police force with a strength of 220 men.[8] The Shanghai puppet police now had a total roster of 6,125.[9] At the same time, two other reorganizations were effected. The Nanjing Ministry of the Interior ordered that all branch bureaus (*fenju*) and stations (*suo*) be renamed offices (*shu*).[10] And the Special Branch of the Shanghai government, which was independent from the police, was reorganized under the directorship of Gong Wenfang to report on the movements of anti-Japanese elements.[11]

By September 1939 the puppet detective corps under Guo Shaoyi numbered 300.[12] On October 7, the Japanese instructed Chief Lu Ying to transform this corps into a "special intelligence section" (*te gao ke*) to conduct special operations, handle foreign affairs, censor cultural works, and investigate political dissidents.[13] Simultaneously, the group of guerrillas who had surrendered in the spring of the year to form a Nanhuai Anti-Communist Self Defense Corps in Pudong began to function as a regular police unit of 700 men under Li Jie and Jiang Miaogen. Because the corps had been assessing unpopular taxes on its own in Pudong, it was brought into the regular police structure and paid $30,000 per month.[14] On October 12, 1939, Chief Lu Ying, accompanied by Chief Detective Guo Shaoyi, River Police Chief Bao Ziying, and their Special Services Section adviser Mr. Taketsuchi, inspected the corps—now consisting of 700 constables—by way of bringing these former guerrillas under formal police control.[15]

As the puppet police extended its control over the suburbs, backed up by the Japanese army, confrontations with the Shanghai Municipal Police in the extra-Settlement Western District increased.[16] On August 19, 1939, Settlement police officers fired on puppet police on Jessfield Road, killing a sub-inspector and a sergeant. The Western District Police at 92 Jessfield Road were subsequently exhorted to "adopt a strong and undaunted attitude towards the Settlement Police," and authorized to use force against anyone, regardless of nationality, who dared to interfere with their duties in Huxi.[17] This fresh determination to assert Chinese police— albeit puppet police—sovereignty over the extra-boundary roads was supported by the Japanese once the British declared war against Germany on September 3, 1939.[18] On the night of September 9, 100 members of the puppet police's reserve unit were transferred from the Toyoda cotton mill to 92 Jessfield Road, where they brought the number of Chinese city government police to 360 men. With these new forces, the puppet police began to patrol extra-Settlement streets in that area, including Rockhill Avenue and Avenue Haig.[19]

At the same time, puppet police and Japanese Military Police took over several large residences along Jessfield Road and constructed sandbagged machine-gun emplacements outside their gates.[20] Four days later, the

Japanese Military Police and puppet police expropriated a large house at 448 Avenue Haig (whose Taiwanese owner reputedly had used it as a gambling casino) and turned it into a billet for thirty-five of their members.[21] The next morning, a notice over Wang Delin's signature was posted at the entrance to 92 Jessfield Road announcing that the Western District was now under the jurisdiction of the Reform Government and inviting members of the Shanghai Municipal Police to join the city police at an equivalent amount of pay.[22]

The Settlement authorities and the Western military commanders in the Huxi sector at first refused to recognize the puppet régime's claims. When the Shanghai city police established a traffic post at the corner of Robison and Kiaochow [Qiaozhou] Roads, the Shanghai Municipal Police immediately protested to Count Bentivoglio, commander of the Italian Marines. In less than three hours the post was removed.[23] Tensions heightened, however, after Chinese and Sikh constables were shot on traffic duty on the outside roads. On October 22, in the early hours of the morning, a thirty-minute gun battle broke out between Shanghai Municipal Police sergeants and elements of the puppet secret police from 76 Jessfield Road.[24]

By then, both the Japanese and puppet organs were vehemently arguing that the combination of anti-Japanese terrorism and the continuing crime wave in the International Settlement proved that the Shanghai Municipal Police was incapable of ensuring law and order, thus making it necessary for the Chinese to police Huxi themselves and even to recover the foreign concessions.[25] Reviving arguments that the foreign concessions provided criminals with a secure haven of operations, the puppet press claimed that the Shanghai city police had successfully overcome crime and disorder in the areas under its jurisdiction:

> So far no alarming cases of robbery have occurred in the areas under the jurisdiction of the Shanghai City Government, and peace and order is more efficiently maintained there than in the Foreign Settlements. This demonstrates that the Chinese government is capable of maintaining peace and order in the areas under its jurisdiction. We hope that for the sake of the lives and property of the several million Chinese residents in the Foreign Settlements of Shanghai, the City Government will make every endeavor to secure the return of the foreign settlements.[26]

The Wang Jingwei régime and police rights

The claim of law and order in Huxi was ludicrous, of course, but it was made—as the last sentence in the quotation suggests—in the context of negotiations between Wang Jingwei and the Japanese to form a new

Nationalist government. One of the key points of those negotiations, designed to buttress the patriotic claims of the Wang régime, was restoration, after ninety-eight years of foreign dominion, of Chinese sovereignty over the concessions. A major assertion, in this regard, was the linkage between extraterritoriality and crime:[27]

> From the time that they came into existence, the Settlements have been a den of all kinds of evil and bandits and gangsters make a living on crime in the Settlements. Due to the special circumstances prevailing in the area, bandits are more audacious, so much so that they have even staged fighting with the police. . . . In this connection we earnestly hope that after its inauguration the new Central Government will regard the retrocession of foreign settlements as its primary task. The Settlements constitute the number one shelter for crime in China, and in order to purge the city of lawless elements, the retrocession of all foreign settlements should be given immediate attention. So long as the foreign settlements remain unrecovered, Shanghai will never have peace or security.[28]

At war in Europe and keenly aware that the soon-to-be established Wang Jingwei régime would have much more leverage than the Reform Government when it came to the disposition of the foreign concessions, the British authorities in the International Settlement were increasingly disposed to negotiate an agreement with lame-duck Mayor Fu Xiaoan over police jurisdiction in the badlands.[29]

Discussions opened just after New Year's day, 1940, between Godfrey Phillips, secretary and commissioner general of the Shanghai Municipal Council, and Mayor Fu's representatives.[30] The talks progressed well—so well, in fact, that secret service elements from 76 Jessfield Road tried to delay a compromise settlement by attempting to assassinate Phillips. Shortly before 9:00 a.m. on January 6, 1940, Phillips's chauffeur drove into an ambush on Avenue Haig in the British Defence Sector. Three rickshas blocked the road, forcing the chauffeur to brake to a halt and giving three assailants the opportunity to draw their Mausers and fire upon the car point-blank. Phillips miraculously escaped being wounded. The three shooters, who were probably Japanese Special Services Section agents, escaped altogether.[31] Another three backup agents fled down an alley, but were seized by armed guards in front of a badlands casino. The agents identified themselves as being from "76" and so were turned over to the puppet Special Services Corps, and then eventually to the Japanese, who kept them in protective custody.[32]

Undaunted, Phillips went on to the negotiations in Ambassador A. C. Kerr's official armored car, and that very day worked out an agreement "in principle" with Mayor Fu to form a special Western District police force with "certain principal officers" to be appointed from among candidates recommended by the Shanghai Municipal Council. These "principal officers" would act in any cases involving foreign nationals. That so-called modus vivendi agreement (*linshi xieding*) was signed by the Chinese mayor and the Shanghai Municipal Council on February 17, 1940.[33] It was hailed by *Xin shenbao* as "a satisfactory solution of the outstanding extra-settlement roads question. . . . The goal of new China is to work for her independence, to remove all aggressive influence, and to abolish all the unequal treaties. The settlement of the outside roads question in the Western District marks the beginning of this."[34]

On March 30, 1940, Wang Jingwei formally inaugurated the new national puppet government in Nanjing.[35] Nominally under the control of Wang Jingwei's "orthodox" Guomindang, its second most important figure was Zhou Fohai, who wore five different hats: vice-president of the Executive Yuán, minister of finance, minister of police, vice-chairman of the Military Affairs Commission, and general director of the Central Reserve Bank.[36] Zhou, who also was responsible for the secret police, had an excellent Japanese secondary and university education, having graduated from Kyoto Imperial University in 1924.[37] Once back in China, where he helped found the Chinese Communist Party, Zhou was tapped to run the Propaganda Department of the Guomindang in Canton. From that position, which also meant teaching political study classes at Whampoa Academy, he rose—narrowly surviving the 1927 purge—to become "valet to the star actor" (*paolongtao de jiaoshe*), Chiang Kai-shek. Serving as editor of *New Life Monthly,* Zhou Fohai systematized Sun Yat-sen's writings in his work *Sanminzhuyi zhi lilun de tixi* (Theoretical system of the Three People's Principles; 1928), which was translated into Japanese by Inukai Ken and helped establish Zhou's reputation among Japanese intellectuals.[38]

Zhou Fohai had begun recruiting and training personnel in Shanghai in late 1939, before the Nanjing government was actually even organized, so the new puppet government was already a prominent presence by the time of its formal inauguration on March 30.[39] Responding to its existence, *Xin shenbao* took on a new tone as early as April 1, criticizing the failure of the authorities in the two foreign settlements to check the "terroristic elements in the employ of the Chungking [Chongqing] authorities" who were trying to block "the progressive development of the peace movement."[40] On April 10, the puppet newspaper decried both Chiang Kai-shek's "running dogs" and the Communists for shouting about recovery of the foreign settlements but doing virtually nothing about it. "Our new central government is now in existence. Not only does our government desire to recover the foreign settlements in China, but our friendly nation

Japan has given indication of a desire to render assistance to China in the retrocession of these settlements."[41]

76 Jessfield Road

Claims for the peaceful police administration of the badlands were belied by the activities of the Special Services Section at 76 Jessfield Road, which also compromised the distinction Wang Jingwei's supporters wished to draw between opportunistic "bad" collaborators such as members of Liang Hongzhi's Reform Government, and idealistic "good" collaborators such as themselves, who supposedly cooperated with the Japanese to bring about peace and protect the Chinese people.[42] After the war was over, a Chinese political commentator remarked:

> Wang Kemin's Provisional Government and Liang Hongzhi's Reform Government were the senior generation operating in the past under the sign, "traitor" (*jian*). In the occupied zone everyone called them the "former traitors" (*qianhan*). Naturally enough, Wang Jingwei's collaborationist régime was called the "latter traitors" (*houhan*). Many of these treacherous scoundrels verbally acknowledged that they were "latter traitors," but quite unabashedly saw no cause for shame. But ever since the "latter traitors" took the "former traitors'" place as Japanese puppets, the people gnashed their teeth and hated them bitterly. This was because the "former" were actually no match for the "latter" in heinousness, especially since the "latter" had their den of monsters at No. 76 (the puppet secret service organ)—the mere mention of which turned one pale—where people were mowed down like fields of hemp.[43]

Wang Jingwei's deputy, Zhou Fohai, may have been given ultimate responsibility for the puppet secret police, but the real authority within that palace of horrors was in the hands of Li Shiqun and Ding Mocun, the two former Communist renegades who had joined Nationalist intelligence only to betray their new secret service masters by defecting to the Japanese.[44]

Li Shiqun was originally an agent of the Bureau of Statistics and Investigation under the Central Committee of the Nationalist Party (Zhongguo Guomindang zhongyang weiyuanhui tongji diaocha ju, or "Zhongtong") assigned by Chen Lifu to head the special services brigade (*dui*) for the Shanghai region. Later Zhongtong assigned him to a post in Jiangxi, which he abandoned in 1938 to go to Hong Kong. In Hong Kong he contacted Japanese Consul General Nakamura, who referred him to First Secretary Shimizu. Li Shiqun thus began gathering intelligence for the Japanese in the late summer of 1938.[45]

Li had excellent contacts in Shanghai, where he had joined the Green Gang in the early 1930s as a disciple of Ji Yunqing. Returning that fall, Li Shiqun quickly realized that he could use the informers and agents that he had run as a Zhongtong officer to expand his operation from a small intelligence-gathering outfit into a large gang of mercenaries to conduct special operations for the Japanese.[46] Working through Wang Manyun, a former Guomindang Municipal Committee member and a sworn disciple of Du Yuesheng, Li earned Du's favor by sending the Green Gang leader in Hong Kong a copy of the latter's voluminous police file, purloined by the Japanese.[47] Li also quickly gathered a core of seven former Zhongtong and "CC clique" members to serve as his backbone cadres.[48] In addition he secured the allegiance of Wu Shibao, another Green Gang member, who enlisted local gangsters to serve as bodyguards for Wang Jingwei and other prominent collaborators.[49] Wu Shibao, thickset and swarthy, was a notoriously sadistic murderer, whose wife was a celebrated if hard-hearted Shanghai beauty.[50]

Ding Mocun, who had supervised Li Shiqun's work as an editor of the "CC clique's" *Shehui xinwen* (Social News) in Shanghai during 1933, held an even more prominent position under Chen Lifu in Zhongtong, being chief of the Third Department until that section was reorganized in August 1938 and handed over to Dai Li.[51] At that time "Little Devil Ding" (who was only five foot one) ostensibly retired from intelligence work to get another job in Hankou.[52] According to Chen Lifu himself, Chiang Kai-shek suspected Ding Mocun of treachery because Dai Li had intercepted telegraphic communications between Ding and "certain Japanese in Shanghai." But when the Generalissimo suggested that Chen Lifu arrest Ding, Chen replied that Ding had already reported these contacts to him. Chiang Kai-shek simply wrote *yue* (read) on the memorandum and returned it to Chen Lifu.[53]

Shortly after this, Ding Mocun left Hankou without permission to go to Hong Kong.[54] Chiang Kai-shek reprimanded Chen Lifu for letting Ding leave and asked him who had recommended Ding to join the party. When Chen responded that the recommenders were Dai Jitao and Zhou Fohai, who was a fellow Hunanese, Chiang said nothing "except that I should be on guard." In retrospect, twenty years later, Chen Lifu felt that the Generalissimo had been absolutely correct. "When Ting Mo-ts'un [Ding Mocun] went to Shanghai he destroyed both Chün-t'ung [Juntong] and Chung-t'ung [Zhongtong] organizations."[55]

In early 1939 Li Shiqun invited Ding Mocun to Shanghai. After he arrived, the two men together went to see General Doihara Kenji in the Special Services Section's headquarters in Hongkou. As Professor Wen-hsin Yeh has pointed out, the assassination of Chen Lu had already convinced the Japanese that they needed to create their own Chinese secret service in order to protect prominent collaborators such as Wang Jingwei:[56]

> Ding and Li offered their services to help "assemble a group of Nationalist comrades and to facilitate peace." The Japanese were pleased to procure an instrument that would permit them to penetrate the seemingly impenetrable web of Chinese social networks—"the complicated Chinese social scene of personal relationships" that Chongqing agents had so skillfully exploited in the past. Doihara's plan to support a puppet secret service was approved on February 10, 1939, by the army general staff in Tokyo, and Li and Ding's operations were formally launched on March 1. Colonel Haruke Yoshitane[57] was appointed the liaison officer from the Plum Blossom Agency (*Ume Kikan*), Colonel Kagesa Sadaaki's military intelligence unit directing the Nanjing puppet government of Wang Jingwei. Ding and Li agreed to clear their operating details with the Japanese Military Police in advance and to submit daily intelligence reports. In return they received a steady supply of weapons, ammunition, and money.[58]

Shortly afterwards the Li–Ding operation moved into 76 Jessfield Road, from whence it encouraged the defection of such key Juntong agents as Wang Tianmu and Chen Mingchu, while simultaneously crushing organizational units of that selfsame service.[59] It was Chen Mingchu who perhaps betrayed some of Chen Lu's assassins to the Japanese consular police and who later delivered Liu Geqing to the puppet secret service.[60]

A few days after the murder of Chen Lu on February 19, 1939, Xu Guoqi, one of the leaders of the Juntong assassination team, had arranged with Ping Fuchang and You Pinshan to leave Shanghai for safe harbor in Hong Kong. Their steamer had sailed on February 28. Tan Baoyi, warned by Zhu Shanyuan that Shanghai was now too dangerous and supplied with $80 for the boat ticket, sailed twelve days later, arriving in Hong Kong on March 15. Xu Guoqi, who had left instructions with Tan's cousin telling him to check in to the Tai Lai Hotel, stopped by the next day and took him to an afternoon banquet at the Jinlong (Golden Dragon) restaurant. The other members of the team—Ping Fuchang, You Pinshan, and Liu Geqing—were all present. Their host, a medium-built man about 5'4" tall in his late thirties, was Dai Li. Although Liu Geqing was later to be rewarded by Dai Li and praised as a national hero for having killed Chen Lu, nothing at all was said about the assassination at the reception. Dai Li, who was accompanied by two aides, merely gave each of the men a $20 fountain pen and wished them well. This was the first and last time that Ping Fuchang and Tan Baoyi saw their secret service chief.[61]

The Wang Jingwei assassination mission

Tan Baoyi and his Juntong comrades—Ping Fuchang, Zhu Shanyuan, You Pingshan—spent the next two months in Hong Kong, awaiting reassignment. In late May 1939, Liu Geqing finally gave them their new orders. Their mission was to return to Shanghai under the command of Mao Wanli and Wang Luzhao, and prepare to assassinate Wang Jingwei.[62] The team traveled separately: the four agents by one boat, and the two leaders by another. When they arrived in Shanghai on June 1, the agents took rooms in the Yafei [Xiafei] boarding house at 66 rue Paul Beau, while the leaders stayed at the Dah Tsoong and Dah Faung Hotels.[63]

At 5:00 a.m. on June 29, Sergeant Major Katoda and another member of the Japanese Military Police came to the central branch headquarters of the Shanghai Municipal Police and said they had "information" that two members of the Chen Lu assassination team were staying in Room 14 of the Xiafei boarding house. They did not reveal the source of the tip, but they indicated that it was reliable enough to justify a raid. The Shanghai Municipal Police inspectors agreed to cooperate, and went together with the two Japanese gendarmes to the Lokawei police station in the French Concession where they secured the assent of Chief Inspector Délormé to a joint operation. It was thus a combined force of Japanese, British, and French police that descended upon Tan Baoyi and Ping Fuchang's lodging shortly after dawn that same morning.[64]

When Tan and Ping were arrested on June 29, the police found guns and ammunition in Room 14.[65] Nevertheless, the Shanghai Municipal Police—which assumed jurisdiction over the prisoners with the consent of the French authorities—were initially unable to get the two men to confess to any wrongdoing. During the formal interrogations that began the following day, both secret agents insisted that they had no connection whatsoever with the Nationalist government.[66] The Japanese consular police and Military Police, however, were convinced that their informants had told them the truth, and that the two prisoners were indeed members of the squad that assassinated Foreign Minister Chen Lu. On July 3, 1939, Sergeant Major Katoda submitted a formal request to the Shanghai Municipal Police to hand over Tan Baoyi and Ping Fuchang for Japanese Military Police interrogation.[67]

The Shanghai Municipal Police was not eager to comply, since Sergeant Major (later Sub-lieutenant) Katoda's unit already had an infamous reputation for torture, especially when it came to questioning suspects in the Chen Lu case.[68] On March 16, 1939, for example, the Shanghai Municipal Police had been asked to help Sergeant Major Katoda arrest Shao Fusheng, the night watchman who had been missing from his post in front

of Chen Lu's mansion the night of the assassination. Katoda was acting on the usual anonymous tip, in this case stemming from a complicated business arrangement involving loan sharks, theater owners, and a couple of ex-policemen, including a former Chinese detective sergeant who had worked out of the Gordon Road station. The latter was the part-owner of the Dalai Theater (where Shao Fusheng worked as a ticket collector) who had recommended Shao to Wu Tiecheng's secretary for the night watchman's position at Chen Lu's house.[69]

The business deal had gone sour; fist fights had broken out more than once over welshed loans; and in the end one of the partners had made Shao Fusheng's whereabouts known to the Japanese Military Police, who donned Chinese clothing and accompanied Shanghai Municipal Police officers to Guizhou Road to pick up the suspect. At 3:00 that same afternoon, the Japanese Military Policemen spotted Shao Fusheng walking along the street near the Amoy Road intersection, and they pointed him out for the Shanghai Municipal Police officers to arrest.[70]

Sergeant Major Katoda appeared convinced that Shao Fusheng was a member of the assassination conspiracy.[71] The Shanghai Municipal Police detectives were not so sure, especially when his alibis for February 19 (morning tea at a story-telling club, afternoon ticket taking in the Dalai Theater, and so on) were independently corroborated by witnesses' depositions.[72] But even though the Shanghai Municipal Police officers were fairly certain that Shao Fusheng was innocent, they handed him over to the custody of Sergeant Major Katoda for an interrogation period of three days from March 21 to March 24. The interrogation period—which turned out to be four days—was to seem interminable.[73]

That first afternoon, Katoda and his military policemen took Shao Fusheng across Garden Bridge—the "Bridge of Sighs"—to Bridge House. On the fifth floor he was taken into a room occupied by three Japanese who began beating him, especially about the eyes, when he denied any knowledge of the Chen Lu case. "I still denied that I knew of this case, and eventually they tied me down on a long form and for what I took to be half an hour poured cold water down my nostrils."[74] The second day, after spending the night in a downstairs cell with captured Chinese guerrillas, Shao Fusheng was taken back to the fifth-floor interrogation room, where he was grilled but not tortured.[75] The third day he was taken to a different interrogation room on the sixth floor, where the three Japanese interrogators had been joined by a Chinese Shanghai Municipal Police detective who threatened to shoot him if he did not tell the truth:[76]

I then told [the Chinese detective] that I truly did not know of this case, whereupon I was seized by the Japanese and tied down to a form and had

water poured down my nose again. After about twenty minutes, they released me and again questioned me as to whether or not I knew [a suspect who was Shao Fusheng's neighbor]. I at first denied I did, but when they produced a large knife and threatened to behead me, I admitted that I knew this man. During this time, the [Chinese detective] was present. I was again returned downstairs.[77]

During the fourth day Shao Fusheng was again interrogated but not tortured. On the afternoon of the final day, Shao was removed from his cell and taken upstairs where a Japanese threatened to kill him with a pistol if he did not talk: "I told him I had nothing further to say and that if he wanted to kill me he could do so. He then commenced laughing and said that I was being returned to the Shanghai Municipal Police. I was returned to the Shanghai Municipal Police at 5:00 p.m. 25-3-39."[78]

When Shao Fusheng was returned to Central Police headquarters on March 25 by Sergeant Major Katoda, the Shanghai Municipal Police officers noted a "fairly bad abrasion of the left eye" and bruises on the body and legs.[79] Regarding him as the victim of a "frameup," Special Branch officers soon discerned that the ordeal had left Shao "mentally unbalanced" and suicidal.[80] Now, less than four months later, they were hardly about to hand over two new assassination suspects, Tan Baoyi and Ping Fuchang, to Sergeant Major Katoda and his men without some consideration. Fully ten days after Katoda's formal request, the Shanghai Municipal Police finally informed the Japanese Military Police that they could have Tan and Ping for five days' questioning and no more. But by then, July 13, the Japanese felt that this was not enough time for their "specialists" at Bridge House to conduct the kind of extended interrogation they had not been able to inflict upon Shao Fusheng. They turned down the offer.[81]

Two days later, however, the Shanghai Municipal Police helped the Japanese consular police make a raid on House 17, Lane 317, rue Frélupt.[82] In the house they discovered a report by one You Heqing—that is, Liu Geqing—to his superiors "on the successful assassination of Chen Loh [Chen Lu]." The report listed five agents responsible for the Nationalist triumph: Xu Guoqi, You Pinshan, Zhu Shanyuan, Ping Fuchang, and Tan Baoyi.[83] Whether or not the Shanghai Municipal Police realized the significance of the report at the time is unclear. What does seem evident in retrospect is that the Shanghai Municipal Police and the Japanese Military Police were beginning to identify the Chen Lu suspects with a new Juntong conspiracy to assassinate Wang Jingwei. During the late summer and fall of 1939 there were numerous rumors of Communist and Nationalist plots to dispatch Wang, and the presence of suspected Juntong agents such as Ping Fuchang and Tan Baoyi in Shanghai seemed no mere

coincidence.[84] That concern, plus full recognition of the damning significance of the rue Frélupt report when it was presented to them by the Japanese Military Police in a formal request on October 6 that Ping and Tan be handed over for interrogation, finally led the Shanghai Municipal Police to "loan [the two prisoners] to the Japanese Gendarmerie for enquiries."[85] At 4:30 p.m. on October 18, Ping Fuchang and Tan Baoyi "were handed over to the Japanese Gendarmerie . . . for a period of two weeks."[86]

During their sixteen weeks in Shanghai Municipal Police captivity, Ping and Tan had refused to talk.[87] The Japanese interrogators broke them in six days. By October 24 the two seasoned field agents—graduates of Juntong's top training unit—had divulged the organizational structure and recruitment procedures of Juntong;[88] the names of ten senior Linli Depot graduates working as underground agents in Shanghai;[89] Juntong's responsibility for the assassinations of Zhou Jitang and Tang Shaoyi, and for several major bombing incidents;[90] the identities of the other members of their assassination squad;[91] and the existence of a secret wireless apparatus in the International Settlement that maintained daily communications with Kunming, Chongqing, Tianjin, and Hong Kong.[92]

Their Japanese interrogators were interested, furthermore, in learning of better ways to "mop up" Juntong agents in Shanghai, of more details about Dai Li's personality, of other terrorist units in the city, and of other Linli Depot graduates "who have approached the Reformed Government circles by ostensibly presenting themselves as pro-Japanese figures."[93] Ping and Tan's answers to these questions were vague, though not evasive. There was no way to "mop up" Juntong agents "except buying them off," first by "brib[ing] the low-class members" and then "arrest[ing] the high-class members by their information."[94] Dai Li was the most "prominent" Juntong leader, but he always stayed in Hong Kong and they "know little about him."[95] Because he had "no lateral connections," Tan Baoyi could tell the Japanese nothing about other Juntong squads in Shanghai.[96] And while both men "thought it possible" that the Reform Government had been burrowed into by Juntong moles, they knew none by name.[97]

Above all, the Japanese were concerned about a plot to assassinate Wang Jingwei. Both Ping Fuchang and Tan Baoyi admitted that that was their major mission.[98] But they also confessed that no steps had yet been taken to implement the mission. They did not know the procedures planned, nor the details of the bodyguard, nor even Wang Jingwei's address. In other words, the assassination had been premeditated, but it was not "in progress concretely."[99]

Ping Fuchang and Tan Baoyi of course also admitted their involvement in Chen Lu's assassination.[100] On October 26, recently promoted Second

Sub-Lieutenant Katoda informed the Shanghai Municipal Police that Tan and Ping had confessed to the murder, and that he was going to take them to the scene of the crime in order to reconstruct the assassination. Special Branch officers then accompanied them to Chen Lu's former mansion and observed the reenactment, which was quite convincing.[101] Two days later, Tan Baoyi and Ping Fuchang were returned "from loan" to the Shanghai Municipal Police.[102] Their guilt by now was firmly established in the eyes of the Special Branch, and at 11:00 on the morning of November 8, Tan and Ping were returned to Sub-Lieutenant Katoda, being fully remanded to the custody of the Japanese Military Police.[103] Seven months later, on June 11, 1940, the two Juntong agents were sentenced to the death penalty by court martial at the headquarters of the Japanese Military Police.[104]

Solving the Chen Lu murder case and preventing Wang Jingwei's assassination were triumphs for Japanese counterespionage. They occurred just as several other Juntong special service teams were also being rounded up early in October 1939 by the puppet secret service at 76 Jessfield Road. On October 5 Shanghai newspapers reported that more than twenty terrorists were being arrested by Japanese consular police after months of investigation. These twenty included Tan Baoyi and Ping Fuchang along with more than a dozen other Juntong agents accused of numerous assassination plots, including the poisoning incident at the Japanese Consulate General on June 18, 1939.[105] For the moment, it seemed, the Japanese and their Chinese collaborators in the badlands were winning the terrorist wars.[106]

8

Terrorism and crime

The conclusion of the Chen Lu murder case and the breakup of the Wang Jingwei assassination conspiracy were also a triumph for 76 Jessfield Road. Credit for many of these arrests, including the capture of another group of secret agents sent from Chongqing to kill Wang Jingwei, was given by Japanese newspapers such as *Tokyo nichinichi* to Messrs. Ding Mocun and Li Shiqun of the Reform Government special services group. Li Shiqun was thus able to boast, when he visited Tokyo later in the fall, that he had destroyed or utterly undermined Nationalist military intelligence (Juntong) throughout Shanghai, Nanjing, Jiangsu, Zhejiang, and Anhui. "With the left hand we annihilate the Blue Shirts, with the right hand we knock down the C.C. clique."[1]

According to Shanghai Municipal Police reports, however, "76" was also responsible for a series of assassination attempts itself, including the brutal murder of Miss Mao Liying, chair of the Chinese Women's Vocational Joint Friendship Society (Zhongguo funü zhiye lianyi hui), on December 12, 1939, by a group of five men who fought off police with pistols before brazenly driving back to 76 Jessfield Road to report in.[2]

G. Godfrey Phillips, the secretary of the Shanghai Municipal Council who had himself been fired on, felt obliged to turn to the consular authorities by writing a letter on April 29, 1940, to Commander L. Neyrone, the Italian consul general who was dean of the Shanghai Diplomatic Corps. In the letter he expressed grave anxiety about the activities of the Special Services Corps of the China Guomindang Anti-Comintern and National Salvation Army headquarters at "76." This group, he said, "constitutes an appallingly grave menace to peace and order in Shanghai." The headquarters corps consisted of over 500 intelligence workers and armed guards, and there were an additional seven branches, each with 10 to 20 members, throughout the city.[3] Phillips believed that unless the organization was curbed, it was doubtful that the newly envisaged Western District police force was going to be able to bring law and order to the badlands.[4]

Indiscriminate terrorism and police subversion

Part of the terrorist problem was its indiscriminacy. The Japanese authorities continued to express concern about the "rampant" attacks on "the lives of Chinese personages having some connection with Japanese enterprises."[5] But it was the "affray" on May 10, 1940, that aggravated them the most, precisely because it was perpetrated by "76" elements nominally under their control. That day, at 6:00 p.m., five men armed with Mausers tried to hold up a motorcar at the Bund. The automobile was carrying $170,000 in customs receipts to the Yokohama Specie Bank—funds that were being doled out by the Japanese Special Services organ to Zhou Fohai.[6] After the robbery attempt failed, one of the robbers tried to make his getaway up Jiujiang Road, firing at guards outside the Mitsui Bank, who shot him down. Another tried to commandeer a taxi on Sichuan Road, and eventually engaged in a gunfight outside of the Palace Hotel, where he was subdued and captured. During the shooting spree, a Sikh Shanghai Municipal Police constable, two Chinese, a Swiss newspaper employee, and two Japanese bank clerks were wounded.[7]

That night, at 12:40 a.m. on the 11th, Major General Miura, commander of the Japanese Military Police, came to Shanghai Municipal Police headquarters, accompanied by two Japanese officers in uniform, to see Commissioner of Police Bourne. The interview, which included Consul Buttrick, lasted until 4:00 a.m. General Miura "spoke energetically," saying that if the Shanghai Municipal Police did not stamp out pro-Chongqing armed activity in the next month, "the Japanese army might take drastic steps." Bourne carefully asked the livid Japanese Military Police commander whether or not this was a warning to be conveyed to the U.S. and British defense commanders, at which point Deputy Commissioner Akagi (appointed, of course, to represent Imperial Japan's interests in the Shanghai Municipal Police) discreetly intervened. Deputy Commissioner Akagi explained that the Japanese Military Police wished to do nothing offensive, but that they were hard pressed by their military authorities to take some action. At this point, a somewhat mollified General Miura told Bourne in confidence that Tokyo had instructed him to discontinue the Wang Jingwei anti-Chongqing assassinations in Shanghai. Consul Buttrick suggested, by way of response, that it might be opportune to have the U.S. Embassy again suggest to the Chinese government in Chongqing the advisability of suppressing terrorism in Shanghai in order to maintain peace and order. The U.S. Embassy in Tokyo might also bring the matter to the attention of the Japanese government, advising them to do away with the "76" Special Services Corps gangsters operating under the orders of the Wang Jingwei régime. Commissioner Bourne noted in this context that the criminals who tried to rob the customs receipts were connected with a Japanese-sponsored gambling house on Jessfield Road:

> I laid very strong emphasis on the fact that I have foretold to the gendarmeries [i.e. the Japanese Military Police] again and again in the last eighteen months the danger of these gambling houses, opium houses, and groups of hired assassins at 76 Jessfield Road, 22 Singapore Road, 35 Edinburgh Road, and other localities.[8]

On May 14, nonetheless, Ambassador Johnson expressed to the Chinese minister of foreign affairs in Chongqing the concern of the U.S. consulate in Shanghai, and he said he hoped that the central government "would use its influence with patriotic Chinese to prevent occurrence of such incidents which could only serve to disturb the situation at Shanghai." The minister promised to take the matter up with the military.[9] And the following day, the Shanghai Municipal Council passed a resolution asking the consular body to take all the steps it could to get the lawless bodies in the badlands suppressed, singling out 76 Jessfield Road for special attention because of its role in assassinations and kidnappings. However, Italian Consul General Neyrone, with the backing of the Japanese consul general, refused to support an intervention on the grounds that the Shanghai Municipal Council had already signed a de facto agreement with Mayor Fu Xiaoan on February 16. The British and U.S. consuls expressed their own doubt that establishing a special Western District police force per the February 16 agreement was likely to prove effective in reestablishing orderly conditions in the badlands or the Settlement. But the consuls remained deadlocked, and though the British and U.S. officials' prediction proved in the long run to be quite accurate, there were no subsequent steps taken by the consular body.[10]

In the short run, terrorist incidents, at least, were much reduced. The period from June 1939 to June 1940 had the lowest incidence of terrorism throughout the entire period of "island Shanghai." The Japanese press service Domei noted on May 18, 1940, that there had been a sharp drop in anti-Japanese terrorism: only four assassinations in April compared with fourteen in March.[11] But the worst was yet to come. Beginning on June 28, 1940, with the assassination in the International Settlement of Mu Shiying (one of Wang Jingwei's most important propagandists) by Chongqing loyalists, and continuing on July 1 with the retaliatory killing of Shao Xubai (a pro-Nationalist journalist) by Nanjing puppets, terrorism suddenly redoubled.[12]

Because of the fall of France, the wraps of neutrality were almost completely off in the French Concession. In June 1940, the new Vichy French authorities turned over the policing of Xujiahui to the puppets, and allowed puppet agents to operate in the French Concession against pro-Chongqing terrorists.[13] This new arrangement with the local Wang Jing-wei régime was one of the factors inspiring the effort in the late summer and early fall of 1940 to suborn the International Settlement's Shanghai Municipal Police.[14]

Police subversion

On September 16, 1940, Deputy Commissioner R. W. Yorke, chief of the Shanghai Municipal Police Special Branch, was leaving his house off of Yuyuan Road when two Chinese shot at him. He returned the fire and drove them off.[15] Yorke's attempted assassination took place the day after the Shanghai Municipal Police had suspended over sixty policemen on suspicion of being suborned. Since Yorke was in charge of the investigation of this subversion, and since his counterpart in the French Concession Police, Lieutenant Blanchet, had nearly been killed by assassins from 76 Jessfield Road three weeks earlier, the connection was obvious enough.[16] As Consul General A. H. George explained to the British ambassador:

> It appears that the Shanghai office of the Ministry of Police of the Nanking "government" situated at number 76 Jessfield Road is making determined attempts to suborn members of the French and Shanghai Municipal police forces, with the apparent object of inducing members of the two foreign-controlled police forces to render full facilities to the members of the Special Services Group attached to the Shanghai office of the Ministry of Police in the execution of their "duties" in the foreign-controlled areas prior to the actual "recovery" of these areas by the *de facto* authorities. As a *quid pro quo,* members of the foreign police forces are promised employment after the foreign areas have been "recovered," and necessary relief should they be dismissed in the event of their political activities being discovered by the foreign police authorities.[17]

The person in charge of this subornation was Pan Zhijie, chief of the Fourth Department at 76 Jessfield Road and for the preceding nine years an inspector in the Shanghai Municipal Police Specials. A chartered accountant in civilian life, Pan Zhijie—also known as Pan Da and C. C. Pan—was said to have suborned 400 constables and 60 detectives of the Shanghai Municipal Police and French police with monthly retainers of $20 and $60. Pan Zhijie was designated by the city government as commissioner of the special police force for the Western District that the puppets expected to establish.[18]

Whether suborned or not, it was still in the common interest of the foreign settlements' police to keep the anniversary of the 1911 Revolution, October 10, from getting out of control. Both sides naturally wished to claim the national holiday, and the question of whether to fly a pro–Wang Jingwei or a pro-Chongqing banner was particularly sensitive. The Shanghai Municipal Police took especially careful precautions this year, given the recent rise in terrorist incidents, including the assassination of Liu Yuying, a high official in a Japanese-operated textile firm.[19] At 6:00 p.m. on October 9, 1940, the Specials were mobilized, and Japanese residents were warned by the Japanese authorities to remain north of Suzhou Creek during the entire emergency period. At midnight all roads were closed, with the exception of main arteries. Beginning at 5 a.m. on the morning of the 10th, barricades were set up on the southern and western boundaries of the Settlement and intersections were blocked by barrier search parties. All vehicular and pedestrian traffic was subject to search on suspicion only. The defense forces (U.S. Marine Corps, Royal Italian Marines, Shanghai Volunteer Corps, and so forth) posted guards on bridges and afforded special protection to Japanese mills and mill quarters in the Settlement.[20]

The precautions seemed to work, although there was the expected battle of posters and flags with the advantage overwhelmingly on the side of the puppet régime.[21] Paper flags with pennants bearing pro–Wang Jingwei and anti-Comintern slogans were posted on buses, electric lightpoles, and trolleys. The Anti-Communist Chinese Youth League (Fangong qingnian tuan) handed out pro-régime handbills. In the badlands, a bamboo *pailou* (ceremonial archway) was erected outside 76 Jessfield Road bearing a blue-sky red-ground national flag with pennant inscribed: "National Construction by Means of Peace and Opposition to Communism." At Nandao, the district administrative office held a meeting attended by representatives of various official organs and eighty primary school students who heard speeches extolling Japan and berating Chiang Kai-shek. In opposition, Chinese loyalists merely posted a few anti-Japanese slogans on walls along Seymour Road and near the department stores on Nanking Road, and surreptitiously distributed a handful of anti–Wang Jingwei pamphlets. The controls imposed by the International Settlement Shanghai Municipal Police were so tight that it was completely foolhardy to come out in the open and oppose the Japanese and their puppets publicly.[22]

The only recourse left, therefore, was terrorism. Early on the morning of October 11, puppet Mayor Fu Xiaoan's cook slipped by the sleeping man's bodyguards to slash him to death in the face and head with a butcher's cleaver.[23] The cook, Zhu Shengyuan, had worked for Fu for twelve years, but was secretly recruited by Dai Li.[24]

The assassination of Mayor Fu Xiaoan "precipitated a deadly struggle between two factions in the Wang camp to control the taxes and revenues from vice and crime in the Shanghai district."[25] The two contenders for the former mayor's empty seat were Chen Gongbo and Zhou Fohai. Wang Jingwei sent Zhou to Shanghai to test the waters, but foreign and Chinese reaction to his appointment as mayor was so negative that the post instead went to Chen Gongbo.[26] A critical factor may have been the response of General Doihara's Special Services Organ. The assassination on November 9 in Nanjing of Yuan Zhi'an, an ardent supporter of Zhou's claims to the mayor's post, and on November 12 in Shanghai of Ling Tse-chuen [Lin Zechuan], another Zhou backer, together suggest that the Japanese Imperial Army staff backed Chen Gongbo's claim.[27]

The administration of Chen Gongbo

When Chen Gongbo was appointed mayor of Shanghai after Fu Xiaoan's death, one of his first acts was to declare solemnly that he was determined to clean up the areas under his control. He promised this when he was sworn in, repeated it several weeks later at a press conference, and reiterated the pledge in his New Year's message on December 31, 1940.[28] The New Year's season, when debts were due and crime rates traditionally climbed, was a rash time to make such a promise. Within the week, on Monday, January 6, 1941, a particularly cold-blooded murder occurred in the badlands. H. Latham, a British employee at the Kung Yik Cotton Mill, was purchasing stamps in the Brenan Road post office at 1:20 p.m. when three armed men walked in. One stood at the door as a lookout. The other two accosted Latham and a Russian woman, demanding their money and valuables in broken English. Latham only had a little more than a dollar in his pocket, but he impulsively pushed the man away and shouted to the clerk to telephone the police. At that moment, the gangster robbing the Russian woman turned and calmly shot Latham through the back. After the robbers left the post office the clerk called the Shanghai Fire Brigade, which arrived at 1:25 p.m. Latham was dead by the time the ambulance reached the hospital.[29] And it was not just the badlands, either. As Vanya Oakes reported:

> Elsewhere in Shanghai, in an area at least nominally international, people in automobiles were held up at the point of a pistol for bogus license fees, and buses operated without either franchises or trained drivers. Shanghai had become a city where there might easily be a corpse on the sidewalk on Saturday which would still be there on Monday.[30]

Throughout the city kidnapping reached a new high.[31] Police arrested a gang of 131 men and women who had collected $10 million in the course of a couple of years. "Their operations ranged from snatching children and shipping them by the dozen to Canton, where there was a big demand for household slaves, to kidnapping rich and uncomplaining merchants and bankers."[32]

But this year's New Year's crime wave seemed qualitatively worse than usual, as documented by the *China Weekly Review*:[33]

> While political terrorism continued to hold Shanghai in its ruthless grip last week, armed robbery and petty crime swept towards its [*sic*] annual peak with the approach of the Spring festival. Last Thursday actually marked the beginning of the wave of robberies which usually precedes each Chinese New Year, and before noon seven robberies had been reported in the Settlement alone. Gangsters, hold-up men, terrorists maintained the pace throughout the day, according to the police records.[34]

To a degree, political assassinations provided a kind of mask for criminal homicides. Businessmen were killed much more casually for purposes of extortion; bombs were hurled into shops much more indifferently for failing to buy protection.[35]

A new form of crime was the robbing of bus passengers. This appeared to have begun in the badlands where hoodlums connected with 76 Jessfield Road refused to pay bus fares and assaulted China General Omnibus Company conductors when they insisted upon payment.[36] It was an easy step from assaulting fare collectors to shaking down passengers, and that practice soon spread to the settlements, where buses were boarded by pistol-packing robbers who forced the passengers to hand over their valuables. One of the most spectacular of these New Year's urban highway robberies took place on January 27, when ten armed men boarded an omnibus on Connaught Road and forced the passengers to give up their overcoats and festival gowns.[37]

The foreign concession readers of *China Weekly Review* were repeatedly told that the source of their daily hazards was the badlands and that they would continue to live in peril unless proper measures were taken to police the Western District according to the agreement reached in February 1940 between the now-late Mayor Fu Xiaoan and Cornell S. Franklin, then chairman of the Shanghai Municipal Council:

> Crime and vice are rampant and more and more gambling dens openly flaunt their banners in the face of Chen [Gongbo]'s puppet police. Settlement police have traced practically every holdup in the recent crime wave to various hideouts in the western area, and airy assurances to the contrary, Chen has placed every possible obstruction in the way of the satisfactory settlement in the long outstanding policing question. Although the Shanghai Municipal Council authorities met on Wednesday [January 8, 1941] to discuss the results of negotiations with Chen on the outside roads special police force, the latter's terms were found to be such to render an agreement impossible.[38]

But Major Kenneth Bourne of the Shanghai Municipal Police and Colonel Lu Ying of the Shanghai municipal government puppet police had continued to negotiate, and—given the tremendous public outcry over the January crime wave—soon managed to come to a tentative agreement for forming a special police force for the badlands, mainly composed of Shanghai municipal government rank and file, but officered by a combination of Settlement, puppet, and Japanese inspectors.[39] The tentative agreement reached by Lu and Bourne in January 1941 was submitted to the Shanghai Municipal Council and to the Chinese authorities in Nanjing for approval, which was forthcoming.[40]

The Hayashi affair

The Shanghai Municipal Police force was a colossal burden on the budget of the International Settlement. For years the Shanghai Municipal Police had been living off the Ch.$81 million reserve fund generated by the sale of the muncipal electric power plant in 1929. In order to avoid another annual deficit, the Council had tried to raise land taxes in 1936 from 14 to 16 percent, but the Japanese ratepayers had strenuously objected.[41] Since the International Settlement's net indebtedness—which was secured by the $67 million worth of land and buildings owned by the Shanghai Municipal Council—had already been $39,692,284 before the war with Japan broke out, the Council had had no choice but to dip into its electricity plant reserves for another $2 million to balance the 1936 budget. The same was true for the 1937 budget, which ate up another $3.25 million of the rapidly diminishing reserve fund, despite a police pay cut of 8 percent and the reduction of various police allowances.[42]

The war only worsened fiscal matters, which took on an increasingly irksome political tone as the Settlement came more and more to depend upon the rates or taxes paid by the growing Japanese population of Shanghai's international sector (which of course incorporated "Little Tokyo" in Hongkou). By January 1941 there were about 87,000 Japanese subjects living in Shanghai proper: roughly 79,000 Japanese, 5,000 Koreans, and 3,000 Taiwanese.[43] At the Municipal Council's annual public meeting in 1940 the ratepayers among Shanghai's Japanese residents had sought to increase their representation on the Shanghai Municipal Council, but their proposal was defeated.[44] This year, however, the municipality was in such dire financial straits that a special meeting of the ratepayers was called for January 23, 1941, to consider a proposal to levy a 40 percent surcharge on the land tax municipal rates and special rates retroactive to January 1, 1940, and to increase general license fees.[45]

The Japanese ratepayers association and amalgamated street unions of retail merchants, led by their seventy-year-old chairman, Hayashi Yukichi, were strongly opposed to this tax increase, which would fall most heavily upon them. Given the rigged composition of the Council, however, the Japanese ratepayers had little hope of defeating the proposed tax increase, not to speak of getting an amendment passed that would seek refinancing of the Settlement's debt through bank loans.[46] In an interview with the Shanghai *Mainichi* a few hours before the meeting, Mr. Hayashi said:

> It is obvious how the municipal ratepayers meeting today will end. I am now in the same mental condition as Mr. Masahiga Kusunoki (a famed Japanese general who committed suicide following his defeat on the field of battle). . . . I am willing to come and display a spirit that is worthy of the true Japanese. There must be a limit to forbearance on our part. We may be obliged to meet violence with violence. I am willing to become a stepping-stone for our future advance. I shall attend the meeting today joyously and courageously.[47]

The chairman of the Shanghai Municipal Council was W. J. Keswick, who was the head of Jardine, Matheson, & Co. "Tony" Keswick was considered by some to be, at worst, an appeaser for having handed over to the Japanese on July 5 the land records and title deeds of the Chinese municipality, which had been stored in the International Settlement for safekeeping.[48] Others deemed him, at best, a momentary friend of Japan, keen upon cultivating favor in order to protect his company's interests in East Asia at a time when Jardine, Matheson desperately needed access to Chinese resources under Japanese control.[49]

Though chairman of the Shanghai Municipal Council, Keswick did not convene the meeting of 2,084 local residents (representing 13,066 votes) that gathered in the open grandstand facing the track at the race club on Thursday, January 23. Instead, the senior diplomat in Shanghai, Consul General Poul Scheel of Denmark (officially without portfolio since Hitler had taken over his country) chaired the meeting. The tax increase proposal passed handily if provocatively, Consul General Scheel having simply identified the ayes with non-Japanese faces without actually counting the nays—an unconsciously racist act that produced an uproar of whistling and stamping among the Japanese in the bleachers. Chairman Hayashi then introduced the Japanese ratepayers' amendment, declaring in a deep and angry tone that the present system of taxation was unjust; and insisting, nonetheless, that "certain banks" were prepared to meet any requirements of the Shanghai Municipal Council on a commercial basis.[50] Since the crowd knew that the Council had reached the end of its credit tether, many laughed aloud. Hayashi flushed and ended his speech with a thinly veiled threat:

> Should these important recommendations unfortunately be defeated through opposition by a powerful minority group who, as is still fresh in our memories, took advantage of the shortcomings of our election rules to create several thousand decisive votes at the last general election of the councillors . . . and should the measure for tax increases pass over the opposition of several million vitally affected Chinese and Japanese, I must point out that the responsibility for the repercussions must fall on this group and the municipal authorities alone.[51]

After Hayashi returned to his seat beside the speaker's platform, Keswick came to the podium to rebut the Japanese amendment for being an "unsound suggestion," and concluded by saying, "By all the force of my command I ask you to reject this amendment." As Scheel got up to put the amendment to the vote, Hayashi also rose and began to climb toward the podium. Everyone watched the slight form of the seventy-year-old as he slowly ascended the stairway. When he reached the platform, he suddenly drew a .32 caliber revolver from his side pocket, aimed at Keswick, and fired two shots through the Englishman's heavy overcoat and into the fleshy part of his chest. As Keswick fell, pandemonium broke out. Three other men on the stage—Council member I. Okamoto, and K. Ikeda and K. Noguchi of the Secretariat—wrestled the gun out of Hayashi's hands. Chairs and cushions were flung through the air. Commissioner Kenneth Bourne stood at the head of the steps holding off other Japanese who tried to climb up the stairs to the speaker's platform, while police hustled Hayashi off to detention and carried Keswick down to an ambulance for Country Hospital.[52]

Tony Keswick readily survived the attack. Hayashi Yukichi, a hero to his community, surrendered himself to the Japanese Consulate, which announced that Hayashi would be sent to Nagasaki for trial.[53] The Japanese diplomatic spokesman said that it would not be "compulsory" for Shanghai witnesses to appear before the Nagasaki court. "No one"—except, of course, for the *China Weekly Review* itself—"noted the irony of the Japanese shooting Mr. Keswick, who has been for the past year the leader of attempted appeasement of the Japanese."[54] No one could know then, either, that Tony Keswick would end up, after the Japanese attack on Pearl Harbor, as the head of Britain's wartime secret service, the Special Operations Executive, in the China theater.

Although two Japanese tried to burn down the Shanghai race club's public stands on February 2, the Shanghai ratepayers—less the Japanese who boycotted the meeting—convened under the chairmanship of a recuperating Tony Keswick three days later and approved the 40 percent surcharge by a vote of 7,055 to 5.[55] The new taxes would help defray the Council's additional costs of paying for a special force to patrol the western suburbs—an assignment that brought British police officers into direct daily contact with the casino mobsters and vicious secret service killers of Shanghai's notorious badlands.

9

Rackets

On Saturday, February 1, 1941, Mayor Chen Gongbo and Shanghai Municipal Council Chairman W. J. Keswick had met at the Chinese city hall in Jiangwan and signed a police agreement in a blaze of flashbulbs amidst champagne toasts.[1] The arrangement, which implemented the "modus vivendi" agreement signed a year earlier, announced regulations for the establishment of a Western Shanghai Area Special Police Force (WASP for short) or Huxi tebie jingcha zongshu to control the area next to the two concessions, the area formerly under the jurisdiction of the West Shanghai police division, a section of the jurisdiction of the Xujiahui police division, and districts presently guarded by the Shanghai foreign defense forces.[2]

The new WASP was to be composed of the existing police main corps, the whole West Shanghai division, part of the Xujiahui division, and officers of the detective branch corps together with officers recommended by the Municipal Council. According to the regulations, it was to be the only organization to exercise police power in the above areas, and it would do so under the direction of the Shanghai city police bureau.[3] The maximum strength was to be 1,466 men with an additional reserve of 12 men, grouped into five police divisions and a number of stations and substations.[4] The WASP would also have seven branches: police affairs, executive, special, foreign affairs, crime, internal affairs, and a secretariat.[5]

Officers in charge of divisions where most of the residents were foreign nationals would be appointed by the Shanghai municipal government (that is, the puppet city government) from a list of 197 candidates (including men of Chinese nationality) recommended by the Shanghai Municipal Council. Any police officer dismissed from the Shanghai Municipal Police or French Concession Police for improper conduct would be ineligible for appointment to the WASP. Basically each division would have a mixture of nationalities with a preponderance of Europeans and Japanese in command. Cases involving foreign nationals would be handled by the foreign affairs branch of the WASP, although foreigners without treaty rights would be dealt with according to Chinese law. In cases such as these, it was agreed, the deputy commissioners would refer matters to the commissioner before their final disposal. If there were disagreement then the matter would be settled by the commissioners of the Shanghai municipal government police and of the Shanghai Municipal Police; if that failed, then a final decision would be made by the mayor and the chairman of the Shanghai Municipal Council.[6]

Cooperation with the police forces of the city government and of the International Settlement in matters concerning intelligence, searches, and extradition would be facilitated by special liaison officers. With regard to "close pursuit," members of all three police forces could cross city boundaries. A person committing a crime in Huxi who escaped into the Settlement, or vice-versa, and was arrested by his pursuers, would be taken to the nearest police station for booking only "and at once" handed over to the pursuing police agents. In the investigation of a crime, if the WASP had "reasonable suspicion" that confederates of a criminal gang were hiding in the Settlement, then the suspects were to be handed over directly. The WASP would in that event have to report evidence of guilt within a week or return the accused to the custody of the Shanghai Municipal Police "in good condition."[7]

These various agreements notwithstanding, a major impediment to the actual formation of the new badlands police force was a special annex, which had delayed the signing of the agreements in the first place, stipulating that "all illegitimate businesses (such as the running of gambling dens, trafficking in opium and narcotics, and providing addicts with such narcotics) shall be forbidden to exist within the area under its jurisdiction."[8] The obvious reluctance of the puppet authorities even to pretend to honor this stipulation continued to hold up the actual establishment of the WASP, even though the sheer confusion of jurisdiction between the Japanese Military Police, Li Shiqun's "sorry imitation of the Gestapo," and the municipal puppet police abetted the lawless violence of the badlands.[9] Finally, it was announced that the WASP would open its station doors at 57A Great Western Road and send its constables out on patrol in their new police uniforms on March 17, 1941.[10] The newly appointed WASP chief was none other than Mr. C. C. Pan (Pan Zhijie), the Specials inspector whose job it had been to suborn the foreign concessions' police.[11] Needless to say, gambling and drug trafficking continued to flourish in the badlands, the more so because of Shanghai Municipal Police efforts to drive such rackets out of the International Settlement.[12] They had to go someplace.

The crackdown on gambling in the International Settlement

In November and December 1940 the Shanghai Municipal Police launched a drive against gambling in the International Settlement.[13] One of the first targets was the colorful slot machine king of Shanghai, Jack Riley. Riley had already served ten of twenty-five years for robbery in the Oklahoma State Penitentiary when he was named a trusty and allowed to join the prison baseball team. At the first out-of-pen game, Riley let his teammates head back to jail and took a train in the opposite direction, ending up many months and maritime miles later on the docks of Shanghai. Under the name of Becker he used his adept handling of dice in the penny ante crap shooting along the Bund to accumulate the stake for a real game, in which he won the Manhattan Bar in the French Concession. That was when he began importing slot machines. By December 1940, Riley's slot machines were all over town. Even the U.S. Marines Club paid its rent and a lion's share of its expenses with the kickback from Riley's slots. Riley also banked his own crap table at Joe Farren's big casino out in the badlands, holding a share of ownership in the gambling joint as well.[14]

The Shanghai Municipal Council issued a formal complaint against Jack Riley in a letter sent to the U.S. consul general. Charles Richardson, Jr., special assistant to the district attorney of the U.S. Court of China, was given the case. Richardson, a Princeton graduate trained in law at Harvard and Berkeley, quickly determined there was no question that Riley was violating the laws against gambling set forth in the District of Columbia code governing Americans living in China. Jack Riley was arrested.[15]

The arrest was most unpopular; among many expatriates in Shanghai Riley was a hail-fellow-well-met who was simply supplying a harmless demand for slot machines. When the police booked him, however, they discovered that his fingerprints had been partially obliterated with acid. Richardson therefore asked the U.S. Court of China for the highest bail ever set there: $500,000, or U.S.$25,000. Riley had the cash deposited in the court clerk's hands less than two days after he had been locked up. Meanwhile, every slot machine in the Settlement disappeared.[16]

Jack Riley's attorneys disclaimed U.S. citizenship for their client, who had no passport in his name. Richardson promptly sent what the Shanghai Municipal Police had taken of Riley's seared fingerprints to the FBI, which discovered a wanted card giving his real name as Becker, and listing his birthplace, real mother, and doctor at birth. There was no doubt that Jack Riley was an American. When Riley confidently sauntered into court on December 4, he was stunned by Richardson's dramatic presentation of proof of his U.S. citizenship. Just before the court recessed for "tiffin," Riley left the courtroom and never returned, forfeiting the $25,000 bond.[17]

The Shanghai Municipal Police moved on from slot machines to target the five or six major gambling dens operating in the International Settlement. These gamblers were said to have divided the Settlement into "spheres of influence," and to have agreed to cooperate so that if one den was raided its owner could reopen in one of the other den's sectors. On January 11 the Shanghai Municipal Police raided the notorious Denis Apartments at 1477 Bubbling Well Road, arresting the owner of the "37427 Club," Antonio Perpetuo. Charges were brought against him in the Portuguese Consular Court, which was the second instance of arraigning a foreigner before that person's own consular authorities. The police hoped to shut down the other five dens as well. "We've been campaigning against them for the past ten years, but this time we'll drive them out of the Settlement."[18]

This next phase of the Shanghai Municipal Police's campaign was conducted in February 1941 under a special vice squad led by Inspector Dick Moir and carried out by a flying squad under Assistant Commissioner Victor Sharman. The police had already closed down a number of "lower-class dens" in private apartments and houses, and they continued to carry out mass roundups of unorganized gamblers (e.g., the twenty-five men accused of playing after-hours poker in the Stock Exchange on Jiujiang Road), but the major emphasis was on the rest of the big dens, such as the luxurious Silver Palace on Avenue Foch, or the roulette joint in the Burlington Hotel, whose foreign and Chinese operators were arrested and fined.[19] By March 29, 1941, it was possible for the Shanghai Municipal Police to announce that the three-month campaign had succeeded. "For the first time in five years, the police are aware of no operation of public gambling dens."[20] But that was only in the International Settlement. Elsewhere, the vices boomed.[21]

Wang Jingwei's "Monte Carlo régime"

The Shanghai Municipal Police raids of January–February 1941 simply drove the major Settlement gamblers into the badlands, where some of them had been long ensconced in several of the English-style country houses with imposing gates and long driveways lying off of Edinburgh Road and Avenue Haig.[22] Gambling and opium smoking had thrived under the Japanese occupation of Huxi, when "a miscellaneous crowd of Japanese carpetbaggers and gangsters" moved in, along with Cantonese gamblers who had been operating casinos in Shenzhen on the border of Hong Kong's New Territory and who swarmed into the Western District on the heels of the Japanese troops.[23] Shanghai natives were not far behind.[24]

The underworld operators of the vice-dens in the badlands recognized two authorities. For Japanese gangsters it was the Special Services Section of the Japanese Army, and for the Chinese it was 76 Jessfield Road.[25] Although Li Shiqun routinely denied any connection whatsoever between his secret police and gambling, it was common knowledge that vice constituted a major and growing source of revenue for both the local puppet regime and Wang Jingwei's government in Nanjing:[26]

> It is well known to the Settlement authorities that the operators of gambling dens in the Western area contribute heavily toward Nanking's revenue, and it would be manifestly absurd to believe that these people would have not been informed by Nanking were their places going to be closed down. Far from showing any recent signs of nervousness as they would have done had they been warned, on the contrary a good many of the establishments have been spending heavily on "improvements," and some new places have been opened. It may be concluded reasonably, therefore, that the gambling dens, with their accompanying dope divans and other accessories, are going to continue. And so long as the vice dens exist, No. 76 Jessfield Road will remain—if only to collect the spoils.[27]

This was why the Wang Jingwei puppet regime was sometimes called a "Monte Carlo government," and why Mayor Chen Gongbo found it so difficult to clamp down on vice in the badlands—all of his public promises notwithstanding.[28]

On Boxing Day, 1940, for instance, "yet another luxury gambling club," the Union Club, opened its gates for business directly across from the Bubbling Well Road fire station at the corner of Yuyuan and Tifeng Roads.[29] Close by was the Paramount Arcade, then celebrating its second anniversary with banners announcing "National Happiness" (Guo le) streaming from a specially erected *pailou* (ceremonial archway).[30] In early January 1941, the Six Nations gambling club, off Avenue Haig in the badlands, began expanding its quarters in order to accommodate a growing clientele by making the casino "the largest and most luxurious in the Far East."[31]

Though business was good, competition for Shanghai's high-strung and war-weary gambling clientele was intense. In early February there were rumors that a new casino was going to open on the corner of Great Western and Edinburgh Roads not far from WASP Commissioner C. C. Pan's residence. This new gambling club was supposedly connected with the notorious Jack Riley, who had not after all left Shanghai when he jumped bail in December. Instead he had gone into hiding with "good friends" paid off to keep him out of the hands of the police. Now, Riley and a group of other foreigners, including Japanese and Korean gangsters, had approached Joe Farren and told the ageing, baldish nightclub owner that he had better restrict his gambling to one room with two roulette tables. Farren refused.[32]

On Saturday February 15 around midnight, a group of Korean gamblers—about ten men in Western suits—entered the ballroom on the ground floor of Farren's singly or in pairs. At a given signal they split into two groups, one covering the ballroom and the other going upstairs to the single entrance to the gambling rooms. Drawing Mausers, the gang shouted wildly in Korean, firing shots at the ceiling. Panic ensued. Patrons dived under tables or huddled behind pillars. One wild shot killed Alice Daisy Simmons, an English stockbroker. Another volley of shots brought down Walter Lunzer, an Austrian security guard hired by Farren's after fleeing Nazis at home. A shrill whistle sounded, and the Korean gunmen backed out of the gambling rooms, turned, and ran through the ballroom out to four cars that roared away in the night.[33]

Jack Riley was eventually caught in a raid led by U.S. Marshal Sam Titlebaum, who brought him back in shackles on the S.S. *President Cleveland* to serve time at McNeil's Island Federal Penitentiary.[34] The spectacular shooting did close down gambling at Farren's, whose owner removed the roulette tables in the name of peace and safety.[35] But there were plenty of other casinos for gamblers to frequent that continued to operate under the routine protection of the puppet police.[36]

Nonetheless crimes continued to flourish in the most unusual ways.[37] Teenagers posing as members of an "anti-traitors' battalion" extorted money from a native banker; a foreign woman was robbed of her fur coat along Great Western Road at 3:00 in the afternoon; someone tried to hold up the Chinese Stock Exchange; a Swiss outlaw working in cahoots with the Japanese stole millions of dollars' worth of confiscated U.S. copper; rival thugs smashed up posh ballrooms; a casino owner was shot down walking along Canton Road; twenty-three gangsters, including two girl guides, tried to kidnap a Chinese millionaire in the dye business; other mobsters snatched children for ransom from schoolyards in the badlands, with one petty hoodlum demanding $13 in exchange for the boy he had grabbed off a bicycle on Baikao Road.[38]

Kidnapping was assuming epidemic proportions:

> The manager of one of the larger non-governmental Chinese banks had been kidnapped by the Japanese and was being held for ransom. This, by the way, was a favorite method of keeping the puppet régimes in funds. The Japanese were disinclined to give more than occasional stray pennies from their own funds to maintain the utilitarian puppets, so that when a puppet began clamoring for money or the item of an extra military engagement appeared on the swindle sheet, it was the custom to look at a carefully compiled list and

kidnap some individual who could be calculated to be ransomed for the sum required.[39]

Between early February and early April 1941 kidnappers seized the vice-president of the Shanghai Gold Stock Exchange, the general manager of the Chung Mei Chemical Works, the manager of the Nee Tai Shing Coal Company, and one of the leading members of the Chinese Cotton Brokers Association.[40] "Terrorism of a strange, foreign type is the 'order of the day' in this city as incidents of murder, kidnapping, and bombing have occurred one after the other in these recent days."[41]

It was, in other words, becoming increasingly difficult to distinguish crime from conspiracy as the two converged to pulverize whatever shreds remained of Shanghai's civic society.[42] Precisely because Shanghai was a city of nightlife, for instance, its cabarets became prime targets for both sides in the terrorist wars, and especially for pro-Nanjing elements who combined extortion with terrorism. Over lunar New Year's festival in 1941, eight different cabarets were bombed—five within a single hour on the night of January 25: Ciro's, the Nee Kau Mei Ballroom, the Paradise, the Green Spot, the Paramount, the Lambeth Bar, the Lambeth Annex, and a cabaret on Avenue Edward VII near Mohawk Road. Most of the bombs were of the "nuisance" type, phosphorous or gasoline, but the explosion at Ciro's drove pieces of flying glass into the son of an International Settlement Chinese police officer and killed him.[43] As always, if pro-Nanjing elements were detected and pursued by the police, the terrorists simply fled into safe houses in the badlands or bolted back to 76 Jessfield Road, where they could not be followed by the regular police because of the protection extended them by the Japanese.[44]

Wu Shibao

Number 76 Jessfield Road was in new hands now because of the feud within the Wang Jingwei régime between Zhou Fohai and Li Shiqun, who relinquished his position as head of the Shanghai Special Services Section (Tegong zongbu) in January 1941 to Wu Shibao.[45] Li Shiqun continued to remain very powerful in the Wang Jingwei secret service apparatus by serving as minister of police in Nanjing, while Ding Mocun was named minister of social welfare. But the two men no longer ran "76," and the regular Shanghai Special Municipality Police (Shanghai tebie shi jingcha shu) was reorganized as the Shanghai City Government Police Bureau (Shanghai shi jingcha shu) and brought more directly under the new mayor's control.[46] Yet when it came to Mayor Chen Gongbo's crackdown on vice, the new head of "76," Wu Shibao, who was popularly called the "king of racketeers," was in some ways even more difficult to control than Li Shiqun had been.

In early March 1941 Mayor Chen ordered all of the gambling dens in the badlands closed. At least four major casinos continued to keep their doors open.[47] The owners of these four gambling dens had an "understanding" with Wu Shibao and the Japanese Military Police whereby a daily protection fee of $12,000 was paid over to the "East Asia Charity Association" (Lane 1032, 25 Yuyuan Road), headed by one of the senior Japanese police officers. Wu Shibao in turn told Chinese police chief Colonel Lu Ying that any attempt on the part of the city government to close the dens could result in unpleasant consequences.[48] He asked Colonel Lu to explain to Mayor Chen that the gambling house owners had stockpiled firearms at the China Club and were prepared to offer armed resistance, backed by the Japanese Military Police, if the city tried to close them down. Chen Gongbo still wanted them shut, but the casino owners had increased their daily protection fees to $15,000 in order to be sure of Japanese and puppet armed support in the event of a conflict with the Chinese city government.[49]

Meanwhile, other rackets were flourishing in occupied Shanghai too. Prostitution continued to increase, and eventually, in November 1941, Wang Jingwei's puppet government lifted the ban on prostitution altogether and Shanghai was flooded with unlicensed streetwalkers.[50] The drug trade also soared, both nationally and in Shanghai.[51] After the Japanese occupied Nanjing in 1937, the Japanese special services organs began to carry out a "narcotization" policy, which was expected to raise $300 million per year when fully implemented. Pistol-packing Chinese peddlers working for Japanese narcotics dealers sold heroin in paper packets for as little as five Chinese cents.[52] In Shanghai's badlands, two years later, there were said to be forty-two opium hongs that were securing permission from the Japanese and city government authorities to operate legally in exchange for certain fees.[53]

By May or June 1941 the gambling houses and opium dispensing dives in the badlands constituted a chief source of income for the puppet Nanjing government. Monthly receipts from these rackets came to about $3,750,000, of which $750,000 was contributed in the form of "special taxes" to the Treasury in Nanjing. Smaller sums were given to local municipal officials. For example, it was said that two officials received $50,000 each per month from one foreign-operated house. The Six Nations Club on Avenue Haig paid over $10,000 per day; the Union Club, $3,000; the China Club, $3,000; and the Eventail, $3,000.[54] Journalists estimated that these payments amounted to 50 percent of the gross income of the gambling houses.[55]

At just this same time, however, the Japanese home government in Tokyo was becoming concerned about the extent of crime, narcotics addiction, and other vices in the Shanghai areas controlled by the Nanjing régime. In May 1941 the Tokyo *Asahi* published an editorial arguing that the most effective way to strengthen the Nanjing régime would be to do away with China's long-standing ills, including gambling and opium smoking; and it urged the Japanese authorities to press Wang Jingwei to introduce these reforms. This was followed by talks among Japanese politicians about ways of "strengthening" Nanjing. As a result Ambassador Honda Kumataro returned to Tokyo where he publicly urged support for the puppet government. The upshot of this flurry was growing Japanese pressure on Wang Jingwei, during his June 1941 visit to Tokyo, to clean up some of Shanghai's more egregious vices.[56]

Even before setting sail for Japan, Wang Jingwei had ordered WASP chief C. C. Pan to close all of the gambling houses between May 31 and June 2. Mayor Chen Gongbo firmly supported this resolution. Nonetheless, Special Services chief Wu Shibao managed to thwart Wang's plans. On June 15 Nanjing's vice-minister of police, Teng Tsu-yu (Deng Zuyou), came to inspect the arrangements in Shanghai, and his lavish welcome by Wu included a night out at the Argentine (a new nightclub started by European gambling entrepreneurs), where croupiers reopened the roulette wheels downstairs and chemin-de-fer and slot machines were played upstairs.[57]

The very next day, June 16, 1941, Commissioner Pan was informed that the gambling houses had been reopened, and he promptly promised to punish those responsible. Five days later he personally led a raid on the Eventail and the Welcome Cafe, but other nearby casinos operating full-blast were not at all disturbed.[58] Moreover, only parts of the gambling paraphernalia were seized, and the "joints" themselves were never forced to close.[59] It was actually reported that a major new casino was opening on Columbia Road in one of Shanghai's best residential districts.[60]

Even so, the puppet newspaper *Shanghai* continued to make outlandish claims about the success of Mayor Chen's campaign against gambling. It declared that as of May 31 all the Chinese-operated gambling dens had been closed, "never to re-open again," and that Commissioner Pan had permanently shut down the foreign-owned clubs in Huxi, while also taking action against the popular *huahui* lottery establishments. "Thus, what once were notoriously known as the 'Badlands' have reverted to 'Goodlands'—an ideal residential area with excellent roads, and various special areas for growing industries."[61]

The Nationalist government tried to make the best propaganda use it could of the Wang Jingwei régime's toleration of massive vice activities in

Shanghai. Chiang Kai-shek personally autographed a note in July 1941 to the Shanghai press excoriating the puppets and calling for a fight against gambling and opium. Mayor Chen Gongbo subsequently insisted upon closing down foreign-operated gambling houses in the concessions (by that time there was only one fly-by-night venture mounted by a Frenchman), and then supported an effort by the regular Chinese police to take over the badlands operations.[62]

In late July 1941 General Lu Ying, director of the Shanghai Special Municipality Police headquartered in Nandao, finally moved in on Commissioner C. C. Pan's bailiwick in the badlands. General Lu sent his assistants to the headquarters of the WASP with instructions to serve as liaison between Commissioner Pan's office and the police establishment downtown. The coup thereby succeeded. On August 16, Captain Wu Shibao was ordered to give up his position at 76 Jessfield Road and report to the town of Changzhou to do rural pacification work. Wu had to resign his police post, but he refused to depart from Shanghai, where he continued his racketeering activities until Li Shiqun finally arranged to have him poisoned.[63]

Patriot wars

Nationalist China was at war with Japan, and her soldiers had no qualms about conveying the conflict into "island Shanghai." As Dai Li's Juntong began to recover its footing in the city after losing the secret service wars of 1939, "clandestine work" (*qianfu gongzuo*) increased markedly, with terrorist incidents rising to a crescendo in the winter and spring of 1941.

On January 20, 1941, Tong Yui, the prominent lawyer who had been instrumental in transferring the Second District Court in the French Concession to the Wang Jingwei régime the previous November, was shot four times as he sat in his car waiting to go to work.[64]

On January 25, a Chinese gunman attempted to kill Gimitsu Shozo, the Japanese supervisor of the Japan–China Silk and Cotton Mill, as he was walking along Robison Road. The agent's gun jammed after one shot, and the mill supervisor escaped with his life.[65]

On February 16, Tuan Bien-shun [Duan Bianshun], director of the pro-Nanjing "Morality Relief Association," was wounded by a gunman while having a morning cup of tea at a café on boulevard de Montigny.[66]

On February 25, Chinese agents killed one Japanese noncommissioned officer and wounded another. Several hours later, a third Japanese officer was fired on. Shortly after that, a Chinese gunman critically wounded a Chinese working in a factory connected with the puppet police.[67]

On February 26, a Japanese soldier was killed, another soldier was wounded, and a Japanese sailor was shot at by gunmen in broad daylight. That same evening, a Chinese agent pumped several shots into the abdomen of Wang Yung [Wang Yong], a member of the puppet police, as he was leaving his home in Caojiadu in the badlands.[68]

On March 12, Wu Zung-an [Wu Zongan], the twenty-three-year-old son of a collaborationist banker married to a Japanese, was abducted as he left the Eventail Nightclub on Yuyuan Road.[69]

On March 14, Chinese terrorists attacked two Wang régime officials in the badlands, killing one and wounding the other.[70]

On March 16, Shen Ming, the director of the consolidated tax bureau for Zhejiang and Jiangsu, was gunned down in his car in the lane in front of his Yuyuan Road home by a band of six armed Chinese agents.[71]

On March 17, Pan Tse-tung [Pan Zedong], the head of Wang Jingwei's bodyguards, was shot in the neck on Avenue Road.[72]

On March 30, a young Chinese shot Shen Chu-hseng [Shen Zhusheng], an official in the Shanghai tax bureau, twice in the chest.[73]

On April 9, Chinese gunmen killed one Japanese military policeman and wounded another in Yangshupu north of Suzhou Creek.[74]

On April 12, two Chinese terrorists killed two Japanese Military Police corporals in Yangshupu.[75]

On April 15, Chen Hu-hwei [Chen Huhui], a tax bureau employee, was wounded by a Chinese agent while he was waiting to catch a bus.[76]

On April 30, a lone Chinese gunman on Old Stone Bridge shot a Japanese naval sentry in the stomach.[77]

On May 1, Kuo Tse-yuen [Guo Ziyuan], former member of the Nandao police presently working for the Wang régime, was shot dead at the corner of Yunnan Road and Avenue Edward VII.[78]

The targets of these Nationalist assassination attempts were almost always Japanese soldiers and sailors, often on sentry duty, and Chinese collaborators, usually working for the police, the tax authorities, or one of the numerous Sino-Japanese companies spawned by the Occupation.[79] Many of the attacks were successful, and a relatively small number of Juntong assailants were captured, while many escaped into the International Settlement afterwards. But the Nationalists' "clandestine work" was not unchallenged. As we shall see in the next chapter, their erstwhile opponents among the terrorists fighting on behalf of the Nanjing régime concentrated the warfare in three highly contested arenas: newspapers, law courts, and banks.

10

Terrorist wars

Just as soon as the Japanese forces defeated the Chinese defenders of Shanghai in November 1937, the Imperial Army took over the Guomindang censor's office in the International Settlement and announced that all Chinese newspapers would have to be submitted for examination.[1] In order to avoid such a demeaning and disgraceful submission to Japanese censorship, many Chinese newspapers hired British or U.S. citizens as publishers in order to register with the Settlement authorities as a foreign publication. *Shen bao,* for instance, became a U.S.-registered concern, ostensibly being published by N. F. Allman, the U.S. lawyer who was also a member of the Shanghai Municipal Council. In this way, "foreign-published newspapers" and their literary supplements became the most important forum for intellectual resistance during the period of "island Shanghai."[2]

Newspaper wars

Since the Japanese and puppet authorities could not manipulate these "foreign-published newspapers" through censorship, they resorted to terrorism.[3] Beginning in early February 1938 staff members and editors of foreign-registered papers, such as L. Z. Yuan at the *Evening Post* or Director Samuel Chang at the *Damei wanbao* (the Chinese edition of the *Evening Post and Mercury*), received threatening letters—or in some cases packages with decayed human hands inside—that in one way or another warned them to cease anti-Japanese activities or face the consequences.[4]

   Those who refused to shut up were likely to be bombed or shot, as was Samuel Chang on July 16, 1940, as he sat having coffee and a sandwich in a German restaurant on Nanjing Road:[5]

> Wang Ching-wei's [Wang Jingwei's] Japanese-paid gunmen dashed about casually shooting up Chinese who refused or hesitated to cooperate with the

New Order in East Asia. Foreign publications presumed to be critical of Japanese tactics were liable to find hand grenades flying through their windows. Randall Gould, the editor of the American-owned evening newspaper, received almost daily communications threatening all manners of reprisals.[6]

As Shanghai's biggest daily, and a fierce supporter of the anti-Japanese resistance, *Shen bao* was specially targeted. Its "publisher," N. F. Allman, was one of seven foreign newspapermen threatened with deportation by the Nanjing puppet government, and its supervising editor, Chu Yueh [Zhu Yue], was shot and wounded by a terrorist in June 1940.[7] Two masked and armed Japanese also roughed up *New York Times* correspondent Hallett Abend in his apartment.[8] Among the eighty-three educators, artists, writers, editors, and journalists blacklisted by the Wang Jingwei régime in July 1940, ten were *Shen bao* employees.[9]

Every one of the eighty-three names on the blacklist was marked for death, and many went into hiding or left for Chongqing. One journalist on the list later reported that each morning when he left for work, deliberately getting off the tramway a stop ahead or a stop behind his destination, he would write out instructions for his family in the event of his death at the hands of *daitu* or thugs; and once at work in his newspaper, published behind steel doors, its printing press protected by steel grills, he would remain in a continuing state of profound anxiety, not knowing whether he would get back to his family that evening or not.[10]

Of all the periodicals singled out for attack, *Shen bao* remained the primary target.[11] The newspaper was bombed three times. The first outrage was committed in July 1940 by three men who threw four hand grenades, killing one and wounding nineteen, including a Chinese constable. One of the terrorists was captured and confessed to being a member of a "certain" political organization under the *tegong zongbu* (special work headquarters) of the Nanjing régime.[12]

The second bombing of *Shen bao,* after a failed attempt in September, occurred in November 1940.[13] The terrorists used potato-masher bombs, which caused severe damage but no deaths.[14]

The third bombing was a curiously botched affair. On January 6, 1941, a Chinese constable of the Shanghai Municipal Police found three potato-masher hand grenades on the ground at the intersection of Hankou and Shandong Roads. It was discovered that the grenades, which were carefully wrapped up in newspapers, had been thrown by a Chinese from the roof of a building adjoining 309 Hankou Road, the site of the *Shen bao* building. None had gone off. Some speculated that they might have been left there to frighten workers into leaving the newspaper. Others thought they were intended to be a retaliation for the bombing of the pro–

Wang Jingwei organ, *Bing bao*, a week earlier, or that *Shen bao* was being punished for publishing a searing analysis of the local monetary situation as a result of the opening of the puppets' Central Reserve Bank. Whatever the real reason, the incident led the police to increase patrols in the neighborhood, and the very next day, January 7, constables were on hand to seize a twenty-one-year-old "thug" and former puppet policeman when he exploded a grenade against the newspaper building at the corner of Henan and Shandong Roads. The terrorist, Tian Liang, still had the grenade release pin on his finger when he was apprehended.[15]

Tian Liang, a farmer before he became a policeman in Nandao and Pudong, had joined Chen Gongbo's Special Services Section a month earlier. For the attempted Sunday bombing, he and two accomplices had each received $20. For the Monday assault, Tian was paid $50. Together these constituted his first (and last) secret mission for 76 Jessfield Road.[16]

If bombing the *Shen bao* offices did not work, then assassination might be more effective. One of the most prominent names on the blacklist was King Hua-ting [Jin Huating], the Chinese editor of *Shen bao*. At 4:30 a.m. on February 2, Jin walked out of a ballroom on Avenue Edward VII. A man posing as his bodyguard stepped forward and shot him three times, in the forehead, abdomen, and right side. Jin collapsed and died on the pavement.[17] The assassin was a member of the *tegong zongbu* of the Wang Jingwei government—the same puppet special services unit that also killed Zhu Xinggong and Cheng Zhenzhang, the editors of *Damei wanbao*.[18] And of course there were always the kidnappings. By April 19 fifteen Chinese journalists had been abducted by Nanjing terrorists, including the advertising manager of *Shen bao* and the editors of two prominent pro-Chongqing newspapers.[19]

Court wars

The Shanghai First Special District Court's judges were originally appointed by Chiang Kai-shek's government. Although efforts were made to discredit them, virtually all of them remained loyal to the Nationalist régime after the wartime capital was transferred to Chongqing.[20] The most stalwart was Qian Hongye, presiding judge of the criminal division of the First Special District Court, who was thought to be the only judge who could deal fairly with political criminals in court. At noon on July 29, 1940, Judge Qian was assassinated by unidentified gunmen at the corner of Weihaiwei Road and Avenue Foch. Few doubted that this was the handiwork of 76 Jessfield Road.[21]

In September of that same year a letter was sent from "76" to judges, court interpreters, and other officials at the First Special District Court.

Signed by the "Kuomintang [Guomindang] Anti-Red Party," it read in part:

> There is no hope for China today in her war with Japan. The British government's removal of her troops from China shows that Britain realizes the actual position of China. The American marines stationed in Shanghai are powerless to act or do any good for the Chinese people. Cooperate with us in making an established peace in China and conclude this bloody war. We urge you to report at 76 Jessfield Road within a week, where you will be warmly welcomed. Should you fail to do so, harm will be done to you by a third party.[22]

As a result of this threatening note, the judges took up temporary residence in the court building on North Zhejiang Road.[23]

In November 1940 the French surrendered jurisdiction of the Second Special District Court to the Nanjing government, thereby, incidentally, giving the Nanjing authorities a certain discretionary control over the vice industries of the Concession.[24] This left the First Court's judges virtually alone in their defiance of the puppet régime:[25]

> The agents of disorder are doing everything possible to paralyze the activities of the First Special District Court by threatening the lives of judges and other court officials and bringing pressure upon all parties concerned. What has happened to the Second Special District Court, surrendered by the French, was indicated by the recent judgments sentencing a poor exchange shop proprietor for refusing to accept Chow fu-hai's [Zhou Fohai's] phony banknotes.[26]

At 4:30 a.m. on Monday, February 3, a taxi commandeered by three Chinese in Hongkou drove by the civil court on Weihaiwei Road. Three grenades were thrown, damaging the secretariat's offices. The cab drove on to the criminal court on North Zhejiang Road and three more grenades were hurled. Only one went off, causing slight damage to the building. The taxi sped on to Jessfield Road where the three terrorists descended.[27]

Just as in the case of the newspaper wars, bombing was less effective than attacks upon the person. On March 4, 1941, Dr. Hsu Wei-tseng [Xu Weizeng], presiding judge of the Second District High Court, was abducted in front of his home on route Voyron in the French Concession by five men armed with Mausers.[28] In mid-April Judge Hong Shide's home was bombed with hand grenades by four men.[29] At the same time there were threats to the safety of the president, presiding judge, and chief procurator of the First Special District Court; and on April 22 there were unsuccessful attempts to kidnap two of the court judges who suffered hand grenade and pistol attacks but escaped uninjured.[30] Even court clerks or secretaries were liable to be seized.[31]

As the offices of the First Special District Court began to resemble a rooming house, with all judges and senior officers living on the premises, a British intelligence report remarked: "Nanking adherents have, by means of kidnappings, been bringing strong pressure to bear on the judges of the Chinese courts in the International Settlement, who [it] is feared will not resist for much longer."[32] Or, as the *China Weekly Review* put it: "This wave of atrocities against Chungking [Chongqing]-appointed judges is part of the Japanese attempt to drive all Chungking [Chongqing] courts out of the International Settlement."[33]

Bank wars

Part of the larger history of the War of Resistance against Japan was the financial war: banks fighting banks, and especially the furious competition between the Nationalists and Wang Jingwei's régime to have their respective currencies displace their rival's.[34] In Shanghai that competition took the form of armed struggle, conducted guerrilla-fashion with urban terror tactics:[35]

> A few weeks ago, newspaper men were the objects of assassins' bullets and bombs. Now it is innocent bank clerks who are being mercilessly massacred by Nanking hired gunmen or are being kidnapped by Japanese gendarmes and their puppet assistants. . . . Attempts are being made to dominate local finance and banking circles, through organized speculation, hoarding of commodities, a tax of local bank officials, and more recently the mass murder of bank employees and bombing of their premises, in order to force them to submit to the control of political gangsters and their superiors.[36]

Both sides engaged in this terrorism. Indeed, some of the first killings of bank officials were assassinations of collaborators by pro-Chongqing agents.[37] And one of the most spectacular bombings—the attack on February 20 on the Central Reserve Bank on the Bund—was also probably the work of Nationalist terrorists.[38]

At 10:30 that morning, which was a Thursday, six men dressed in Chinese long gowns entered the Central Reserve Bank on the Bund.[39] One of them made for the manager's office on the second floor, but was alarmed by the appearance of an accountant. He and the other men drew their guns, fired, and then threw four homemade bombs, only two of which exploded. The assailants then rushed back down the main staircase where a bank guard sought to impede them and was shot down and killed. The agents then made their escape.[40]

The puppet authorities tried to make the best propaganda use they could of this brazen daylight attack by Nationalist agents on the Wang régime's central currency-issuing bank. On February 25, Minister of Police Li Shiqun announced from 76 Jessfield Road in the badlands that "we must put a stop immediately to the recurrence of terrorism committed by Chungking [Chongqing] agents." It was "a known fact" that Chongqing terrorists had been engaged in numerous assassination attempts during the past two or three years. Such terrorism, "the most depraved form of instrument to use in any political struggle," posed a terrible threat to the coexistence of the international communities in Shanghai and was making it impossible to revive business and trade prosperity.[41]

Referring to the bombing of the Central Reserve Bank, Li said that there were still many banks in Shanghai that belonged to the Chongqing régime, but the Reform Government had never tried to destroy them. Many bankers and financiers were now tending toward the Reform régime and the "peace movement," and Li wished to encourage that trend. He added, more ominously, that "there are also many Chungking [Chongqing] agents in this city. We have allowed them to move freely. Neither have we resorted to killing for the sake of killing. These Chungking [Chongqing] agents are still regarded by us as Chinese nationals so long as they are peace-loving and law-abiding." If, on the other hand, Chongqing agents were to engage in terrorism, then that was another kettle of fish. It would be Li Shiqun's duty as a public security official to swiftly carry forward the work of restoring peace and order. "As minister of police, I am unwilling that Shanghai should come under the spell of a reign of terror."[42]

Li Shiqun's speech notwithstanding, there was an attempt on the life of Fu Yung-ping [Fu Yongbing], an assistant secretary of the Central Reserve Bank, during the noon-hour rush on March 3, and the successful assassination by Chongqing agents of a senior manager of that same puppet institution on March 21, 1941. Given Li Shiqun's implicit warning, the Nationalists had every reason to expect retaliations, but no one foresaw the severity of the Japanese and puppet response.[43]

On the night of March 21, while puppet terrorists were throwing grenades and bombs into three pro-Chongqing bank buildings, a gang of six gunmen posing as policemen pushed their way past the night watchman guarding the dormitory of the Jiangsu Farmers Bank. The gunmen flipped on the lights and began shooting at random into the beds, killing five bank clerks and badly wounding six more who were left comatose in blood-saturated blankets.[44] Later that night—actually in the early hours of Saturday morning, March 22—police cars descended upon Centro Terrace, the residence compound of the Bank of China at 96 Jessfield Road in the badlands. The plainclothes puppet police, accompanied by a few Japanese military police, dragged bank clerks and other employees out of their beds and at 3:00 a.m. took 128 of them to dreaded 76 Jessfield Road, where they were incarcerated.[45]

The next day, March 23, Minister of Police Li Shiqun admitted the detention of 128 employees of the Bank of China. He said that the ministry was reluctant to take reprisals against "Chungking [Chongqing] terrorists," but those attacks had steadily increased and the authorities of the two foreign-controlled areas had failed to take any action. Therefore, the ministry had had no choice but to order the arrest of employees of the Chongqing-controlled banks in the city. Li said that the prisoners would be given all possible protection and comforts, and that they would be "released as soon as the Chungking [Chongqing] régime shows repentance, and local peace and order have been definitely established. . . . Should this warning be unheeded, we shall be forced to take similar measures to deal with the entire staff members of all the financial establishments operated by the Chungking [Chongqing] régime in Shanghai."[46]

To reinforce Li Shiqun's warning, Nanjing terrorists unleashed their bomb squads on March 24. That afternoon, a frantic employee of the Farmers Bank of China on Avenue Road called the Shanghai Municipal Police and reported that a messenger had left a package that ticked. Detective Sub-Inspector F. A. Ewins rushed to the bank and gingerly dismantled the bomb, which was wired for both time and contact explosion.[47] At about the same time, shortly before 4 p.m., the Burkill Road branch of the Central Bank of China erupted. The TNT blast destroyed most of the second story, killing one person and wounding thirty-eight.[48] Another explosion thundered across the boundary in the French Concession, where the Canidrome branch of the Central Bank of China was also blown apart by TNT. Seven were killed and twenty-one wounded, most of them clerks and accountants.[49]

Shanghai banks opened for business as usual on March 25, 1941, but there was frantic behind-the-scene maneuvering:[50]

> It is reliably learned that officials of Chinese banks including government banks, except the Central Bank of China, are negotiating with representatives of [the] Nanking régime for: firstly, a modus vivendi whereby Chinese banks in Shanghai will not be subject to further molestation; secondly, the release of arrested staff members. Chinese bankers are hopeful that successful arrangements may be made so that the financial activities of Shanghai may proceed, thus avoiding a general breakdown.[51]

For the first time, Nationalist foreign affairs representative Dr. Tuan Mao-lan [Duan Maolan] came to see U.S. Consul General Lockhart to ask for more support from the municipal authorities of the International Settlement. Dr. Tuan said that without adequate protection the banks would have to evacuate Shanghai and withdraw support of the Nationalist currency there. Lockhart promised to communicate his concerns to the U.S. authorities.[52]

On March 28 the U.S. Embassy in Chongqing received a note from the Ministry of Foreign Affairs reporting the Bank of China kidnapping, the bombing of the Farmers Bank, and the bombings of the Central Bank of China branches. "The Ministry observes that this flagrant trampling on various Chinese banks where the wholesale slaughter of their personnel and the concessionaries at Shanghai by the Japanese and puppets is not only aimed at disturbing the monetary markets of Shanghai but also at destroying the peace and order of the entire Concession areas." The Americans were asked to transmit a telegram to the International Settlement authorities ordering them "to render adequate protection to the various Chinese banks in the Settlement." Other than urge the Shanghai Municipal Police to take more stringent measures, however, there was not much that the U.S. State Department could do to ameliorate the situation.[53]

As of April 5, 1941, there was no indication of how soon the 128 Bank of China employees would be released from their detention at 76 Jessfield Road.[54] Three days later, however, the accountants and clerks were taken back to Centro Terrace at 96 Jessfield Road and put under house arrest on "shop security."[55] But the puppet police, backed by Japanese Military Police, told the Bank of China employees that they were being held hostage to the good behavior of Chongqing authorities. In the case of the assassination of any one of their bank staff members, the police would kill three of the Bank of China members selected by lot from the 128 employees now under guard.[56]

These threats—if they even knew of them—failed to deter Chongqing terrorists, perhaps Juntong agents, on April 16 from shooting and hacking to death an assistant chief of accounting of the Central Reserve Bank, while he lay—already wounded from a previous attack, and in front of his family—in his bed in Dah hwa [Dahua] Hospital.[57] Not only did that provoke a counterterrorist attack half-an-hour later, when Nanjing agents shot the chief cashier of the Bank of China's main office in Shanghai; it also led to an immediate reaction in the exchange market. "Market sentiment and persistent terrorism and the resulting counter-terrorism may result in the removal of Chungking [Chongqing] official banks from Shanghai, none of which opened today."[58]

That same day, April 16, 1941, the police authorities at 76 Jessfield Road invited nine senior accountants from the Bank of China hostage group to come to their headquarters, where they were cordially entertained for a considerable time. Finally, six of the nine persons were ordered to leave. The other three—the head of the Sinza Road sub-branch, the chief cashier of the main office, and a third man—were escorted to the staff quarters of the bank by armed police, lined up, and shot. As soon as the police departed Centro Terrace, leaving the three corpses behind, the seventy-seven families living in the bank compound moved. Thereafter the deserted premises of the much coveted compound were taken over by employees of the puppet Central Reserve Bank.[59]

It was widely believed in Shanghai that the motive behind the killing of the three bankers was not just retribution, but also the determination to force acceptance of worthless Central Reserve Bank currency in the French Concession and the International Settlement. This did not succeed. The Chinese dollar nosedived, and Chongqing bank doors were closed until they could get better police protection.[60]

And still the bank wars continued. On April 21 the chief auditor of the Central Reserve Bank, Li Ting-mu [Li Dingmu], was shot in the back and killed on the steps of the Zhongnan Hotel on Avenue Edward VII.[61] The following week six terrorists bombed the Lieneyih Commercial Bank on Tientsin Road.[62] Although the four Chongqing banks reopened on April 28, 1941, the local foreign community and many members of the Chinese community were convinced that unless the violence encouraged by Chongqing and Nanjing ceased, Shanghai could not continue in its present status.[63] In a very strong editorial the *Shanghai Evening Post and Mercury* called upon Chongqing to make "an open public statement that it eschews public violence," and to give "explicit and unmistakable orders to its adherents there to call off the guerrilla warfare in this city."[64]

Weariness

A weary pall was settling over the city amidst this unending violence that emanated from the badlands or arrived in the form of Dai Li's Blue Shirts from Juntong training depots in Free China. A good deal of the terrorism was unmistakably patriotic, being clearly directed against the Japanese Occupation forces. Beginning in early April in Nanjing, and then later that month in Shanghai, Nationalist agents bombed restaurants and theaters frequented by Japanese soldiers.[65] On April 26, time bombs were detonated in two of the largest theaters in Hongkou's "Little Tokyo," injuring sixteen Japanese.[66] But even so, there was still a sense of wanton randomness about the terrorism of March and April 1941. During the week of March 22–29, 14 Shanghainese were killed, 60 wounded, and 128 kidnapped.[67] During April 19–26 "gangsters . . . assassinated four bank employees, Japanese gendarmes attempted to take over the Chinese Ratepayers Association, policemen shot and killed by mistake a bodyguard of the Commissioner of Police of Greater Shanghai, and thugs threw a bomb in the home of the judge of the Kiangsu [Jiangsu] High Court."[68]

That sense of randomness and pall of weariness created a certain longing for order, or at least conditioned Shanghai residents, including the foreigners, to accept new political arrangements. In April, after the Japanese Military Police and the Shanghai Municipal Police had a standoff at the Chinese Ratepayers Association, their respective authorities worked out a new modus vivendi where the Shanghai Municipal Council was to be replaced by a larger "Provisional Council" appointed by governments and not elected by ratepayers.[69] This was a major change in the governance of the Settlement. The representation of the British and Chinese was reduced, U.S. and Japanese representation was increased, and a Swiss, a Hollander, and a German were added for diplomatic reasons. The high-ranking police officers of the Shanghai Municipal Police remained British, but the police, finance, and public works departments began to be reorganized along Japanese lines.[70]

The presence of a new Provisional Council had little effect on Chongqing terrorism, which only worsened. During May and June 1941, there were three prominent cases of assassination: two of police officers and one of a famous French lawyer and author.[71]

The first victim was Ying Tsan-ching [Ying Zanjing], senior Chinese detective of the WASP. Detective Ying, forty-three years old and a native of Nantong, had served on the Shanghai Municipal Police for sixteen years, but resigned on December 1, 1939, to join the "peace movement" led by Wang Jingwei. Well liked by his colleagues on the Shanghai Municipal Police, Ying had taken a job with the newly formed badlands WASP. On May 27, he was just stepping out of his automobile at the front door of his home on Wenchow [Wenzhou] Road in the International Settlement, when two gunmen dressed like students shot him. Ying Zanjing was rushed to the Paulun Hospital, but he died without recovering consciousness.[72]

Baron R. d'Auxion de Ruffe—a tall, well-built man of imposing appearance—was the oldest resident French lawyer in Shanghai. Scion of a patrician family from southwestern France, he had come to the city in 1910, where he practiced law until the world war broke out. After serving with distinction in the French army, which awarded him the *croix de guerre* and the *médaille militaire,* he returned to Shanghai in 1918 to resume his law practice. Baron d'Auxion was also a man of letters who collected Chinese antiquities, edited *Extrême-Orient,* and contributed articles to a leading French daily. Many of these articles were quite critical of the Chongqing régime. The baron, who was sixty-six years old and president of both the French Club and the Cercle français, had been very close to the late mayor Fu Xiaoan, who had appointed him an "honorary advisor" to the municipal puppet government.[73] Although some speculated about his involvement in Vichy and de Gaullist quarrels, and there was talk of a personal grudge connected with an important lawsuit, it was probably Baron d'Auxion's friendship with Mayor Fu that put him in harm's way.[74]

Shortly before 9:00 on the morning of June 13, Baron d'Auxion left his home at 56 rue Massenet and drove to his offices in the St. Anne building at 25–41 rue du Consulat, opposite the French Consulate General and just a short distance from the Bund. As he entered the building he was followed by two Chinese in foreign attire. The baron's offices were on the third floor, and he was just about to reach the second floor landing when the two gunmen fired their .38 caliber pistols, striking him in the back three times. D'Auxion collapsed on the stairs, falling back until his foot caught in the stair railing. The assailants dashed out of the building and down rue Laguerre, heading for the Nandao. The baron, meanwhile, was taken by emergency ambulance to the Sainte-Marie Hospital, but he was dead on arrival, leaving a widow, the Baroness Selina d'Auxion de Ruffe, a daughter, the Countess Beatrice du Bus de Warnaffe, and four grandchildren vacationing at that time of year in Qingdao. The French community of Shanghai was profoundly stunned by his murder.[75]

The third victim was Special Deputy Commissioner Akagi Chikayuki, who had done so much to conciliate Shanghai Municipal Police activities with the aims of the Japanese consular police and Military Police. On June 17, 1941, four days after the murder of Baron d'Auxion, Akagi left his house on Yuyuan Road to drive his wife to the hospital for routine medical treatment. As his car turned onto Tifeng Road, two gunmen opened fire. Akagi was hit in the head, but he still managed to get out of the automobile to return the fire before he was shot again in the arm and back. The assailants fled.[76] Akagi had enough strength to get back in the car and tell his chauffeur to take him to the Country Hospital.[77] There he died on the operating table despite a transfusion of blood donated by three Japanese. His wife fortunately escaped injury. On June 24 a funeral parade was held in Commissioner Akagi's honor. The procession wound its way from the race course near the intersection of Bubbling Well and Nanking Roads the full distance to Boone Road, where the hearse stopped at the Nippon Club for a Buddhist ceremony. Thousands of spectators lined the sidewalks along the way.[78]

The three assassinations were unequivocally the work of pro-Chongqing terrorists or Blue Shirt Juntong agents.[79] In many cases, however, there was a certain ambiguousness. Sometimes, as in the case of the

Central Reserve Bank bombing, contemporaries wondered aloud if the terrorist incident was not the work of an agent provocateur.[80] In other cases, the motivation of the agents, even to their own superiors, was dubious—as Wen-hsin Yeh has explored in the Liu Geqing affair.[81] Part of the problem was that the Nationalist intelligence services had adopted a policy of intertwinement: the so-called *quxian jiuguo* ("saving the nation in a devious way") strategy of working through and with enemy intelligence services:[82]

> Dai Li adopted a strategy of entering [the enemy's ranks] and dragging [their people into his] so that the number of middle- and lower-ranking special agents who had been infiltrated in the puppet Special Work organization would have to be counted in the thousands. We were among you and you were among us. The goal of this was to carry out the so-called *quxian jiuguo*—"saving the nation in a devious way."[83]

According to mainland Chinese sources, Chiang Kai-shek had ordered Dai Li to cooperate secretly with Wang Jingwei's secret services in order to oppose the Communist New Fourth Army before the *Wannan shibian* ("Southern Anhui [or New Fourth Army] incident") of January 1941. The same orders had been given to Chen Lifu and Xu Enzeng (director of Zhongtong), who set up a special communications channel with Ding Mocun, former Zhongtong agent and now one of the heads of the Special Work headquarters of the Nanjing régime. Coded wireless messages received by the Zhongtong Code Section in Chongqing were taken directly to Director Xu, who decoded them personally and kept them in a special file numbered 0042 (42 being the multiplication of 7 times 6 or "76") in a green safe in his office.[84]

Dai Li had a similar setup with wireless communications direct to Zhou Fohai, and with a number of key agents well placed in the police and security services of the Nanjing administration, sometimes serving Juntong ends, sometimes serving puppet roles, including the arrest, torture, and execution of Chinese patriots.[85] As a consequence, the question of ultimate loyalty remained very much in question among patriots and collaborators throughout the war, and there was not quite the same clarity of choice—Marcel Ophuls's *The Sorrow and the Pity* to the contrary notwithstanding—as one could imagine in the case of the French resistance to the Nazis.[86] Historians in China have never fully confronted the question of collaborators (in part because there were so very many of them), although the issue was the main subject of a long-running television series in mainland China in the 1980s about wartime Beiping.[87] But when Chinese historians do address the subject, they will have to grapple with the question of clarity of choice, if only to show how mixed people's aims were at the time, and how unclear were the distinctions between friend and foe when the agents of at least three seats of government—the Nationalist party-state in Chongqing, the Reform puppet-state in Nanjing, and the Communist rebel-state in Yan'an—competed among themselves in the lower Yangzi and coastal provinces both vis-à-vis the Japanese Occupation forces and for positional advantage in whatever postwar settlement was likely to occur.[88] There were necessary compromises to be made on all sides, which is one reason so many intellectuals who remained behind in Shanghai felt at best ambivalent, at worst guilty, about their common plight.[89]

11

Dimout

One paradoxically vivid element in all this grayness was the emergence in middle and late 1941 of Dai Li's Blue Shirts. The paradox simply rested in the name itself, which was the term applied by the Shanghainese, the Japanese, and the Westerners to members either of Juntong or of the Loyal and Patriotic National Salvation Army working underground in Shanghai against the puppet and Occupation forces.[1] As we have seen, the Blue Shirts were formally disbanded in 1935 at the behest of the Japanese after the Tangku Agreement was signed with the Nationalist government.[2] Former members of the Blue Shirts working in security and intelligence under Dai Li were shifted over into the Second Department and eventually became the backbone cadres of the Military Statistics Bureau, or Juntong. The name "Blue Shirts" stuck with them, however, on the tongues of others, and so the term was used more and more frequently in 1941 to designate the resurgent Nationalist secret service networks operating with increasing impunity in both "island" and occupied Shanghai.[3]

Blue Shirts and day-to-day terrorism

In the fall of 1941, for example, five Shanghai newspapers published a purportedly complete roster of eight executive detachments of the Blue Shirts Society in Shanghai, giving the noms de guerre of squad chiefs and deputy chiefs, as well as of intelligence and communication officers.[4] The extent of the Blue Shirts organization was made plausible in the public's eye by signs of growing guerrilla activity around Shanghai (and especially along the Shanghai–Ningbo railroad) in mid-April before the Japanese initiated their "model peace zone" policy later that July.[5] During the week of May 3–10, the Japanese Naval Landing Party and Military Police announced that they had arrested a large number of Chinese agents from Chongqing infiltrated into Hongkou:

Honkew [Hongkou] has been penetrated so thoroughly by them that Japanese soldiers and sailors seldom dare to move about in the area except in parties of two or more. Sentries on duty have even become fearful of the terrorists following recent successful attacks. Japanese authorities state that these terrorists have entered the district by disguising themselves as common people. Beggars' rags, the clerk's own gown, and vendors' garments have frequently been found to conceal anti-Japanese pro-Chungking [Chongqing] agents.[6]

The level of Chongqing-sponsored terrorism rose accordingly.

On June 20, 1941, two Chinese puppet policemen were found murdered in the badlands near Hongqiao Road.[7] Three days later, ten Chinese guerrillas wounded a Japanese motorist and killed the Japan Tourist Bureau employee who tried to save him.[8] On July 1, one of the Chinese translators for the Japanese Military Police was shot down in front of his home just off Haining Road.[9] Five days later a lone Chinese gunman shot the Japanese cook for the Naval Attaché's office while he was walking along Kinchow [Jinzhou] Road about forty yards north of Ward Road.[10]

On July 7, the anniversary of the Marco Polo Bridge incident, the Shanghai Municipal Police and French police congratulated themselves for preventing any major shootings or bombings; but outside the foreign concessions a huge time bomb blew up forty-eight meters of the Shanghai–Nanjing railroad tracks, destroying fifteen sleeping cars.[11] Another time bomb went off at the pro-Nanjing newspaper offices of *Guo bao* (National News) at 1926 Bubbling Well Road in the badlands, wounding one Chinese, deafening another, and setting the building on fire. And a hand grenade was thrown at the Japanese Military Police barracks on Poong Lai [Penglai] Road in Nandao.[12]

The next two weeks in July were relatively quiet, except for the murder of a Nanjing collaborator, Hwa Kang [Hua Gang], as he was cooling himself in front of his house on Lane 82, Brenan Road.[13] On July 21, however, the Japanese Military Police went into a kind of panic. It all began when a member of the Nanjing Peace Preservation Corps, Wang Teh-chow [Wang Dezhou], was killed. Wang had been stationed in Songjiang, where Chongqing terrorists had already murdered several members of his family. He had come to Shanghai seeking protective refuge. Early on the morning of the 21st, however, his time ran out. As he was leaving his residence on Lane 51, route de Grochy, a team of eight gunmen shot him down.[14]

Just as the Japanese Military Police received the report of Wang's death, they got wind of the murder of Sergeant D. B. Simajin, a Russian policeman with the Shanghai Municipal Police.[15] And at about that same time they also learned from one of the Chinese spies working for the Japanese navy that a "dangerous band of armed terrorists" was on a mission to attack the residents of a house in Hongkou. The Chinese informant, upon leaving the Japanese Military Police headquarters on North Sichuan Road, thought he saw one of the terrorists walking along the street. He drew his pistol and fired into the air. As a result, orders were issued to close all bridges into Hongkou, and for five hours all transportation was stopped while long lines of trucks and motorcars were halted in their positions down the Bund.[16]

The same closing down was ordered on July 26 when a Japanese naval sentry was shot as he tried to inspect the belongings of a Chinese man at the corner of Kunming and Baoding Roads in Yangshupu.[17] Three days later, after the bridges were reopened, Chongqing terrorists shot and killed a mechanic for the French Tramway Company who was a leading officer in the Nanjing-sponsored Tramworkers Union.[18] This was followed by a relatively tranquil ten-day hiatus until August 9 when an incendiary bomb went off in the four-story building that housed the official mouthpiece of the Nanjing régime, the puppet *Zhongyang ribao* (Central Daily News).[19] Five members of the staff were injured and the building was completely gutted, forcing the newspaper to publish much abbreviated issues printed thereafter in the plant of *Xin shenbao,* the Japanese-sponsored Chinese daily at 288 Seward Road in Hongkou.[20]

The burning of *Central Daily News* was the harbinger of an oncoming firestorm, a "fury of terrorism" that began shortly after the fourth anniversary of the Japanese invasion of Shanghai on August 13. The anniversary itself was uneventful because the Shanghai Municipal Police and Japanese authorities took so many precautions to prevent disorder. Barricades were erected, patrols were increased with the use of the Shanghai Volunteer Corps and the Police Specials (i.e., reserves), search parties were stationed at major intersections and all police leaves were canceled, the U.S. Fourth Marines were confined to barracks ready for an emergency, and the Japanese flew airplanes low overhead "to impress the Chinese with Japan's military power."[21] Two days later a prominent banker was killed and wholesale slaughter prevailed thereafter.

The banker was twenty-nine-year-old Kennson Gee (Ji Kunsheng), son of a prominent Sichuan official and the local manager of a *qianzhuang* (native bank). Ji, who lived in the American Club seventy-five yards from Shanghai Municipal Police headquarters on Foochow [Fuzhou] Road, had several days earlier published an article in the magazine *Finance and Commerce* calling for investments in Free China.[22] The piece had infuriated the puppet banking authorities.[23] On August 15 Ji stepped out of the American Club and started to cross the street to his car. Five gunmen in a sedan shot him to death in front of the club. Before they could escape, police poured out of the police headquarters and opened fire on the assassins. In the frantic gunfight that followed one Chinese constable shot out the engine of the car—which had been stolen a week before while parked outside the Paramount Ballroom on the fringe of the badlands—and the assassins had to flee westward toward Jessfield Road on foot. The police pursued them on motorcycles, firing as they went, as far as the Louza district, where one of the terrorists was killed and three others were captured along with their weapons. Along the way three civilians and two policemen were killed, and eight pedestrians and three policemen were wounded.[24]

That same day a WASP patrolman was shot and killed on Brenan Road in the badlands when he attempted to search two men's baskets. On August 16, a lone gunman wounded the prominent lawyer Wang Zeshing [Wang Zexing], a friend of Wu Shibao, "gangster chief of the Nanking political police headquarters at 76 Jessfield Road." Two terrorists shot a Japanese employee of the Toyoda Cotton Mill in the chest as he was pumping up a flat bicycle tire. The manager of a coal importing firm was kidnapped outside his home on rue Frélupt. And a powerful explosion rocked the Huangpu ferry boat *Kiaochow maru* [Chaozhou wan] just after it disembarked passengers on the Bund at the foot of Nanking Road.[25] On August 17 the owner of the Dah Woo Dai [Dawudai] Theater at 663 Kiukiang [Jiujiang] Road was mortally wounded in the back by a single assassin; and during the six days between August 23 and 28 a Japanese staff member of the Hsing Chang [Xingzhang] Cotton Spinning Company was critically wounded near the Japanese Naval Cemetery, two Japanese civilian employees of the Japanese army were ambushed and killed by four Chinese gunmen, the Astro and Lyric Theaters were bombed, one Japanese civilian and one Chinese civilian working for the Japanese army were killed in Hongkou (which was again closed down), bandits in the largest robbery ever staged in the French Concession stole $300,000 in gold from a silver hong, the general manager of the First Trust Bank was kidnapped, terrorists used phosphorous to try to burn down a Mitsubishi Trading Company warehouse, and Chinese gunmen shot down a member of the Peace Preservation Corps in Pudong across the river.[26]

Retaliation

As early as August 17 the Japanese began to erect new barbed wire barricades around the outskirts of Greater Shanghai.[27] Fences were strung around Xujiahui and Hongqiao districts on the perimeter of the badlands, so that many minor roads were blocked, and all bridges across Yangzipu

Creek except two were indefinitely closed.[28] Chinese coming into Shanghai now by land had to enter via military checkpoints, where they were
rigorously searched for concealed weapons. "Little Tokyo" in Hongkou
was turned into an impenetrable fortress. After August 28, 1941, Chinese
were barred from entering "Japantown" between 7:00 p.m. and 5:00
a.m., and when they came across Suzhou Creek during the day their
clothing, parcels, baggage, vehicles, and persons were intensively searched
by sentries whose numbers were doubled and redoubled on the bridges.[29]
"Armored cars patrolled the streets north of Soochow [Suzhou] Creek
throughout the night and all exits and entrances from Hongkew [Hong-
kou] into the south of the creek area were closed."[30]

The puppet authorities took stringent measures of their own, as well. In
late August, the Nanjing government issued a new criminal law for Shanghai. It placed all robbery and banditry cases in the badlands and elsewhere
outside the Settlement and French Concession under the jurisdiction of
local Chinese military organs. That is to say, cases that were formerly tried
in civil courts—and in the case of the badlands, in the South Market
(Nandao) court, per the February "modus vivendi" agreement—were
now by the unilateral decision of the Wang Jingwei régime to be judged
under martial law. In practice this meant that Mayor Chen Gongbo instructed WASP Commissioner C. C. Pan to hand armed gangsters and
kidnappers over to the Peace Preservation Corps.[31]

This militarization, so to speak, of criminal law occurred in a special
new context brought about by the reorganization of the Nanjing government's police system.[32] On August 16, 1941, the Ministry of Police (Jingzheng bu) was downgraded to a Police Headquarters Department (Jingzheng zongshu) and brought under the direct control of the Ministry of
Interior (Neizheng bu). In a move reminiscent of the division within
Chiang Kai-shek's régime between Zhongtong (Central Statistics) and
Juntong (Military Statistics), Wang Jingwei's political police office was
put directly under the Ministry of Investigation and Statistics (Diaocha
tongji bu) of the Military Affairs Committee.[33] At the same time, the
Ministry of Social Affairs was folded into the Social Welfare Promotion
Committee, which was supposed to conduct nonpolice secret service
work by supervising public assemblies, student activities, and labor affairs. The Nanjing authorities felt that by ceasing to exist as a ministry,
this group's activities would not be so visible to the public.[34]

Although these changes were part of a general policy of police central-
ization, they were also driven by political rivalries centered on Li Shiqun,
minister of police, and Ding Mocun, minister of social affairs.[35] Prior to
August 16, Wang Jingwei and Zhou Fohai had both grown increasingly
dissatisfied with the two men, and especially with Li Shiqun. Zhou, who

was minister of finance, was visibly annoyed with Li because few of the illegal revenues pouring into 76 Jessfield Road ever made their way to the central government's coffers. Wang, as head of government, "feared the rising power of Li" and disliked the "open and rather high-handed manner in which certain activities of the police have been carried on, particularly as they have been brought too directly to public attention."[36]

Li Shiqun's free-wheeling independence, both as the person who controlled the badlands renegades at "76" and as full-fledged minister of police, also galled Minister of Interior Chen Qun. As a former Reform Government official, Chen Qun had strong backing from the Japanese, who disliked Li Shiqun and Wu Shibao's errant and intractable behavior.[37] When Chen Qun insisted, consequently, that these two other ministries be brought under his jurisdiction, Wang Jingwei perforce found himself in agreement. Ding Mocun was given another post of equal rank but less power, and Li Shiqun was made general secretary of the Rural Pacification Movement (the "model peace zone" effort to "clean up the villages," or *qing xiang*) with headquarters in Suzhou.[38]

All of this had a discernible impact on the puppet secret service operations at 76 Jessfield Road. Although that ominous office was put under the charge of a former lieutenant of Li Shiqun, vice-minister of police Tong Keming, Li was now out of the picture altogether, and Nanjing's orders were to carry out secret police activities in a "much less obvious fashion."[39] Zhou Fohai's Ministry of Finance now had more direct control over the revenues of "76," including the gambling payoffs; and it was clear that Chen Qun's assertion of Ministry of Interior authority over the entire secret police apparatus was an exertion in parallel with General Lu Ying's move in July as director of the Shanghai Chinese Police now headquartered in Nandao (South Market) to displace C. C. Pan's authority in the badlands as chief of the Western Area Special Police and the bevy of gangsters and collaborators who served as his clandestine agents.[40]

The end of "island Shanghai"

Did the assertion of downtown Nandao's police control over the assorted thugs, secret servicemen, terrorists, and ill-trained constables of 76 Jessfield Road and the WASP actually succeed in turning—to use *Shanghai*'s ludicrous phrase—the "Badlands" into "Goodlands"?[41] The answer is hardly so. Quite apart from Huxi, Nandao itself continued to harbor gambling and drug operations through the fall and winter of 1941.[42] Not long before the attack on Pearl Harbor the Swedish journalist Karl Eskelund wrote an important newspaper piece describing the situation in Nandao "as a cross between a poverty-stricken Chinese village and a poor man's Monte Carlo." Playing a primitive variant of roulette using numbers painted on a table and dice, six large gambling establishments, open day and night, offered their customers free wine, beer, cigarettes, and even milk for their little children. But they more than covered expenses with the opium sold in divans upstairs and the winnings taken in by the house. For adjacent to these gambling and drug dens were numerous pawn shops "where unfortunate gamblers are able to pawn their valuables and even their clothes."[43]

No, imposing Nandao's rule on the "Badlands" failed to turn them into "Goodlands." Terrorist wars continued to rage, especially over banks and currency controls and over domination of the press.[44] Homicide and crime rates spiraled upwards. In spite of by-now complete cooperation between the Shanghai Municipal Police and the Japanese Military Police in rounding up Blue Shirts, the last directors of the Shanghai Municipal Council continued wearily to negotiate with the Japanese consul general over final control of the Settlement police.[45] If and when war broke out with Japan—as now seemed obvious to many—the International Settlement (already appearing to many Chinese living under its protection an independent entity in name only) would be turned over to the puppets, which would be a hollow victory for Chinese sovereignty indeed.[46]

Meanwhile the gap continued to grow between rich and poor, while both staggered under the weight of a growing wartime inflation. For Chinese workers prices had risen tenfold since just before the War of Resistance began in 1937, and for foreigners, the cost of living was climbing at a rate of nearly 9 percent a month.[47] During the two months before December 8, 1941, and the fall of the entire city to the Japanese, beggars and thieves brazenly stole food off of street stands while policemen stood idly by, until vendors had nothing to sell. The Settlement authorities tried to hold the price of rice at 130 yuan a *picul,* but profiteers flourished and even the upper middle class began to realize that the struggle for existence in time to come would be over food and daily necessities. "It seemed as though the isolated island was going to sink into a boundless bitter sea."[48]

We began with Percy Finch's blazing description of Shanghai under early Japanese occupation, when the terrorist wars were just beginning. Let us end with Vanya Oakes's somber reflections on the city just before Pearl Harbor:

> Shanghai was a city of vice and violence, of opulence wildly juxtaposed to unbelievable poverty, of whirling roulette wheels and exploding shotguns and crying beggars. No longer a center of the world upheaval which had begun there in 1937, Shanghai now was living in a state of perpetual alarum and excursions, aftermath of bombings and destruction, abnormalities of trade, currency dislocation, the sly infiltrations of the Japanese, the influx of

refugees, an ever-soaring cost of living, the outbreak of war in Europe, and its reverberations along Bubbling Well Road. Shanghai had become a tawdry city of refugees and rackets.[49]

The experiences of four years of "island Shanghai" amounted in most people's eyes to a "terrorist nightmare."[50] "For many months past," the chairman of the Shanghai Municipal Council, J. H. Liddell, said in September 1941, "the Settlement has been the scene of periodic acts of terrorism, the sufferers having been for the most part Chinese." Asking the gunmen to put down their weapons, Liddell added:

> I make this appeal in the hope that I will be heard and have the support of every section of the community and of all political groups and parties. I request to use wholeheartedly all the influence that they possess so that law and order may again prevail, that the people who live here may do so in peace, which is their greatest desire.[51]

No doubt that desire for peace and for law and order after the chaos of the badlands made it easier for the Japanese to take over direct rule of the city once the U.S. fleet was sunk at Pearl Harbor on December 7, 1941. Imperial Japanese rule was draconian, to be sure. Applying a modified *baojia* (*hokô*) system, perfected on colonial Taiwan by putting civilian mutual responsibility units under direct police control, the Japanese and their puppets punished entire neighborhoods with isolation and even starvation for acts of resistance.[52] The Occupation created bitter memories among the Shanghainese, but there were, after all, virtually no urban uprisings, no overt confrontations, after the Japanese imposed their version of the New Order (Xin zhixu) on all of Shanghai.[53] One reason for the ease of takeover and domination from 1942 to 1945 of China's largest city may be the ambiguous disorder that characterized the years of trauma from 1937 to 1941. Weariness and wariness were never far apart, and, as the popular Shanghai expression at one time mockingly put it: "It was tough to live in peace for so long."[54] The Japanese ruled Shanghai securely not because they were politically nimble, but because the Chinese in the city were psychologically devastated.

Epilogue: Outcomes

Shanghai: Just after Japan's surrender, August 1945

Chungking troops in town. Cheering crowds line up and hail their heroes. The harbor wakes up. When planes are circling overhead steamers hoot, firecrackers greet the roaring engines, and everybody runs to see the newcomers. The Japanese have lost. They know it and they take it nicely. Their guards stand silent at their posts and cooperate in keeping order.

Around them is China victorious and only over the Japanese Embassy flutters "the rising sun." Gradually the Japanese soldiers and civilians disappear from the street picture. Their shops are closed. They fade out. Their embassy goes down. They will go away: Japan for the Japanese! American boys, British boys, Shanghai girls, do your duty! They do. Every nightclub is full. Life begins at sunset and never ends. Who cares about the curfew. The war is won. May peace be preserved! Two world wars is enough in any century.[1]

Shanghai: The Communist liberation, May 25, 1949

Communist partisans went wild with enthusiasm. The Great World in the French concession, the city's largest amusement resort, hosted a mammoth picture of Mao Tse-tung, which obviously had been weeks in the making. The red flag appeared over buildings and flew outside stores which twenty-two years earlier had quite as enthusiastically flown the Kuomintang flag. Sympathizers who found themselves without Communist emblems hastily manufactured them by tearing the blue sky and white sun quarter from the red field of the Nationalist flag. Madly jubilant and easily moved students danced the *yang-ko* in the streets, welcoming Mao's men with all the fervor another generation had welcomed Chiang's. It was like a Hollywood remake with Marxian inflections.[2]

Shanghai: Nine days after the Communist liberation, June 3, 1949

After the wiping out of the military forces of the Guomindang reactionaries, a period of military control must be exercised in the principal city. . . . This system will prove useful to the task of the continuous fight for the obliteration of the remnant reactionary forces and the protection and consolidation of the people's own interest. For this reason, during the period of military control, the Military Control Committee is the highest authority in the city. The municipal government is the principal constituent portion of the Military Control Committee.[3]

Abbreviations

BFOR—British Foreign Office Records. London: Her Majesty's Public Record Office.

BWOR—British War Office Records. London: Her Majesty's Public Record Office.

CC—*China Critic.*

CP—*China Press.*

CSDCF—Confidential U.S. State Department Central Files. China: Internal Affairs, 1940–1944.

CWR—*China Weekly Review.*

FRUS 1939—*Foreign Relations of the United States: Diplomatic Papers, 1939, vol. 4, The Far East, the Near East, and Africa.* U.S. Department of State. Washington: U.S. Government Printing Office, 1955.

FRUS 1940—*Foreign Relations of the United States. Diplomatic Papers, 1940, vol. 4, The Far East.* U.S. Department of State. Washington: U.S. Government Printing Office, 1955.

MG—*Municipal Gazette of the Council for the Foreign Settlement of Shanghai.* Shanghai: Municipal Council, 1941.

NCDN—*North China Daily News.*

NCH—*North China Herald.*

OSS—Office of Strategic Services Archives, U.S. Army. U.S. National Archives, Military Reference Division.

RDS—*Records of the Department of State Relating to the Internal Affairs of China, 1930–1939.* Government Documents Library, microfilm 31217.

RWSSZ—Shanghai shi dang'an guan, comp. *Ri wei Shanghai shi zhengfu* [The Japanese puppet government of Shanghai]. Shanghai: Dang'an chubanshe, 1986.

SAM—Shanghai Archives Microfilms. Microfilms of selected documents that the Berkeley Center for Chinese Studies acquired from the Shanghai Municipal Archives in 1994.

SB—Shen bao.

SEPM—Shanghai Evening Post and Mercury.

SMA—Shanghai Municipal Archives.

SMP—Shanghai Municipal Police (International Settlement) Files. Microfilms from the U.S. National Archives.

SS—Shanghai shenghuo.

ST—Shanghai Times.

TS—Tairiku shimpo.

USMIR—U.S. Military Intelligence Reports, China, 1911–1941.

XSB—Xin shenbao.

ZR—Zhongyang ribao.

Notes

Prologue: Consequences

1. "Nationalist and Communist agents were able to assassinate a few collaborators and Japanese but the Shanghai occupation and its puppets largely prevented this from happening in the city. Many Chinese migrated westward rather than staying in Shanghai resisting. At least before World War II broke out in Europe, leaders in the British and American parts of the International Settlement were also willing to cooperate somewhat with the Japanese occupation," claims White, "Non-governmentalism in the Historical Development of Modern Shanghai," 48.

2. "Every known crime, petty, political, and legal, was bred there." Oakes, *White Man's Folly*, 362. "Policing of this disputed area had always been the major cause of conflict between the Settlement and the Chinese authorities, and on several occasions these disputes assumed serious proportions." "Shanghai Mayor Keeps His Promise to the Public," 2–3. The term "badlands," which was widely used in the U.S.-edited *China Weekly Review*, was rendered in Chinese by a neologism, *dai3tu3* (vicious land), which was nearly homonymic with the term for rogue (literally, "vicious follower"), *dai3tu2*.

3. Xia Yan, *Baoshen gong* (reprint Beijing, 1978), 26, cited in Wakeman and Yeh, "Introduction," 5.

4. The super-stratification of wealthy collaborators became even more pronounced after Pearl Harbor, when "if life meant misery for the many, it was a carnival for a few." Fu, *Passivity, Resistance, and Collaboration*, 125.

5. Ch'ien, *Fortress Besieged*, 325.

6. After the Vichy régime was established in France, as we shall see, the Japanese worked out a separate earlier arrangement with the authorities in the French Concession.

1. Island Shanghai

1. The battle is ably summarized in Fu, *Passivity, Resistance, and Collaboration*, 2–5; and expertly analyzed in Williamsen, "The Military Dimension, 1937–1941," 142–144. A competent, though ideologically tendentious account, can

also be found in He Li, *Kangri zhanzheng shi,* 101–103. The best diplomatic account of these events is to be found in Borg, *The United States and the Far Eastern Crisis of 1933–1938,* 300–317.

2. Yu Zidao, "Lun kangzhan chuqi zhengmian zhanchang zuozhan zhongxin zhi zhuanyi," 1.

3. Chiang Kai-shek ordered General Zhang Zhizhong on 16 August to "wipe out the enemy army in one stroke." Sun, *China and the Origins of the Pacific War,* 91. For the effective Chinese use of powerful German 15-cm howitzers in this battle, see Coox, *Year of the Tiger,* 8–9.

4. Ch'i, *Nationalist China at War,* 40–47.

5. The Generalissimo was convinced that the only possible way the Chinese could defeat the enemy, which controlled the air and had superior artillery, was by engaging his infantry in close encounters and standing firm. He believed that Chinese soldiers were superior in will, determination, and resistance to faster-moving and better-equipped Japanese troops. See his 13 September 1937 despatch to battlefield commanders in Qin Xiaoyi, ed. *Zhonghua minguo zhongyao shiliao chubian—Dui Ri zhanzheng shiqi. Di er bian: Zuozhan jingguo,* 50–51. For the more general strategy, see his uncharacteristically long statement of 18 August 1937 on strategic principles in ibid., 44–48. This is qualified by Dorn, *The Sino-Japanese War, 1937–41,* 72; and by Garver, "China's Wartime Diplomacy," 8.

6. Sun, *China and the Origins of the Pacific War,* 91.

7. The Japanese lost forty-seven aircraft, mostly heavy bombers, to Chinese anti-aircraft fire and fighters throughout China during the first four days of the Shanghai offensive. They confined their bombing to the Shanghai area until 31 August, when enough fighter reinforcements arrived from Japan to give them air supremacy. Hsü, *The War Conduct of the Japanese,* 2.

8. Pan Ling, *Old Shanghai,* 60.

9. Ibid., 4–11. Although Japanese officers fighting the crack 88th Division claimed that the Chinese "have no idea of teamwork," they never questioned their bravery. Ruffé, *La bataille de Shanghai,* 23–24. The bombing of Zhabei was regarded by many Europeans and Americans as an act beyond the pale of civilization. Dower, *War without Mercy,* 38.

10. Li Enhan, *Riben jun zhanzheng baoxing,* 341; Boyle, *China and Japan at War, 1937–1945,* 69; Hata Ikuhito, *Nitchū sensō shi,* 280–283.

11. Dorn, *The Sino-Japanese War, 1937–41,* 76–77; Cook and Cook, *Japan at War,* 31–32.

12. Hsi-sheng Ch'i, *Nationalist China at War,* 42–43; Snow, *The Battle for Asia,* 48–51; Coox, *Year of the Tiger,* 18.

13. Coble, "Chinese Capitalists," 3.

14. Except for a few warehouses whose massive stone walls had resisted the flames, the entire quarter was in ruins. Thomasson, "Prise de vues à Shanghai," 283. See also "Shanghai in Torment," 132.

15. Fifty percent of all industrial properties in the Shanghai area were destroyed. Coble, "Chinese Capitalists," 4.

16. The machinery industry, which lost 360 firms to fighting and another 66 to

inland migration, did not fully recover until after 1949. Reed, "Gutenberg in Shanghai," 55.

17. Li Enhan, *Riben jun zhanzheng baoxing,* 342.
18. "The chairman of the British Chamber of Commerce estimated the material damage to British property at £500,000, adding that consequential losses were probably fifteen to twenty times as great." Clifford, *Retreat from China,* 69.
19. Finch, *Shanghai and Beyond,* 259. See also Hauser, *Shanghai: City for Sale,* 313; Henriot, "Le gouvernement municipal de Shanghai," 324; Henriot, *Shanghai, 1927–1937,* 230. The loss of China's major banking assets was a tremendous blow to the Nationalist régime. On the eve of the war, China's banks' holdings amounted to Ch.$5,918,350,357, of which $5,593,794,057 fell into enemy hands, leaving "Free China" $324,556,300, or 0.54 percent of the total. Han Qitong, *Zhongguo dui Ri zhanshi juanshi zhi guji (1937–1943),* 48–49.
20. See, for the special refugee zone set up by Father Robert Jacquinot de Besange, Finch, *Shanghai and Beyond,* 269–275.
21. Hauser, *Shanghai: City for Sale,* 306–307; Feng Yi, "Le problème des réfugiés à Shanghai (1937–1940)," 9. On 22 August 1937 Chiang Kai-shek ordered his brother-in-law, T. V. Soong, to use Bank of China funds to succor Shanghai's *nanmin* (refugees). Qin Xiaoyi, ed., *Zhonghua minguo zhongyao shiliao chubian—Dui Ri zhanzheng shiqi. Di er bian: Zuozhan jingguo,* 50.
22. Finch, *Shanghai and Beyond,* 261–262; Candlin, *The Breach in the Wall,* 301.
23. Fu, "Intellectual Resistance in Shanghai," 3–4.
24. Production levels in Shanghai in 1939 were greater or equal to those in 1936 for silk weaving, flour milling, and cotton weaving. Coble, "Chinese Capitalists," 5.
25. Honig, "Women Cotton Mill Workers in Shanghai," 27–28; Honig, *Sisters and Strangers,* 34.
26. As of fall 1938, industrial production had recovered its prewar levels. Roux, "The Guomindang and the Workers of Shanghai (1938–1948)," 5.
27. Oakes, *White Man's Folly,* 372–373. Needless to say, the trade in Chinese antiques thrived too. Bari, "Helen D. Ling," 5.
28. Coble, "Chinese Capitalists," 6; Ristaino, "White Russian and Jewish Refugees in Shanghai," 62–64; Heppner, *Shanghai Refuge,* 42.
29. Oakes, *White Man's Folly,* 374; Eastman, "Facets of an Ambivalent Relationship," 278.
30. Oakes, *White Man's Folly,* 348–349. After Germany and the Soviet Union signed their nonaggression pact on 23–24 August 1939 and before Hitler invaded Russia in June 1941, the Germans were shipping 100,000 tons a month of products over the Trans-Siberian railway. In 1940, German–Chinese trade amounted to U.S.$9.7 million, with Shanghai accounting for about half of that amount. Shanghai's exports to the United States by February 1939 amounted to approximately U.S.$1 million per month, which was

roughly half the amount exported in February 1937 before hostilities began. *RDS*, 893.00 P.R. Shanghai/125 (Feb. 1939), 17.

31. Yu Hongjun remained the official mayor throughout the war. Henriot, "Le gouvernement municipal de Shanghai," 428.

32. SMP, D-8194, 21/12/37. Yu Xiaqing, whose San Bei Steamship Navigation Company had lost a tremendous amount of shipping during the Battle of Shanghai, recouped his costs by using freighters under the Norwegian, Panamanian, and Italian flags to transport rice from Saigon and Rangoon to sell in Shanghai. Yu died in Chongqing in 1945. His coffin was shipped back to Shanghai where he was buried with high honors (Tibet Road was renamed after him) in November 1946. Coble, "Chinese Capitalists," 7; Tsao, "On the Nature of Chinese Capitalists," 6.

33. Wang Fangnan, "Wo zai juntong shisinian de qinli he jianwen," 143. Nonetheless, Lu Bohong was assassinated by Nationalist Juntong (Military Statistics) agents on 30 December 1937. Ch'eng, *The Banker*, 255. The "local self-government committees" were linked by the Dadao puppet police to neighborhood *zianhui* (self-pacification committees), which were made responsible for protecting prominent local collaborators, such as Han Zidong in Pudong. SMA, Wang 1.1.137—Dadao government—Jiaobu daofei qizei an [Cases of Exterminating and Arresting Bandits and Thieves], 3–5 Jan. 1938, 4b and 14. This file also has a complete report of military conditions in Pudong, including the extent of piracy in the coastal marshes, where so many goods were being transported to Hangzhou Bay and thence inland via Jinhua and Jiangshan, on pp. 51–52.

34. Fu's original name was Zongyao. He was from Zhenhai (Zhejiang) and had been a client of the warlord Sun Chuanfang. He was also head of the board of directors of the Shanghai French Commercial Tramway Company (Shanghai fashang dianche gongsi): Zhang Weihan, "Dai Li yu 'Juntong ju'," 138.

35. Finch, *Shanghai and Beyond*," 312; *RWSSZ*, 1–2 (see also the first illustration in the frontispiece, which displays a photographic copy of the founding announcement); White, "Non-governmentalism in the Historical Development of Modern Shanghai," 48.

36. Su Xiwen, forty-seven years old, was originally from Amoy and had been head of the Fujian Finance Bureau. *RWSSZ*, 13.

37. SMA, Wang 1.1.10—Dadao government, cover sheet dated in both lunar and solar (24 Feb. 1938) figures—Jingchaju xiang zhangze [Rules and regulations of the Police Bureau], 2, 5–7. Photographs of the flag are to be found in the frontispiece photographs in *RWSSZ*, and in *China Weekly Review* (hereafter *CWR*), 8 Jan. 1938, 152. To justify its rule, the puppet government accused both the Guomindang and Chinese Communist Party of spreading civil war across the country and promised to restore peace and tranquility. *RWSSZ*, 6.

38. SMA, Wang 1.1.10—Dadao government, cover sheet dated in both lunar and solar (24 Feb. 1938) figures—Jingchaju xiang zhangze, 5, 9b, 18, 24a. The head of the public health section was Fan Jimin, 36 *sui*, who had a degree in medicine from the Zhejiang Specialized Medical School (Yiyao zhuanmen

xuexiao). He had been head of the Songjiang county hospital. SMA, Wang
1.1.58—Dadao government (April 1938)—Guanyu jingju neiwai yuanjing
[Long-term perspectives for the police], 2b. The chief adviser for the detective
squad was Li Jinbiao, a gangster who had been a detective in the Song–Hu
police department (Song–Hu jingcha ting). Li was later assassinated by Nationalist agents on 28 October 1939. *SB*, 29 Oct. 1939, 9. For an organizational chart of the Dadao government, see *RWSSZ*, 3–5.

39. *RWSSZ*, 12.

40. Ibid.

41. SMA, Wang 1.1.58—Dadao government—Guanyu jingju neiwai yuanjing,
19. There is a complete roster of the Dadao police bureau for March 1938 in
SMA, Wang 1.1.226—Dadao government—Jingchaju sanyuefen qingce [Po-
lice roster in March]. The inspectorate (including Chief Inspector Liu Wanqing and Chief Investigator Xu Wenbing) is listed in SMA, Wang 1.1.34—
Dadao government—Jingchaju weiren ji renmian [Police department appointments and dismissals], 66a; and other important positions (Hu
Zhenggu, head of the Detective Brigade, and his deputy, Huo Liangchen) are
noted in SMA, Wang 1.1.29—Dadao government—Jingchaju cunren [Police
department personnel assignments], 2b–3b. When people heard the term
"Dadao Municipal Government" (Dadao shi zhengfu), they invariably smiled
because *dao4* (way) was a homophone for the character *dao4* (robber), making the phrase mean "The Municipal Government of the Big Robbers." Zhu
Zijia, *Wang Zhengquan de kaichang yu shouchang*, vol. 4, 32.

42. Wang Zihui later served as minister of industry (*shiye buzhang*) in the Reform
Government. Qin Xiaoyi, *Zhonghua minguo zhongyao shiliao chubian—
Dui Ri zhanzheng shiqi. Di liu bian: Kuilei zuzhi*, 139.

43. Cao Zhenwei, "Liang Hongzhi," 406–407; Zhu Zijia, *Wang Zhengquan de
kaichang yu shouchang*, vol. 5, 108–109. For an intimate and artfully written
portrait of Liang, see ibid., vol. 4, 36–37.

44. *Zhonghua minguo weixin zhengfu zhenggang*, "Weixin zhengfu zuzhi xitong
ji zhongyao zhiyuan biao" [Table of organization and important personnel of
the Reform Government] (10 Sept. 1939), attachment to p. 311; Qin Xiaoyi,
*Zhonghua minguo zhongyao shiliao chubian—Dui Ri zhanzheng shiqi. Di
liu bian: Kuilei zuzhi*, 127–128, 132–138; Nashimoto Yûhei, *Chûgoku no
naka no Nihonjin*, vol. 2, 65–74; Liu Qikui, "Wang Kemin," 342–343; Epstein, *The Unfinished Revolution in China*, 315; Koo, "Some Economic
Documents Relating to the Genesis of the Japanese-Sponsored Regime in
North China," 66; Boyle, *China and Japan at War, 1937–1945*, 88–89 and
110–111; Jones, *Japan's New Order in East Asia*, 72; Imai Takeo, *Shina jihen
no kaisô*, 282–283.

45. *Zhonghua minguo weixin zhengfu zhenggang*, 1. See also Qin Xiaoyi,
*Zhonghua minguo zhongyao shiliao chubian—Dui Ri zhanzheng shiqi. Di
liu bian: Kuilei zuzhi*, 140–141. For the "cleansing of villages" policy, see
ibid., 142–143; Huang Meizhen, *Wei ting yin ying lu*, 52–53.

46. Zhu Zijia, *Wang Zhengquan de kaichang yu shouchang*, vol. 4, 33. The
Reform Government initially operated out of the New Asia Hotel in Hongkou

because the Japanese Army had commandeered most important government buildings in Nanjing. Boyle, *China and Japan at War, 1937–1945,* 112.

47. SMP, D-8155D, 30/3/38. "The real masters," Michael has pointed out, "are the Japanese Special Service Bureau and the Military Police." Michael, "The Significance of Puppet Governments," 411.

48. *RWSSZ,* 18–20. For the regulations governing the relationship between the Nanjing central government and the Shanghai Special Municipality (Shanghai tebie shi), see *Zhonghua minguo weixin zhengfu zhenggang,* 79–80; and *RWSSZ,* 18–19. The Supervisory Yamen was not even powerful enough to find office quarters in Shanghai. In October 1938 its representatives were still hunting, having discovered that "the most suitable accommodations [had] already been preempted by the Japanese authorities." *RDS,* 893.00 P.R. Shanghai/121 (Oct. 1938), 15.

49. *RWSSZ,* 31, 38. For the organization of the Shanghai Special Municipality government, which was actually announced on 15 October, see ibid., 43–45; and *SB,* 15 Oct. 1938, 10.

50. *SEPM,* 25 Nov. 1938, 1, in SMP, D-8870, 25/11/38.

51. Japanese sources sometimes distinguish between *tokumubu* (special services units) and *tokumukikan* (special services agencies). Boyle, *China and Japan at War, 1937–1945,* 85. The various *tokumukikan* were responsible to the Imperial Army Staff in Tokyo. The Kempei, or Military Police, was accountable to the local garrison commander. Stephan, *The Russian Fascists,* 64. According to a captured Japanese code clerk, formerly of the Japanese Consulate and interrogated by the Office of Strategic Services in Burma in 1945, Colonel Harada was head of the Shanghai Tokumukikan between April 1938 and April 1939. "POW Interrogation on Japanese Activities in Shanghai," Office of Strategic Services (hereafter OSS), XL11759, 25/6/45, 1–2.

52. See the lurid description of ubiquitous Japanese spies and their Chinese, Mongol, Korean, and White Russian collaborators in Zhong Heming, *Riben qin Hua zhi jiandie shi,* passim.

53. OSS, XL11759, 25/6/45, 3.

54. SMP, D-8597, 12/7/38. See also OSS, XL11759, 25/6/45, 3.

55. The head of the international intelligence section was Chen Gongshu, a former Juntong agent under Dai Li. During his service for the Japanese, Chen wrote *The Inner History of the Blue Shirts* (Lanyishe neimu), which had a tremendous influence on Japanese perceptions of the Chinese secret service. Zhang Weihan, "Dai Li yu 'Juntong ju,'" 146.

56. *CWR,* 14 Jan. 1939, 213.

57. *CC,* 20 Feb. 1936, 177. Proceeds from the Tokumukikan usually went back to
   Tokyo; Kempei profits went into the private pockets of the Japanese military. Stephan, *The Russian Fascists,* 65.

58. The section was originally formed under the auspices of the Special Services Corps at 76 Jessfield Road, and was later placed under the direct control of the Military Police at 94 Jessfield Road. SMP, D-8373/12, 18/11/40. Another arm of the Special Services Corps, commanded by Wang Ziying and also under the direct control of the Military Police, was supposedly instructed to

assassinate local British, U.S., and French nationals who supported China's resistance against Japan. "Political Terrorism Unabated Here," 92.

59. SMP, D-8373/12, 21/5/40; BFOR, F-1534, 4/3/40, FO-371-24682.

60. SMP, D-8373/12, 22/12/39, and 7/6/40.

61. Ibid., 28/11/40.

62. M. R. Nicholson's report, 893.114 Narcotics/2417, cited in Marshall, "Opium and Gangsterism in Nationalist China," 40.

63. In 1938 in Manchuria, the sale of opium generated 28% of the Japanese government's general budget receipts, enough to finance the entire Kuantung Army. Adams, "China: Asia's Profitable Plague," 382; Marshall, "Opium and Gangsterism in Nationalist China," 47; Jones, *Japan's New Order in East Asia,* 85–86.

64. The major opium-growing provinces had, under Nationalist opium suppression laws, dutifully declared the plant was no longer cultivated. Chiang Kai-shek affected belief in these reports, which he conveyed to the League. Madancy, "Propaganda versus Practice," 32.

65. Ibid., 30.

66. Parssinen and Meyer, "International Narcotics Trafficking in the Early Twentieth Century," 49. "Factories were constructed in Hsinking, Mukden, Port Arthur, Tsitsihar, and Harbin (at Sunbei) to produce morphine, heroin, and cocaine. Opium output in Korea and Taiwan was expanded to accommodate massive Manchukuo imports." Stephan, *The Russian Fascists,* 66. By 1940, most of the opium consumed in North China, where in a city such as Taiyuan more than 40% of the population were drug addicts, was grown in Inner Mongolia (Suiyuan). "Opium Profits in North China," 551–552.

67. Chen Qun, principal of a middle school financed by Du Yuesheng, was a close ally of the Shanghai drug lord. In addition to serving as minister of the interior under the Reform Government, Chen was also head of the Youth League, the police academy, and the magistrates' training school. *Zhonghua minguo weixin zhengfu zhenggang,* "Weixin zhengfu zuzhi xitong ji zhongyao zhiyuan biao" [Table of organization and important personnel of the Reform Government] (10 Sept. 1939), attachment to p. 311; Qin Xiaoyi, *Zhonghua minguo zhongyao shiliao chubian—Dui Ri zhanzheng shiqi. Di liu bian: Kuilei zuzhi,* 134. See also Marshall, "Opium and Gangsterism in Nationalist China," 39.

68. Bates, M. S., "The Narcotics Situation in Nanking and Other Occupied Areas," 525–527. The Chongqing authorities accused the Japanese of encouraging this drug abuse for three reasons: (1) revenue; (2) maintaining the livelihoods of undesirable Japanese and Korean elements, thereby keeping them out of Japan; (3) weakening Chinese wartime resistance by poisoning the people. Madancy, "Propaganda versus Practice," 29–30, 33.

69. *CWR,* 25 Dec. 1937, 88–90.

70. Wakeman, *Policing Shanghai,* ch. 15. For Du Yuesheng's role in running Nationalist intelligence activities in Hong Kong, along with his partnership with Dai Li to transport opium from Sichuan to the coast, see Jiang Shaozhen, "Du Yuesheng," 317; Adams, "China: Asia's Profitable Plague," 382.

71. Marshall, "Opium and Gangsterism in Nationalist China," 38–41. There were hopeful rumors in the Japanese press a little over a year later that Du had changed his mind and was sending a delegation of ten followers to reorganize the Green Gang to attack the Guomindang and support the occupation authorities. Although there was a contingent of Shanghai Green Gang leaders— Geng Jiaji, Xie Baosheng, Gao Xinbao—who supported the Japanese, these rumors were groundless. SMP, D-9319, 6/2/40.

72. The Nandao Opium Monopoly tried to extend the licensing system into the foreign areas, but there was strong opposition and negotiations were broken off. *CWR*, 25 Dec. 1937, 88–90, and 19 Mar. 1938, 57–58. See also *RDS*, 893.00 P.R. Shanghai/119 (Aug. 1938), 21.

73. *RDS*, 893.00 P.R. Shanghai/121 (Oct. 1938), 20; Shanghai/123 (Dec. 1938), 22; and Shanghai/125 (Feb. 1939), 17.

74. SMP, D-8292 A (C), 29/1/40.

75. Ibid., 28/5/41.

76. Yu Junqing was appointed to head the new bureau, which was still located in the Broadway Mansions.

77. Colonel Lu Ying, commissioner of the Shanghai Special Municipality police bureau, was among the guests. SMP, D-8292 A(C), 3/6/41.

78. After General Matsui threatened to occupy the entire city, then-Consul General Okamoto on 21 November 1937 presented the International Settlement and French authorities with a list of demands calling for the suppression of Guomindang and anti-Japanese organizations and propaganda, eviction of central government representatives, and censorship of Chinese radio transmissions. Clifford, *Retreat from China*, 70.

79. This was clearly "a warning [to the Chinese population of Shanghai] against engaging in any anti-Japanese movement." Borg, *The United States and the Far Eastern Crisis of 1933–1938*, 506.

80. *CWR*, 11 Dec. 1937, 34–37, and 19 Feb. 1938, 321; Davidson-Houston, *Yellow Creek*, 158. *Shen bao* lists one Indian constable, one Chinese constable, and one Western detective as being wounded. *SB*, 4 Dec. 1937, 1.

81. The assailant could have been a Korean patriotic activist, contemporaries pointed out. *CWR*, 11 Dec. 1937, 34. That evening General Matsui requested Major Gerrard, commissioner of the Shanghai Municipal Police, to sign an agreement permitting Japanese troops to pass freely through the Settlement and act independently there whenever they thought it necessary. However, this request was almost completely disavowed by Consul General Okamoto at a meeting of the consular body on 6 December. Clifford, *Retreat from China*, 71.

82. *CWR*, 1 Jan. 1938, 136.

83. *CWR*, 22 Jan. 1938, 215; Davidson-Houston, *Yellow Creek*, 158. Up to then, the Shanghai Municipal Police roster consisted of 471 Caucasians, 267 Japanese, 561 Sikhs, and 4,223 Chinese. Of these, 21 Chinese, 12 Japanese, and 64 Europeans held the rank of inspector or above. There were 1,762 Chinese, 426 Sikh, and 181 Japanese constables. The 205 detective constables and 144 detective sergeants were all Chinese. Shanghai Municipal Council, *Report for the Year 1937*, 97.

84. Clifford, *Retreat from China,* 72.
85. SMP, D-2381, 23/2/38.
86. There were, nonetheless, seven terrorist incidents directed again Japanese or puppet representatives between 4 January and 9 April 1938. See reports of these incidents in *CWR* and *NCH* during this period. Pro-Japanese terrorists also struck, assassinating Herman Liu (Liu Zhan'en), the president of Hujiang University (former Shanghai Baptist College, the largest missionary school in Shanghai). Liu's murderer was probably the Japanese special agent Konomi, who was an advisor for the Yellow Way Society (see below). Liu was shot with one of twenty-seven pistols sold to the Japanese Special Services Corps by the Shanghai Municipal Police. His death may also have been part of the bitter rivalry between Su Xiwen's Dadao régime and the Reform Government, since Liu was reported to be about to accept the post of governor of Jiangsu under the latter's aegis. Jing Shenghong, *Minguo ansha yaoan,* 305–306; *CWR,* 16 Apr. 1938, 174, and 17 Sept. 1938, 91. See also Finch, *Shanghai and Beyond,* 311; Lutz, "Occupied China and Student Activism in the Christian Colleges," 5. Liu held a Ph.D. degree from Columbia University. *Who's Who in China,* fifth ed., 162; Woodhead, *The China Yearbook,* 242.
87. "Terrorism Again Hits Shanghai," 8–9; *CWR,* 16 Apr, 1938, 202.

2. Blue Shirts

1. *RDS,* 893.00 P.R. Shanghai/117 (June 1938), 11–12.
2. Ibid.
3. Xu Youwei, "Lixingshe yu Riben (1932–1938 nian)," 5; Wu, "Contending political forces during the War of Resistance," 55–56; *Taiheiyô sensô e no michi,* vol. 3, p. 250; Wakeman, "Confucian Fascism," and Chang, *The Chinese Blue Shirt Society,* passim.
4. See Chang, "'Fascism' and Modern China," 553–556; Eastman, "Fascism and Modern China: A Rejoinder," 840–842; Elkins, "'Fascism' in China," 426–433.
5. Coble, *Facing Japan,* 228. According to Thomas Chao, a State Department informant, the Blue Shirts had gained control of "municipal and provincial police organizations in the capital and in important places throughout the country. They practically dominate the armed forces of the government." "Blueshirts Organization," 3–4. *Shanghai nichinichi* reported that the Blue Shirts' 12,000 members were mostly young officers. "'Blue Shirts' to Suspend Anti-Japan Activities," 1. See also Haruke Keiin, *Shanghai tero kôsaku 76 gô,* 33–35.
6. Coble, "Superpatriots and Secret Agents," 6; Elkins, "'Fascism' in China," 433; Shum Kui-kwong, *The Chinese Communists' Road to Power,* 1–22.
7. SMP, D-4685, 27/1/36. See also Coble, "Superpatriots and Secret Agents," 24.
8. "The San Min Chu I Youth Corps," 2, in *Ch'en Li-fu Materials.* See also Coble, "Superpatriots and Secret Agents," 20–21; "Blueshirts Organization," 3. Chiang Kai-shek secretly ordered the dissolution of the Fuxingshe in

early April 1938. Cheng Yiming, "Juntong tewu zuzhi de zhenxiang," 188. This was openly announced to the Guomindang on 9 July 1938, when Chiang ordered that the Blue Shirts and Blue and White Corps (Qingbaishe) be incorporated under the newly formed Three People's Principles Youth Corps (Sanminzhuyi qingnian tuan). "Memorandum on the Blue Shirt Society," 9; Chang and Meyers, "The Storm Clouds Clear over China," 229–230. Because it was, in the vernacular, applied to Juntong agents, I will use the term "Blue Shirts" as it was employed by contemporaries to designate terrorists working for Dai Li and other Chongqing-sponsored action groups related to the Military Statistics Bureau.

9. SMP, D-4685, 4/9/36, 12/1/37, 21/3/37, 3/10/40; "Memorandum on the Blueshirt Society," 6–7. It should be pointed out that there was a general concern among Shanghai parents, during the *gudao* (isolated island) period, about the aimlessness of youth roaming the streets and not attending schools shut down by the exigencies of the Japanese occupation. *SS,* 17 June 1939, 6.

10. Pan Gongzhan, Wu's deputy and successor, did little to revivify the societies. After he and his followers left for Chongqing on government orders early in 1938, the groups were defunct. SMP, D-4685 (C), 3/10/40.

11. Police Department, Japanese Consulate General, "Report on August 13th Anniversary," 6 Aug. 1938, in SMP, D-8615, 22/9/39, 1; *RDS,* 00/14121 (10 June 1937); "Two Sources of Anti-Japanism," 29; Coble, "Superpatriots and Secret Agents," 7.

12. "Terrorism Again Hits Shanghai," 10.

13. For a detailed list of the eight executive detachments of the "Blue Shirts Society," which in this case undoubtedly refers to Dai Li's Military Statistics Bureau (Juntong) organization, in Shanghai, see SMP, D-4685 (E), 29/1/41.

14. Wang Fangnan, "Wo zai juntong shisinian de qinli he jianwen," 144–145; Xu Zhucheng, *Du Yuesheng zhengzhuan,* 95; Zhu Zuotong and Mei Yi, *Shanghai yi ri,* 1.133–136.

15. SMP, D-3648, 27/7/32. See, for the experience of one Baoandui member trying to defend Zhabei under siege, Zhu Zuotong and Mei Yi, *Shanghai yi ri,* 1.8–9.

16. SMP, D-8039A, 10/9/37. For the connection of the officers training unit with the Special Services Department, see Xu Zhucheng, *Du Yuesheng zhengzhuan,* 100.

17. "Emergency Period Service Group Report," 1. We have put the names in pinyin romanization instead of using the original spelling of the intelligence report, for example, Ong Chin-chiu, Loh Ching-dz, and so forth.

18. "Emergency Period Service Group Report," 1–2.

19. Ibid., 2; SMP, D-8039A, 10/9/37, and D-8615, 22/9/39, 1.

20. SMP, D-8039A, 10/9/37.

21. The officer was identified as Shen Xinfu.

22. "Emergency Period Service Group Report," 3–4.

23. On 11 September 1937, the Shanghai Municipal Police received information from the French police, saying that the headquarters of the Special Services Department was at 545 Hwa Ngoh Fang on Jiujiang Road. This was the

address of the Dagong News Agency, closely connected with the Shanghai General Labor Union, headed by Zhu Xuefan. SMP, D-8039A, 12/9/37.

24. Zhang Guoquan, who had worked for the China General Omnibus Company, lived in the Great West Gate area of South Market with a police inspector identified as Chen Bailong, and who probably was the same person as the Chen Bannong mentioned in the text. Zhang was arrested by the Shanghai Municipal Police on 25 August 1937, on a charge of agitation. He was later handed over to the Chinese authorities, who released him. "Emergency Period Service Group Report," 2–3; SMP, D-8039A, 28/9/37.

25. "Emergency Period Service Group Report," 3–4.

26. Fu Duoma, twenty-seven years old and a native of Dinghai, joined the Special Action Corps on 20 August 1937—the very day the Nationalist police requested SMP help in arresting Chinese "traitors" believed to have poisoned public tea urns (a belief that aroused mobs on 17 August to beat several suspects to death). After hostilities had broken out on 13 August Fu Duoma had moved into the closed-down Xinguang Primary School (of which he was the former principal) at Changxingli in Zhabei. Fu was arrested by the SMP on 16 September 1937. SMP, D-8039A, 22/8/37, 26/8/37, and 10/9/37. "[After the August 1937 bombings] patriotism in its most drastic guise ran through the city like fire in the form of 'traitor hunts'; any poor wretch who loitered about for no more nefarious reason than that he had nowhere to go was liable to be trampled or beaten to death. For several days tea vendors were in peril because there was a wild rumor that traitors were poisoning the tea." Oakes, *White Man's Folly,* 174.

27. Xu Zhucheng, *Du Yuesheng zhengzhuan,* 99; Shen Zui, "Wo suo zhidao de Dai Li," 21.

28. Shen Zui, "Wo suo zhidao de Dai Li," 21–22.

29. "Shanghai Special Service Corps Arrest," 3. See also Haruke Keiin, *Shanghai tero kôsaku 76 gô,* 48–50.

30. Zhang Weihan, "Dai Li yu 'Juntong ju,'" 100–101. Liu Zhilu had been in command of Chaomeizhen under Chen Jiongming. After Chen was defeated in 1925, Liu had taken the remnants of the unit by boat to Shandong where he threw himself upon the mercies of warlord Zhang Zongchang. Then when the armies of the Northern Expedition defeated Zhang, Liu tried to negotiate with Chiang Kai-shek, who held this small band of defeated men in contempt. Before long Liu Zhennian, the warlord who had been cordoning off Shandong in the East, attacked Liu Zhilu, who fled south and joined the "officials in exile in Shanghai" (*haishang yu gong*), becoming a representative for Du Yuesheng in the latter's negotiations with warlord representatives. Xu Zhucheng, *Du Yuesheng zhengzhuan,* 99.

31. Zhang Weihan, "Dai Li yu 'Juntong ju,'" 100–101.

32. Xu Zhucheng, *Du Yuesheng zhengzhuan,* 99–100; "Shanghai Special Service Corps Arrest," 2.

33. Zhang Weihan, "Dai Li yu 'Juntong ju,'" 100–101.

34. "Shanghai Special Service Corps Arrest," 1; Zhang Weihan, "Dai Li yu 'Juntong ju,'" 101; Shen Zui, "Wo suo zhidao de Dai Li," 21–22.

35. "Shanghai Special Service Corps Arrest," 3–4; SMP, D-8039K, 25/10/37.

36. SMP, D-8039A, 10/9/37.

37. This detachment was divided into two sections with six subsections each containing twenty members. Five of Section Two's six subsections operated in Nandao, and one in Zhabei. The latter was stationed at Changleli under the command of Wang Yingming, an officer of the 87th Division. Ibid., D-8039A, 10/9/37.

38. Ibid. This, needless to say, provided extraordinary opportunities for robbery. See, e.g., Hahn, *China to Me,* 54–55.

39. Zhue Xuefan's role was well known to the Dadao puppet police. Chief Detective He Zhenggu had summarized recent reports that the Nationalist Wuhan Garrison Command had reorganized special operations groups in Shanghai into two separate forces. One was a central *tixipai* (Chiang Kai-shek's own loyalists) under Dai Li's command and with orders to carry out "Blue Shirts' activities." The second special squad had been set up for the Shanghai area under Zhu Xuefan, using "unemployed elements" (*shiye fenzi*), retired officers, and *liumang* (hoodlums or "loafers"). Their aim was "to create a reign of terror in Shanghai" and to assassinate "elements close to the Japanese" (*qin Ri fenzi*). SMA, Wang 1.1.72—Dadao file—"Diaocha biedongdui" [Investigation of the Special Action Squads], 1 Mar. 1938.

40. "Shanghai Special Service Corps Arrest," 2.

41. Shen Zui, "Wo suo zhidao de Dai Li," 21–22.

42. SMP, D-8039A, 28/9/37.

43. Zhang Weihan, "Dai Li yu 'Juntong ju,'" 103.

44. Xu Zhucheng, *Du Yuesheng zhengzhuan,* 100.

45. Ibid., 101.

46. Commander Xie had led 400 men from the Nineteenth Route Army in a last-ditch defense of the Sihang cangku against the Japanese. The story of their heroism, which was epitomized in the saga of a schoolgirl bringing them a Chinese flag that they hoisted over their bunker, is still taught to school children on Taiwan as an example of heroic martyrdom. For an example of its impact on the defenders of Shanghai in 1937, see Zhu Zuotong and Mei Yi, *Shanghai yi ri,* 1.53–54.

47. Xu Zhucheng, *Du Yuesheng zhengzhuan,* 95.

48. In December 1937 Du went to Wuhan to see Chiang Kai-shek, who made him head of the Ninth Relief District (Hong Kong) of the China Central Relief Committee (Zhongyang zhenji weiyuanhui). Using that along with the Red Cross office he set up in Hong Kong as a cover, Du Yuesheng received $500,000 a month from the Nationalist government to bribe potential collaborators to prevent them from joining the Japanese. In addition to setting up secret peace talks between Dai Li and Wang Xinheng, and the Japanese, Du Yuesheng was also responsible for stealing the documents that revealed Wang Jingwei's agreement with the Japanese. He also arranged the escape of George Yeh from Japanese territory. Yeh later became foreign minister of the Republic of China. Zhang Weihan, "Dai Li yu 'Juntong ju,'" 147; Jonathan Marshall, "Opium and Gangsterism in Nationalist China," 38. For Dai Li's

report to Chiang Kai-shek on Wang Jingwei's agreement with the Japanese, see Qin Xiaoyi, *Zhonghua minguo zhongyao shiliao chubian—Dui Ri zhanzheng shiqi. Di liu bian: Kuilei zuzhi*, 150–151.

49. Shen Zui, "Wo suo zhidao de Dai Li," 22–23.

50. "Woosung–Shanghai Special Chinese Corps Leaves Shanghai," *Da mei wanbao*, 1 Feb., transl. in SMP, D-8039A, 4/2/38. The newspaper commented that "the death of most of the Chinese traitors may have been the work of the corps."

51. Zhang Weihan, "Dai Li yu 'Juntong ju,'" 101.

52. A few guerrillas in the western suburbs continued to resist, however, as the severed head of a puppet police constable found by a foreign businessman near the Hongqiao Golf Club attested in September 1938. *CWR*, 17 Sept. 1938, 78.

53. Ibid. There was one other effort by core elements of the Loyal and Patriotic Army to infiltrate the French Concession. Ibid., 4 Mar. 1939, 12, and 19 July 1941, 221. See also Chen, *Making Revolution*, 37, 43–44; BFOR, 631, 22/11/39, F1005, FO371-24682; Wang Fangnan, "Wo zai juntong shisinian de qinli he jianwen," 145. The Eastern Pudong branch of the Loyal and Patriotic Army maintained control over most villages in that area throughout the war and supervised the smuggling of gasoline and rubber tires across Hangzhou Bay to Zhejiang, where newly reopened trade routes ran up the Qiantang River through Jinhua to "Free China." Gray, "The Loyal Patriotic Army," 22–27. Gray saw only three machine guns among the Loyal and Patriotic Army during her stay in Pudong. Ibid., 25.

54. The five *waiqin* group heads were replaced by officers better equipped to deal with the Japanese. Dai Li also ordered his fellow townsman Jiang Shaomo to organize an underground espionage unit to gather and transmit intelligence after the Japanese took over. This was formally designated the Number Two Zone of the Shanghai Special Zone (Shanghai tequ dier qu). Shen Zui, "Wo suo zhidao de Dai Li," 25.

55. Ibid. From time to time, Dai Li sent in additional teams of agents familiar with the Shanghai situation, including groups led by Zhou Xiliang, Bi Gaokui, and Zhu Shanyuan. Shen Zui, *Juntong neimu*, 29.

56. In 1949 Wang was Shanghai station chief of the Baomi ju (Bureau to Preserve Secrets), one of Juntong's successor organizations. Wang Fangnan, "Wo zai juntong shisinian de qinli he jianwen," 140.

57. Zhu Xiagu served briefly as station chief before Wang took over full command.

58. The personnel chief was Chen Mingchu. Wang Fangnan, "Wo zai juntong shisinian de qinli he jianwen," 143–144; "Blue Shirts Organization [OSS]," 1. Chen Gongshu (of Tianjin) became assistant commander to Fu Yewen (of Jinhua), who headed the intelligence organization in Wang Jingwei's mobile garrison command for Jiangsu, Zhejiang, Anhui and Jiangxi, which directed rural pacification for the Japanese military from its headquarters at 100 East Road (Dongjie lu) in Hangzhou. Fu Yewen, who was a former Chinese Communist Party member, seems to have been in close touch with Communist

agents throughout this period, when he also served as the secretary general at 76 Jessfield Road. Zhang Weihan, "Dai Li yu 'Juntong ju,'" 146. For Fu Yewen's likely contacts with Communist Party agents, see Chen Gongshu, *Kangzhan houqi fanjian huodong*, 304, 329–330, 333.

59. For the same reason Chen Lifu and Chen Guofu also ordered Wu Kaixian, in the summer of 1939, to clear up the party "underground organization" in Shanghai. Wu established the Shanghai Party Political Unification Committee (Shanghai dang zheng tongyi weiyuanhui), and through Du Yuesheng secured the help of racketeer Huang Jinrong to curb or eliminate collaborationist elements. Jiang Shaozhen, "Du Yuesheng," 317.

60. Wang Fangnan, "Wo zai juntong shisinian de qinli he jianwen," 144. General Zhou Fengqi was slated to become minister of defense in the Reform Government when he was killed in the French Concession by two Juntong agents on 7 March 1938. *RDS*, 893.00/14214, report of assistant naval attaché, Shanghai (7 Mar. 1938). Lu Bohong was killed on 30 December 1937, after forming the collaborationist South Market Local Self-Government Committee.

61. More than forty Japanese military officers were also shot down. Chen Gongshu, *Yingxiong wuming: Beiguo chujian*, part 1, 10. There were other operations conducted by the Guomindang's civilian secret service, the Central Statistics Bureau (Zhongtong), quite apart from Dai Li's organization. Huang Meizhen and Zhang Yun, *Wang Jingwei guomin zhengfu chengli*, 297. "Was Juntong more active than Zhongtong in occupied areas? They were both active. Was there more coordination between Juntong and Zhongtong in occupied areas than in free areas? We did not want them to know one another. In case one system was exposed, the other would be exposed also [if there were coordination]. In underground work in enemy areas it is better to keep two systems separate." "Ting Mo-ts'un, Chün-t'ung, and Chung-t'ung during the War," 1, in *Ch'en Li-fu Materials*.

62. "The [Blue Shirt] society, according to Special Branch information, is not active in Shanghai." SMP, D-4685 (C), 3/10/40.

63. "This group of special service agents [sent to assassinate organizers of the new régime] is directly under the control of the Special Service Department of the Chungking Military Affairs Commission." "Arrival in Shanghai of a Large Number of Special Service Agents of the Chungking Government," *XSB*, 1 Nov. 1939, transl. in SMP, D-8116, 7/11/39.

64. "Memorandum on the Blue Shirt Society," 9–10.

65. For example, in September 1941 the SMP handed eight prisoners over to the Japanese Military Police as suspected members of the Blue Shirts Society. SMP, D-8299, 14/9/41.

3. National salvation

1. Although nowhere in his confession does Sun mention Green Gang connections, these should not be ruled out altogether. The Green Gang often used jewelry stores both to fence stolen goods and as gathering places for gang

members. But members of the Communist "dog-killers squad" also operated out of a jewelry store. SMP, D-9319, 1939, 2–3; Shen Zui, *Juntong neimu*, 64.

2. "Deposition of Sung Yah Shing," 1–2.

3. Ibid., 2–3.

4. His family owned estate property in Hankou worth $10,000.

5. "Deposition of Sung Yah Shing," 3–4.

6. Ibid., 4.

7. The Shanghai Citizens Volunteer Corps had thirty sections of thirty to forty members each and was headquartered in the coal merchants guild across from the Small World Amusement Center.

8. At this point, Sun, along with two journalists, a Jinan University student, and a Guomindang branch member, organized a "society to promote the offering of iron and steel to the government," which continued to meet in the guildhall on Ningbo Road. Although the society was not very active, the name has Blue Shirt connotations and it may have been at this time that Sun was recruited by Dai Li's organization. "Deposition of Sung Yah Shing," 5–6.

9. For the Marco Polo Bridge incident, see Jones, *Japan's New Order in East Asia*, 30–37; Morley, *Japan's Road to the Pacific War—The Final Confrontation*, xx–xxi.

10. The shops were sold to a "former tutor," which meant that Sun still had access to them and could use them as a cache for firearms.

11. "Deposition of Sung Yah Shing," 7. The deputy chief was Liang Tongfang.

12. Wang, born outside Ningbo, was the son of a captain in the Republican Army (1915). After primary school in his village, he attended Nanjing Middle School for three years. Then, through an uncle's introduction, he was apprenticed to a machine factory in Pudong, where he had lived and worked until the Marco Polo Bridge incident. He went to the Guandi Temple in response to the newspaper notice, and was posted to Sun Yaxing's section. "Deposition of Wong Tz Koo," 1.

13. Jiang, born in Nanjing, was the son of a Jinjiang shop assistant. He attended primary school in Jinjiang, and then boarded at Shanghai Middle School (Nandao) where he studied Chinese literature from March 1936 to June 1937. The day he left school to move in with a friend of his father, he bought a copy of *Central Daily News* and saw the advertisement. He enrolled in the association without telling his mother. SMP, D-8597, 22/7/38, 1–2.

14. Zhou, a native of Chongming where he received an elementary education, came to Shanghai by himself at the age of fourteen (fifteen *sui*) to serve an apprenticeship at a printing press in the French Concession. He worked in four different printing shops before becoming a printer at the *Zhongguo dabao* (China Herald). "Deposition of Tsou Sue Kong," 1.

15. *CWR*, 19 Feb. 1938, 321.

16. "Deposition of Sung Yah Shing," 8–9; SMP, D-8597, 2–3; "Deposition of Wong Tz Koo," 1–2; "Deposition of Tsou Sue Kong," 2.

17. Each company was divided into three 40-man sections, and Sun Yaxing was given charge of the Third Section.

18. Wang Zhigu returned to Ningbo because of ill health. Zhou Shougang also got

sick and returned to Chongming. "Deposition of Wong Tz Koo," 1–2; "Deposition of Tsou Sue Kong," 1–2.

19. "Deposition of Sung Yah Shing," 9–10.

20. Snow, *The Battle for Asia*, 52. See also Zhu Zuotong and Mei Yi, *Shanghai yi ri*, 1.101–111.

21. In the wake of this internment of special services plainclothesmen, the French police launched a special campaign against urban terrorism. In the first week of December 1937 they commenced recruiting an additional 300 policemen and detectives, some of them from among ex-soldiers and plainclothesmen in the refugee camps. From 1 January to 12 Feb. 1938, the police made 6,000 antiterrorist arrests and seized 182 pistols. *CWR*, 19 February 1938, 321; SMP, D-8598, 8/12/37, 12/12/37, and 17/7/38.

22. "Deposition of Sung Yah Shing," 10–11. The rest were interned, but some of those special services corpsmen, including Jiang Haisheng, escaped from the internment center to one of the regular refugee camps. SMP, D-8957, 22/7/38, 4.

23. "Deposition of Sung Yah Shing," 11–12; *CWR*, 19 Feb. 1938, 321.

24. "Deposition of Sung Yah Shing," 13.

25. SMP, D-8597, 22/7/38, 6–7.

26. Zhao Liang, thirty-four years old, was a native of Hangzhou. He had worked as a cardboard box maker for twelve years in Nandao before war broke out in 1937, and he volunteered to serve under Sun Yaxing. "Deposition of Zau Liang," 1.

27. "Deposition of Sung Yah Shing," 13–14.

28. Zhang Weihan, "Dai Li yu 'Juntong ju,'" p. 132.

29. "Deposition of Wong Tz Koo," 2.

30. SMP, D-8597, 22/7/38, 7–8; "Deposition of Sung Yah Shing," 15.

31. "Deposition of Zau Liang," 2. Jiang Haisheng said that they were explicitly told that they had to carry out Sun's assassination orders directly. SMP, D-8597, 22/7/38, 8.

32. "Deposition of Sung Yah Shing," 15–16.

33. Ibid., 16; "Deposition of Zau Liang," 2.

34. "Ironically, while [assassination team members] must be loyal and courageous, they may be chosen for their lack of outstanding qualities as much as for the qualities they do possess. It is evidently not desirable for them to be overly imaginative, fanatical, or daring: too much imagination is conducive to doubts; too much fanaticism to instability; too much daring to incaution. At the risk of minimizing the problems involved, it seems that a counter-terrorist assassination team has to find answers to only two questions: how to locate the target and how to get away after the hit." Jonas, *Vengeance*, 355.

35. "Deposition of Sung Yah Shing," 17.

36. Ibid., 18–20; *RDS*, 893.00/1423, Shanghai, 11 June 1938.

37. "Deposition of Wong Tz Koo," 3–4.

38. See especially "Deposition of Zau Liang," 6.

39. It is possible that the watchmen's sons were the two Chen brothers, who also

lived on rue Wagner and whose father was a watchman. If this was so, it would explain why the Sun squad admitted them to membership despite their youth and inexperience. But that is only a conjecture.

40. "Deposition of Sung Yah Shing," 20. Zhang Xiaolin, who was collaborating with the Japanese in order to keep his casinos in business, was eventually shot in the throat and chest by another Juntong sniper while he was leaning out of his window on rue Wagner, shouting at his bodyguards who were making a racket outside. Pan Ling, *Old Shanghai,* 133.

41. "Deposition of Sung Yah Shing," 20–22; SMP, D-8597, 22/7/38.

42. "Deposition of Sung Yah Shing," 23.

43. "Deposition of Tsou Sue Kong," 1–2; "Deposition of Zau Liang," 2–3.

44. Zhu, age twenty-five, was a native of Suzhou who came to Shanghai and worked as a school teacher in a primary school in Nandao before the war. In August 1937 he joined the Jiangyin training camp and became a Special Services Corps "plainclothesman" who fought in the defense of Nandao on 11 November, escaping into the French Concession when the Japanese advanced. His brother got him a job at the refugee camp. "Deposition of Tsu Zung Foo," 1–2.

45. Ibid., 3.

46. Alias Chen Yuanliang, he was a native of Shanghai whose parents came from Guangdong. His father was a private watchman in the French Concession. "Deposition of Zong Kwei Kong," 1.

47. Ibid., 2.

48. "Deposition of Zong Kwei Kong," 2–3.

49. "Deposition of Sung Yah Shing," 23–24; "Deposition of Wong Tz Koo," 4–5; SMP, D-8597, 8/7/38.

50. "Deposition of Zong Kwei Kong," 3; "Deposition of Zau Liang," 3–5.

51. "Deposition of Tsou Sue Kong," 3; "Deposition of Zau Liang," 5; "Deposition of Wong Tz Koo," 5; "Deposition of Sung Yah Shing," 24–25.

52. Jin Yingsheng probably was responsible for the bombing in front of the Yokohama Specie Bank. "Twelve Detained in Terrorist Probe."

53. "Deposition of Zong Kwei Kong," 4–5; SMP, D-8597, 22/7/38, 14–15.

54. Three of the wounded were pedestrians or workmen in the vicinity of the "floating restaurant." SMP, D-8597, 8/7/38; "Twelve Detained in Terrorist Probe."

55. *RDS,* 893.102S/1651, 793.94/13408 (8 July 1938).

56. Ibid., 793.94/13395 (7 July 1938).

57. SMP, D-8597, 8/7/38.

58. *RDS,* 893.102S/1651, 793.94/13408 (8 July 1938).

59. SMP, D-8597, 22/7/38.

60. Ibid.

61. *RDS,* 893.102 S/1654 (11 July 1938).

62. SMP, D-8597, 12/7/38.

63. Ibid.

64. Ibid., 10/7/38.

65. Ibid., 11/7/38.

66. On 8 July, when the measure was being bruited about, Lockhart informed the chairman of the Shanghai Municipal Council that he could not accept the proclamation as applying to U.S. nationals or U.S. property in derogation of U.S. extraterritorial rights or jurisdiction. *RDS*, 893.102 S/1653 (8 July 1938). For legal and humanitarian objections, see ibid., 893.00 P.R. Shanghai/118 (July 1938), 12–13.

67. *CWR*, 30 July 1938, 271.

68. Ibid., 6 Aug. 1938, 301–302; SMP, D-8597, 21/7/38 and 22/7/38. The Bridge of Sighs connected the Doge's palace in Venice with the executioner's chambers in the state prison.

69. *CWR*, 30 July 1938, 272.

70. *RDS*, 893.00 P.R. Hankow/133 (July 1938), 21; SMP, D-8597/8, 6/8/38. The Nationalist secret service in Hankou reportedly changed its operational rules as a result of the new expulsion order, commanding all groups to observe three rules in conducting assassinations or bombings in Shanghai: (1) officers in charge of the group should make a thorough investigation before executing the plan in order to avoid members being arrested by the police; (2) if members could not escape after executing a mission, then they should commit suicide by shooting themselves; and (3) members should be supplied with poison pills to take if they are unable to shoot themselves before being arrested. The last two rules were laid down because now that arrest meant eventually being handed over to the Japanese, it was better to die by one's own hand than to be tortured to death by the Military Police. SMP, D-8635, 23/8/38. Japanese police routinely tortured political prisoners for forced confessions. Mitchell, *Janus-Faced Justice*, 126.

71. Chen Kaiyuan was fifteen or sixteen years old, a student. SMP, D-8638, 25/7/38, 1.

72. "Deposition of Zau Liang," 5.

73. Van Chi-sen, or Chi-sung, an attorney, was being considered for the presidency of the special district court in Nandao. "Nine Suspects Arrested for Tseng Killing."

74. Police later found this document, which read: "Zung Yueh Poo, native of Guangdong, age about 60, slim build, gray and white hair, thin face with short beard (gray and white), sunken eyes with keen sight, wears long gown." SMP, D-8638, 25/7/38, 1–2. Zheng worked as an interpreter in a Japanese import and export firm in the Hardoon Building on Nanking Road. *Evening Echo*, 22 July 1938, clipped in SMP, D-8635, 23/7/38.

75. "Deposition of Tsou Sue Kong," 4; "Deposition of Sung Yah Shing," 25; "Deposition of Tsu Zung Foo," 2.

76. Zheng Yuebao died shortly after being admitted to the Chinese Red Cross Hospital on Avenue Haig a few minutes later. "Nine Suspects Arrested for Tseng Killing."

77. "Deposition of Zong Kwei Kong," 6; "Nine Suspects Arrested for Tseng Killing."

78. "Nine Suspects Arrested for Tseng Killing."

79. SMP, D-8638, 25/7/38, 1.

80. "Deposition of Sung Yah Shing," 26; "Deposition of Wong Tz Koo," 6; SMP, D-8638, 25/7/38; "Nine Suspects Arrested for Tseng Killing."
81. "Twenty-four Terrorist Suspects Land in Police Net"; "Twelve Detained in Terrorist Probe." On 19 June, Consul General Hidaka told Frank Lockhart how pleased he was that the Shanghai Municipal Council was cooperating and had issued the expulsion proclamation. He hoped that the French Concession would follow suit. *RDS*, 893.102 Shanghai/1674 (23 July 1938). For hundreds of pages of documentation on Shanghai Municipal Police cooperation with the Japanese Water Police, see SMP, D-8299.
82. SMP, D-8638, 25/7/38, 4–6. The detectives did find a telephone number that led them to Zhou Shougang, and their party also nabbed Zhao Liang when he wandered into the apartment.
83. "Deposition of Sung Yah Shing," 27.
84. *RDS*, 893.102 Shanghai/1663 (10 August 1938).

4. Retaliation: Pro-Japanese terrorism

1. These principles were stated in a document seized by the police in 1941, when the Rehabilitation Society was still functioning. SMP, D-9139, 23/3/41. For the "Construction of a New Order in East Asia" (Jianshe Dongya xin zhixu), announced by the Japanese military authorities on 3 November 1938 after the capture of Canton and the attack on Wuhan, which had so sorely tested Japan's overall military strength, see Qin Xiaoyi, *Zhonghua minguo zhongyao shiliao chubian—Dui Ri zhanzheng shiqi. Di liu bian: Kuilei zuzhi*, 32; Taylor, *The Struggle for North China*, 159–162; Coox, "Effects of Attrition on National War Effort," 57–59; T'ang, *Fundamentals of National Salvation*, ix–x, 174–176.
2. There was a third society, the East Asia Anti-Communist League (Dongya fangong tongmenghui), established in February 1938 with a "pro-Japanese quasi-political" program. The original promoters were Zhu Ding, a returned student from Japan and chief of the Pudong branch of the Great People's Society; and Zhang Xiangyi, a former superintendent of the Shanghai Municipal Police and "a well-known loafer" later assassinated by guerrillas. SMP, D-8477, 22/7/40.
3. Ibid.
4. *CWR*, 17 Sept. 1938, 91.
5. SMP, D-3445, 5/4/32, 7/4/32, 8/4/32, 19/4/32. See also Wakeman, *Policing Shanghai*, ch. 11; Honig, *Creating Chinese Ethnicity*, 94–95.
6. Huang Meizhen and Shi Yuanhua, "Wang wei tegong zongbu shimo," 353. The establishment of the Yellow Way Society and later the Anqing League represented a significant loss of influence by Du Yuesheng, who remained loyal to Chiang Kai-shek from his home in Hong Kong. Marshall, "Opium and Gangsterism in Nationalist China," 40–41.
7. *RDS*, 893.00 P.R. Shanghai/120 (Sept. 1938), 15; *CWR*, 10 Sept. 1938, 57, and 17 Sept. 1938, 91; Marshall, "Opium and Gangsterism in Nationalist China," 40.

8. SMP, D-8458, 10/2/39. The Japanese secret service organs and their puppets exerted increasingly effective control over Shanghai's labor unions through clandestine organizations, bringing the progressive labor movement to a new low—later Communist claims notwithstanding. Huang Meizhen, "Shanghai lunxian shiqi de shehui maodun yu gongyun xingshi," 2, 18.

9. Walter Yang received $50 for luring Cai to the hotel. Liu Song was paid $1,000. *CWR*, 17 Sept. 1938, 91.

10. Ibid.

11. Three other severed heads were found within the week. In each case, a note was found close by the gruesome remains that warned against anti-Japanese activity. *CWR*, 17 Feb. 1938, 80–81.

12. These terrorists, who were sentenced in the First Special District Court on 3 September 1938, were all members of the Yellow Way Society. Yang Zung-yien, who threw the grenade at the China Travel Service, reported directly to Chang Yuqing. He was paid $35 for the bombing. *CWR*, 20 Aug. 1938, 394. See also, for other Yellow Way operations, *CWR*, 10 Sept. 1938, 50, 57

13. *RDS*, 893.00 PR Shanghai/119 (Aug. 1938), 17–18.

14. *CWR*, 20 Aug. 1938, 394.

15. Ibid.

16. *RDS*, 893.00 P.R. Shanghai/120 (Sept. 1938), 15.

17. *CWR*, 17 Sept. 1938, 91, and 24 Sept. 1938, 113.

18. The Rehabilitation Society was revived early in 1939 by a Fujianese named Zhang Ming. The Organization Department's chief, a Cantonese named Tong Zhou, tried to recruit members from among inmates of the refugee camp at 160 Ningbo Road. The inmates were promised $12 to join. After learning of this through an informant, the Shanghai Municipal Police arrested twenty-two persons in April 1939. SMP, D-9139, 24/4/39. On Cantonese vs. Subei collaborators, see the astute comments in Honig, *Creating Chinese Ethnicity*, 103.

19. SMP, D-8458, 14/12/38; Hu Zhusheng, "Qingbang shi chutan," 107; Rowe, "The Qingbang and Collaboration under the Japanese, 1939–1945," 493; Xu Zhucheng, *Du Yuesheng zhengzhuan*, 13; Wang Yangqing and Xu Yinghu, "Shanghai Qing Hong bang gaishu," p. 63.

20. SMP, D-8458, 14/12/38.

21. The Japanese press reported the meeting as having taken place in Shanghai, but that was incorrect. See the press enclosures in ibid.

22. One of the purposes of the Japanese military in this regard was to use Green Gang, now Anqing League, members in Jiangsu, Zhejiang, and Anhui to lead special services squads attached to pacification units "in order to afford members of the League opportunities to contact the guerrillas and persuade them to surrender to the Japanese." Ibid.

23. Nippo dispatch in SMP, D-8458, 14/12/39.

24. Ibid.

25. The Dah Shing, the Yee Foong, and the Kwangsung Company. Ibid., 10/2/39.

26. Ibid.

27. *Shanghai Times* clipping in ibid., 18/8/39.

28. Chen eventually died from his wound. He formerly worked for O. Okamoto, a member of the Shanghai Municipal Council. *CWR*, 3 Sept. 1938, 30. There was also a riot on August 19 in the internment camp for Chinese soldiers who entered the French Concession when Nandao fell. *RDS*, 893.00 P.R. Shanghai/149 (Aug. 1938), 18.

29. *CWR*, 17 Sept. 1938, 90.

30. The grenades were Mills-type bombs and bore what appeared to be a Japanese inscription. The Japanese claimed that the bombs were manufactured in a Chinese munitions plant near Canton. *CWR*, 24 Sept. 1938, 113.

31. *RDS*, 893.00 P.R. Shanghai/120 (Sept. 1938), 14.

32. Boyle, *China and Japan at War, 1937–1945*, 164–165; Bunker, *The Peace Conspiracy*, 64–65. The Tang assassination occurred a few days after Japanese Foreign Minister Ugaki Kazushige had made an offer to Sir Robert Craigie to restore Hongkou and Yangzipu to the authority of the Shanghai Municipal Council in exchange for appointing more Japanese to the Municipal Police and Special District Court. Clifford, *Retreat from China*, 108.

33. Ibid., 64–65, 88; *RDS*, 893.00 P.R. Shanghai/150 (Sept. 1938), 11–12; Yeh, "Dai Li and the Liu Geqing Affair," 551; Boyle, *China and Japan at War, 1937–1945*, 165. Tang Shaoyi's son was a classmate of Prime Minister Konoye.

34. Xiang Qingwei, from Shengxian (Zhejiang), was a disciple of Lou Bingzhang of the Green Gang. Zhang Weihan, "Dai Li yu 'Juntong ju,'" 139.

35. It is not clear who wielded the hatchet: Xiang Qingwei, Lin Zhijiang, or Zhao Lijun, who are each identified as the murderer, respectively, by ibid., 139; Yeh, "The Liu Geqing Affair," 27; and Wang Fangnan, "Wo zai juntong shisinian de qinli he jianwen," 144.

36. *RDS*, 893.00 P.R. Shanghai/120 (Sept. 1938), 14–15; *CWR*, 8 Oct. 1938, 198; Wang Fangnan, "Wo zai Juntong shisinian de qinli he jianwen," 144. Xie Zhipan had a nervous breakdown after he got to Chongqing, and in the hospital he would frequently pull out his pistol, frightening the nurses. A Juntong inspector, Wang Kequan, sent around to investigate the matter, walked into Xie's room, saw him crouching with a pistol, and shot him. After Dai Li angrily dismissed him from his position, Wang, fearing further punishment, killed himself. Zhang Weihan, "Dai Li yu 'Juntong ju,'" 139.

37. *RDS*, 893.00 P.R. Shanghai/121 (Oct. 1938), 14–15; *CWR*, 8 Oct. 1938, 198.

38. *RDS*, 893.00/14274 (4 Nov. 1938), and P.R. Shanghai/122 (Nov. 1938), 11–12; *CWR*, 12 Nov. 1938, 346.

39. *SB* (27 Nov. 1938), enclosed in SMP, D-8870, 1/12/38.

40. Jiang, a native of Hebei, had also been a cadet in the pre-Occupation police academy. Ibid.

41. Chen Jintao, a Yale Ph.D., had formerly served as minister of finance in the Reform Government under Liang Hongzhi. Prior to that he had been appointed minister of finance in Canton by Sun Yat-sen, and after serving a prison term for having been associated with the left-wing regime in Wuhan, he had turned to scholarship. Qin Xiaoyi, *Zhonghua minguo zhongyao shiliao*

chubian—Dui Ri zhanzheng shiqi. Di liu bian: Kuilei zuzhi, 139; Boyle, *China and Japan at War, 1937–1945*, 113.

42. On 28 November, Li Jinbiao, a counselor in the puppet government who had earlier had an outstanding career in the Wusong–Shanghai constabulary, was also arrested, probably because of this same case. *SB* (27 Nov. 1938), enclosed in SMP, D-8870, 1/12/38.

43. Su, who resisted the replacement of his Dadao regime by Fu's Reform Government, had already suffered an assassination attack himself, barely missing death when two grenades were thrown at his automobile in Pudong. *CWR*, 23 Apr. 1938, 212.

44. Ibid.

45. SMP, D-8987, 31/1/39, 1–4.

46. SMP, D-8987, 31/1/39, 5–6; 3/2/39; and 9/2/39. Early in 1935, Chiang Kai-shek had granted Dai Li personal authority over the Main Detective Brigade of the Shanghai–Wusong Garrison Command (Song–Hu jingbei silingbu zhencha dadui), and Wu Naixian—chief then of Juntong's Shanghai Station—was named commander (*daduizhang*) of the entire division, which was housed in the Baiyunguan on Fangxie Road in South Market. Shen Zui, *Juntong neimu*, 43.

47. "Mystery Man Murdered in Local Hotel," *CP*, 30 January 1939; "Mystery Shrouds Shooting," *ST*, 31 Jan. 1931, both clipped in SMP, D-8987, 31/1/39 and 9/2/39.

48. "Murdered Man Was Important Official," *NCDN*, 31 Jan. 1939, and "Murdered Man Identified as Puppet Leader," *CP*, 31 Jan. 1939, both clipped in SMP, D-8987, 9/2/39.

49. SMP, D-8987, 31/1/39, 4.

50. They went to some of these addresses, in one case discovering that the place was an opium den frequently used by members of the Reform Government for meetings. Ibid., 31/1/39 and 2/2/39.

51. Special Branch made a detailed inventory of the forty-seven sets of written materials that they found in the room. They took such pains because they had by then come to suspect that Ma Yuhang was a member of the Japanese special services. See the five-page list in ibid., 2/2/39.

52. Transl. in ibid.

53. Ibid.

54. Ibid.

55. During this time, Ma Yuhang financially supported Cai Xiangsheng. Ibid., 31/1/39, 1–2.

56. From the Dollar Hotel (Dalu fandian) to the Yangzi Hotel, the Far Eastern Hotel, and finally the Sun Sun [Xinxin lüguan]. Ibid., 3.

57. Ibid., 4.

5. Provocation: The Chen Lu assassination

1. Official reports from Hankou for April 1939 stated that since the Japanese occupation, there was virtually no commercial activity. Similarly, in Canton

the Pearl River was closed to navigation and important industries were at a low ebb. Oakes, *White Man's Folly,* 375.

2. Ch'ien, *Fortress Besieged,* 325.

3. Oakes, *White Man's Folly,* 381.

4. Zhang Fangren, *Jinrong manji,* 31. By the following year, however, cotton was in short supply at a reasonable price. There were 250,000 bales of yarn stored in Shanghai's warehouses, but hardly anyone could afford to buy them. Oakes, *White Man's Folly,* 358, 382–383.

5. Oakes, *White Man's Folly,* 359.

6. Ibid., 357. By then many U.S. dependents, including the family members of all U.S. government employees, had left Shanghai. The Department of State dependents departed in October 1940 on the Madsen Line's *Monterey.* Crichton, "Unsung Heroes," 59.

7. "What had cost $100 to buy now cost $365. By comparison, wages had increased only an infinitesimal amount." Ibid., 359.

8. "The High Cost of Living," 13–14.

9. Because of rents that were only one-eighth those of the settlements, Nandao attracted tens of thousands of new inhabitants in the first year after the Japanese occupation.

10. *CWR,* 11 Oct. 1941, 153.

11. Oakes, *White Man's Folly,* 360.

12. Ibid. The distribution of rice to the population of Shanghai had been a major problem ever since hostilities broke out on 13 August 1937. In December that year starvation had threatened, and only the activities of a number of major philanthropists had staved off catastrophe. Finch, *Shanghai and Beyond,* 323–325. High rice prices were blamed upon "underhand control of the rice market by certain traitorous merchants who in conspiracy with the Japanese and puppet authorities are making handsome profits." SMP, D-8039, 7/3/39.

13. BFOR, FO371-24663. "After the murder on November 30 [1940] of a Japanese gendarme by a Chinese gunman, the Japanese military blockaded until December 14 a large district in the western extra-Settlement roads area of Shanghai. . . . Very little food and other supplies were permitted to enter the area." CSDCF, 893.00 P.R. Shanghai/147 (Dec. 1940), 19. See also Tao Juyin, *Tianliang qian de gudao* 59.

14. Ch'eng Nai-shan, *The Banker,* 361–362. See, for rice riots, Heppner, *Shanghai Refuge,* 77.

15. SMP, D-8039, 24/8/39.

16. SMP, D-8039A, 11/1/41. See also Nashimoto Yûhei, *Chûgoku no naka no Nihonjin,* 2:157–166.

17. BWOR, extract from Shanghai Naval and Military Intelligence Summary No. 7, 9/4/41, WO208-246A.

18. "The High Cost of Living," 14–15. The Western District, or badlands police, had begun distributing rice in February 1940. SMP, D-8155(1), 17/2/40.

19. Wakeman, *Policing Shanghai,* ch. 15; Silliman, "Sino-Foreign Conflict and the Extra-Settlement Roads of Shanghai," passim.

20. In 1939 there were sixty-three true cases of murder versus forty-two in 1938, and twenty-two in 1937, in the International Settlement. That same year, 1939, saw 42% of crime cases unsolved, as opposed to 37% in 1937 and percentages around 35% in 1936 and 1935. *Annual Report of the Shanghai Municipal Council, 1939,* 100–101.

21. Notice included in SMP, D-8155, 24/1/39.

22. The police bureau of the Shanghai puppet government had ten branch bureaus, four police stations, and five other units (detective corps headed by Guo Shaoyi, garrison corps, youth corps, police reserve unit, and river police) with a total roster of 3,444. For a complete list of stations and commanders, see ibid., 2/2/39.

23. Of the 230 constables, 42 undertook census returns, 10 looked after public health, 80 were organized into 10-man patrols (4 or 5 in each patrol were armed with one of the 40 rifles and 20 pistols held by the Western Bureau, the rest carrying batons on the beat), 80 tended to traffic and general patrol duties, and 18 were held on guard duty at the branch bureau. Those assigned firearms were only given one round per weapon as a precaution against mutiny. Ibid., 2/2/39, 7/2/39. Local defense groups were also being increased. SMA, Wang 18.141—Reform Government—"Xiang qu fang gong ziwei tuan zuzhi tiaolie" [The regulations for the organization of village and district Self-Defense Guards against the Communists], 7 Jan. 1939, 3. See also *Zhonghua minguo weixin zhengfu zhenggang,* 118–123.

24. SMP, D-8155, 9/2/39. Later, in May 1939, the Japanese responded to Wang Delin's requests for more weapons by providing two rifles and one Mauser pistol to each of the eight substations and outposts in the Western District. Ibid., 14/5/39.

25. Ibid.

26. Ibid., 24/2/39, 22/3/39. In March 1939 the number of police cadets in training at the civic center was increased from 200 to 300. They and their chief, Wang Ruilian, were transferred on 10 March 1939 to Huacaozhen for further training. Their uniforms resembled Japanese military garb. Ibid., 13/3/39.

27. Ibid., 1/5/39.

28. Han Jun was shot four times by a Nationalist assassin as he was leaving his home on route des Soeurs in the French Concession on 14 September 1939, to commute to work in his armored car. *SB,* 16 Sept. 1939, 11; *XSB,* 25 Sept. 1939, 1, transl. in SMP, D-8615, 31/1/40.

29. SMP, D-8155, 1/6/39.

30. There are fairly complete rosters of these gendarmes in the Shanghai Municipal Archives, complete with identity cards and photographs. SMA, Wang 18.151—Huxi—"Zhoujiaqiao zhen ziweituan mingxian mingce," October 1939 to May 1940; SMA, Wang 18.186—Huxi—"Fang gong ziwei tuan tuanyuan zheng," n.d.

31. The new chief of staff was Yao Zhiduan, alias Yao Asheng and Yao Zidu. He had worked for the Criminal Investigation Department. SMP, D-8155(2), 8/6/39; D-8155B, 1/6/39; D-8155G, 7/3/39, 11/4/39, 19/5/39.

32. This kind of incident explains why Dadao police regulations required all

police on patrol, except for plainclothes detectives, to be in uniform. SMA, Wang 1-1-10—Dadao file, cover sheet dated "wuyin 2/24" (February 24, 1938)—"Jingchaju xiang zhangze" [Rules and Regulations of the Police Department], 24b.

33. SMP, D-8155 (2), 22/5/39.
34. *CWR*, 1 Mar. 1941, 462.
35. Ibid., 14 Jan. 1939, 213.
36. Number 76 Jessfield Road, the former mansion of Anhui warlord Chen Diaoyuan, is now the Jiandong Secondary School, at No. 435 Wanhengdu. Yeh, "Dai Li and the Liu Geqing Affair," 552. See also Zhu Zijia, *Wang Zhengquan de kaichang yu shouchang*, vol. 6, 130–131; Pan Ling, *Old Shanghai*, 47; and Haruke Keiin, *Shanghai tero kôsaku 76 gô*, 94 (for a floor plan of "76").
37. *CWR*, 18 Jan. 1941, 229. For the executions carried out within this "killing field," see *CWR*, 26 Apr. 1941, 247.
38. Wong was arrested both because of the coin minting and because one of his colleagues in the American Engineering Corporation, Saucy Chen, was commissioned by Dai Li to assassinate Wang Jingwei. The plot was discovered on 2 October 1940, and Chen was killed. "'Black Hole of Shanghai,'" 1.
39. SMA, Wang 18.285—Huxi—April 1939 to May 1940. This file contains the weapons rosters for these units, plus information on the cadres' backgrounds. See also SMA, Wang 18.282, Wangwei Huxi—Caojiadu zhen zuzhi ziweituan, 1939–1940.
40. SMP, D-697; 28/12/39; BFOR, FO371-24682, F1104, 12/2/40.
41. SMP, D-8477, 22/7/40.
42. *CWR*, 14 Jan. 1939, 213.
43. BWOR, Far Eastern Department, Report No. 22, 13/2/39, WO-208-246A. On 13 February, the Shanghai Municipal Police requested military assistance from British, Japanese, and Italian troops. After a week-long discussion, combined operations were carried out. "No positive results were obtained this time, but it is considered that political and moral effects of cooperation of all forces will be of utmost value in restoration of confidence." Ibid., Commissioner Shanghai Area to GOC Hong Kong, Dispatch 6810, 22/2/39.
44. *SB*, 2 Feb. 1939, 15. Two days earlier, Ma Yuhang, an advisor to the Reform Government, was also assassinated at the Xinxin Hotel. *SB*, 30 Jan. 1939, 9.
45. *SB*, 6 Feb. 1939, 10; 7 Feb. 1939, 10; 8 Feb. 1939, 11; 17 Feb. 1939, 10; *RDS*, 893.00 P.R. Shanghai/155 (February 1939), 13, and 893.00 14329 (2 Jan. 1939); *CWR*, 11 Feb., 1939, 340. It's not certain that all of these were assassinated by Dai Li's men, but certainly Qian Hua was, since Shanghai Municipal Police ballistics tests proved that one of the .38 caliber pistols used by the Juntong team to kill Chen Lu on 19 February 1939 had been used against Qian on 6 February. "Assassination of Reformed Government Official," 6; *NCDN*, 21 Feb. 1939, 1. Zhou Fengqi, former commander of the Nationalist 26th Army and the Nationalist Shanghai Garrison and now minister of pacification (*suijing buzhang*) in Liang Hongzhi's Reform Government, was also killed at this time, gunned down by four of Dai Li's agents

despatched by Shanghai section chief Zhou Weilong. Zhou Fengqi, then in charge of "peace preservation" (*baoan*) activities, was succeeded as minister of pacification by Ren Yuandao: Zhang Weihan, "Dai Li yu 'Juntong ju,'" 140; Yeh, "The Liu Geqing Affair," 27; *Zhonghua minguo weixin zhengfu zhenggang,* "Weixin zhengfu zuzhi xitong ji zhongyao zhiyuan biao" [Table of organization and important personnel of the Reform Government] (10 Sept. 1939), attachment to p. 311; Qin Xiaoyi, *Zhonghua minguo zhongyao shiliao chubian—Dui Ri zhanzheng shiqi. Di liu bian; Kuilei zuzhi,* 134, 139; Zhu Zijia, *Wang Zhengquan de kaichang yu shouchang,* vol. 4, 34.

46. *RDS,* 893.00 P.R. Shanghai/125 (Feb. 1939), 10–12; *CWR,* 25 Feb. 1939, 389; *ST,* 21 Feb. 1939, 1.

47. *NCDN,* 21 Feb. 1939, 1. See also *ST,* 21 Feb. 1939, 1. Tretiak classified it as one of the six major political assassinations of the Republican period. Tretiak, "Political Assassinations in China," 648.

48. "Further Assistance to Japanese Military Police," 1; Woodhead, *The China Yearbook* (1936), 219.

49. Wang was in disfavor at this time because of his turf fight with Zhao Lijun. Yeh, "The Liu Geqing Affair," 25.

50. "Further Assistance to Japanese Military Police," 1; "Further Statement of Ping Foo Chang," made to Japanese Gendarmerie headquarters, SMP, D-9037, 20/10/39, 3.

51. Ibid.

52. Ibid., 1–2.

53. Ibid., 2; "How the Foreign Minister Was Assassinated." *XSB,* 9 Nov. 1939, transl. in SMP, D-9037, 9/11/39. About 300 graduates of the Linli Depot were ordered back to Shanghai to engage in terrorist activities, such as the assassination of the Reform Government Vocational Bureau official Yu Daxiong on 17 October 1938; and of the Jiading puppet police chief, Yu Yaozhang, in the French Concession on 12 November. *SB,* 18 Oct. 1938, 1, and 13 Nov. 1938, 10.

54. "Further Statement of Ping Foh Chong (II)," made to Japanese Gendarmerie headquarters, in SMP, D-9037, 21/10/39, 1–2.

55. "Mao Van Li . . . relative of Tai Lee [Dai Li], age about 40, Chikiang [Zhejiang], stout build, about five feet three inches in height." "Further Statement of Ping Foo Chang," 6–7.

56. *USMIR,* China, 1911–1941, reports no. 9710, 8 Jan. 1939, 4, and no. 9754, 6 Apr., 1939, 1. The Wang Jingwei group was, from the beginning of its arrival in Hanoi, under the surveillance of Dai Li's men operating out of the office of Sinan [Xinan] Airways, next to his hideout. Miwa, "The Wang Ching-Wei Regime and Japanese Efforts to Terminate the China Conflict," 129. See also Wang Jingwei's insistence on 27 March, six days after Zeng's death, that the young man was only carrying out a policy already approved by the highest organs of the Guomindang, in "Ju yige li" [Take, for example], in Qin Xiaoyi, *Zhonghua minguo zhongyao shiliao chubian—Dui Ri zhanzheng shiqi. Di liu bian: Kuilei zuzhi,* 78–84; Wang, *A la mémoire de M. Tsen-Tson-Ming;* T'ang, *Fundamentals of National Salvation,* 44–49; Zhu

Zijia, *Wang Zhengquan de kaichang yu shouchang,* vol. 5, 45–49; Shen Zui, "Wang Jingwei Henei yuci ji," 79; "How the Foreign Minister Was Assassinated"; *NCDN,* 23 Mar. 1939, in SMP, D-9070/6, 24/3/39; *RDS,* 893.00/14353, Hanoi, 1939; Inukai Ken, *Yôsukô wa ima mo nagarete iru,* 121; and Huang Meizhen and Zhang Yun, *Wang Jingwei jituan toudi,* 441–442, 449–451. Wang Luzhao was described as speaking Mandarin, age twenty-eight, 5'5" tall, and having no particular features. "Further Statement of Dan Pao Yee," made to Japanese Gendarmerie headquarters, in SMP, D-9037, 24/10/39, 1. "This assassination was done by our party under the command of Tai Lih [Dai Li], member of the Military Committee, and Yue Loh Sing [Yu Lexing] was the leader of the party and Wong Loo Jao [Wang Luzhao] was the direct leader of the assassination. I was informed of this by [Wang Luzhao] whilst I stayed in Hong Kong about April this year [1939]." "Further Statement of Ping Foh Chong (II)," 1. "[The mistaken assassination of Zeng Zongming] was committed by our followers with Wong Lee Yau [Wang Luzhao] as a ringleader under the direction of Tan Lih [with the characters for Dai Li]. "Statement of Dan Pao Yee," 6. For the impact of the assassination on Wang Jingwei, see Huang Meizhen, "Wang Jingwei," 74.

57. "Deposition of Ping Foh Chang," SMP, D-9037, 3/11/39, 2; "Further Statement of Ping Foo Chang," 3.

58. "Statement of Dan Pao Yee," SMP, D-9037, 23/10/39, 2; "Deposition of Dan Pau Nyi," SMP, D-9037, 3/11/39, 1; "How the Foreign Minister Was Assassinated." *XSB,* Nov. 9, 1939, transl. in SMP, D-9037, 9/11/39.

59. For obvious reasons, Tan Baoyi made this point most persistently to the Japanese Military Police when they were interrogating him about local spy networks. "Further Statement of Dan Pao Yee," 2. The Shanghai Municipal Police identified the assassination unit as the Field Section of the Shanghai branch of the Investigation and Statistics Bureau of the Military Affairs Commission. "Japanese Arrest Nine Men Detailed by Chungking [Chongqing] for Assassination Work," *ZR,* 9 Nov. 1939, transl. in SMP, D-9037, 9/11/39.

60. "Deposition of Dan Pau Nyi," 1–2; "Deposition of Ping Foh Chang," 2.

61. "Further Assistance to Japanese Military Police," 1–3. Another informant may have been the puppet official Zhu Zhengdong, a graduate of Whampoa who claimed, during his trial for collaboration before the Shanghai High Court in March 1946, that he had participated in the Chen Lu assassination. Zhu had served as director of a puppet organization called the Greater East Asia Buddhist Society, which disbursed rice rations. "Alleged Puppet," 1.

62. Chen Lu's three personal bodyguards and three of the six watchmen that he had hired to protect his mansion on Yuyuan Road were from the Northeast (Dongbei). "Assassination of Reformed Government Official," 3–4.

63. Yeh, "The Liu Geqing Affair," 25–26; "Further Statement of Ping Foh Chong (III)," 1–2.

64. "Further Assistance to Japanese Military Police," 3–4; "Assassination of Reformed Government Official," 1–3.

65. "How the Foreign Minister Was Assassinated," 1.

66. "Deposition of Ping Foh Chang," 2.
67. "Further Statement of Ping Foo Chang," 4; "Further Statement of Ping Foh Chong (III)," 5. The pistols were identified in the press as Mauser semi-automatics. The guns were actually a .38 Alamo Ranger revolver, a .380 Colt automatic, two Astra 7.65 automatics, and a .32 long-barreled Belgian revolver. SMP, D-9037, 23/2/39.
68. "Statement of Dan Pao Yee," 3; "Deposition of Dan Pau Nyi," 1–2. Xu Zhihao, age thirty-six and a native of Jinhua (Zhejiang), had joined the Guangdong training depot of General He Yingqin as a sixteen-year-old. In 1933 he resigned his captain's commission and came to Shanghai to seek regular employment. He was unsuccessful and became a huckster. When hostilities broke out in 1937, Xu joined the Chinese National Salvation Corps (Zhongguo jiuwang guo) housed in the Guandi Temple in Nandao under Zhao Gangyi. In February 1938 he went to Hankou with Ping Fuchang, also a corps member, in search of a job. They had no luck and eventually returned to Shanghai. In January 1939 Xu Zhihao met Xu Guoqi, also a member of the corps, who requested him to work for the corps at $30 per month. Ten days later he was taken to meet Liu Geqing and thus became a regular member of the team. Deposition of Zoo Ts Au," SMP, D-9037, 14/12/39, 1–3.
69. The same afternoon He Peng and Zhao Yuding left the Chen mansion and did not return until about 6:00 p.m. "Further Assistance to Japanese Military Police," 5.
70. "Statement of Dan Pao Yee," 4. *Chen* and *Cheng* are nearly indistinguishable in southern Mandarin.
71. "Deposition of Ping Foh Chang," 2–3.
72. "Deposition of Dan Pau Nyi," 3; "Deposition of Ping Foh Chang," 3; "Deposition of Zoo Ts Au," 3; "How the Foreign Minister Was Assassinated."
73. Shao Fusheng had been recommended to Chen Lu by the former secretary to Mayor Wu Tiecheng. Because Shao, who had a long-standing record of absenteeism, was not at Chen Lu's side at the time of the assassination, the bodyguard fell for a time under Victor Chen's suspicion and was later arrested and horribly mistreated by the Japanese Military Police. He turned out to have been working as a ticket taker at the Dalai Theater the night of the killing. See the depositions in SMP, D-9037, 18/3/39, 20/3/39, and 21/3/39.
74. "Assassination of Reformed Government Official," 4–5; *CP*, 21 Feb. 1939, 1; "How the Foreign Minister Was Assassinated." Tan Baoyi claimed, under interrogation, that he had remained in the courtyard with the night watchman. "Deposition of Dan Pau Nyi," 4.
75. The gunman was probably Tan Baoyi, who entered from the northeastern corner of the room. "How the Foreign Minister Was Assassinated."
76. Luo came in through the door at the southeastern corner of the room. Chen Lu was struck in the head and in the right leg. "Assassination of Reformed Government Official." Victor Chen, who seemed to suspect everyone around his father after the assassination, thought it curious that the Luos opened the

door and were not shot themselves. Within one or two days of the shooting, the Luos left for Hong Kong. "Further Assistance to Japanese Military Police," 5–7.

77. The car was waiting on Yuyuan Road. Tan remembered being driven to an unknown address in the French Concession, where he got out and took a ricksha to the Dongchang lodging house on Avenue Joffre. "Deposition of Dan Pau Nyi," 4.

78. "Deposition of Dan Pau Nyi," 3–4; "Further Assistance to Japanese Military Police," 7–8; "Assassination of Reformed Government Official," 4–6; "How the Foreign Minister Was Assassinated"; Yeh, "Dai Li and the Liu Geqing Affair," 551; Yeh, "The Liu Geqing Affair," 23; *CP*, 21 Feb. 1939, 1; *NCDN*, 21 Feb. 1939, 1; *ST*, 21 Feb. 1939, 1; *CWR*, 25 Feb. 1939. Ping Fushang, for instance, took a bus east along Yuyuan Road to the St. George stop where he got off and rented a car at the Ford rental service station. He drove the car back to the small rooming house on rue Marché where he had been staying. "Deposition of Ping Foh Chang," 3–4.

6. Capitulation: The Xi Shitai assassination

1. Yeh, "Dai Li and the Liu Geqing Affair," 551. The Shanghai Municipal Police took care to maintain a close watch over Chen Lu's funeral procession on 24 February to the Happy Garden Cemetery (Leyuan binyiguan), which was guarded by heavily armed puppet police. SMP, D-9037, 24/2/39 and 25/2/39.

2. Eventually, the vice-foreign minister, Lian You, was appointed. *CWR*, 4 Mar. 1939, 10.

3. "Assassination of Reformed Government Official," 7–9.

4. *CWR*, 25 Feb. 1939, 389. It is clear from several reports, including especially "Further Assistance to Japanese Military Police," that the Settlement police had Chen Lu under surveillance the moment he stepped down from his railroad car at North Station. Once he was inside his house, however, the surveillance team—which had to have been driving one or several automobiles—was removed.

5. *ST*, 21 Feb. 1939, 1; *CWR*, 25 Feb. 1939, 389.

6. *RDS*, 893.00 P.R. Shanghai/14333 (22 Feb., 1939).

7. Ibid., 893.00 P.R. Shanghai/125 (Feb. 1939), 14; *Tairiku shimpo*, quoted in *CWR*, 25 Feb. 1939, 389.

8. *RDS*, 893.00 P.R., Shanghai/155 (Feb. 1939), 15–16.

9. *CWR*, 25 Feb. 1939, 389.

10. On the day before, Li Guojie, the eldest grandson of Li Hongzhang, was shot to death at the entrance to the Qinyuancun on Xinzha (Sinza) Road. Li, who had once been manager of the China Merchants Steam Navigation Company, had an unsavory reputation for corrupt practices. He had supported the Reform Government and had hoped to become minister of industry (*shiye buzhang*). SB, 22 Feb. 1939, 10. See also articles translated from other Shanghai newspapers in SMP, D-9037, 24/2/39; and Finch, *Shanghai and Beyond*,

312. For Japanese "landing parties" (*rikusentai*), see Peattie, "Japanese Treaty Port Settlements in China, 1895–1937," 199.

11. *FRUS 1939*, 1–2; *CWR*, 25 Feb. 1939, 389.

12. *Tairiku shimpo* attacked the Shanghai Municipal Police's barricading of alleys, which it called "a cunning attempt to kill two birds with one stone," that is, ward off Japanese demands "and at the same time fan the flames of resentment against Japan among the Chinese population of the Settlement who will be most inconvenienced by this step." *CWR*, 4 Mar. 1939, 12.

13. *RDS*, 893.00 P.R. Shanghai/125 (Feb. 1939), 14–15.

14. *FRUS 1939*, 6.

15. Ibid., 9–10.

16. Ibid., 10.

17. *CWR*, 4 Mar. 1939, 12.

18. Ibid., 11 Mar. 1939, 48; *SB*, 28 Feb. 1939, 11, and 7 Mar. 1939, 11. Zhu, a graduate of the Baoding Military Academy who had served the Beiyang warlords, was one of the leading officials in the Finance Bureau (Caizheng ju) of the Dadao régime. Members of the Liang Hongzhi Reform Government had been promised generous payments to their family survivors should they fall prey to terrorists' guns. *CWR*, 4 Mar. 1939, 10, 47.

19. Regulations of the Shanghai People's Mobilization Society enclosed in *FRUS 1939*, 16 May 1939, 50–51.

20. The Japanese branch of the Shanghai Municipal Police was thirty-three men short of budget strength. U.S. Consul General Gauss and Admiral Harry E. Yarnell, commander in chief, U.S. Asiatic Fleet, made it plain to the Shanghai Municipal Council that they could not acquiesce to the Council permitting the Japanese Military Police and the Japanese consular police to function independently in the Settlement. *FRUS 1939*, 7–8; *CWR*, 4 Mar. 1939, 12.

21. *CWR*, 4 Mar. 1939, 12. Shanghai Municipal Police Assistant Commissioner Kakugawa was to proceed to Tokyo to recruit thirty more Japanese constables for the Settlement police force.

22. See, for examples of extremely close cooperation, especially in the summer of 1939, SMP, D-8987, 16/12/39. However, see also the Nationalist Chinese government's objection to reports on 5 May 1939 that Japanese Military Police had arrested five Chinese in the International Settlement. The Chinese Ministry of Foreign Affairs pointedly reminded the U.S. Embassy that these arrests were "obviously in contempt of the police rights of the Settlement." *FRUS 1939*, 52.

23. *RDS*, 893.00 P.R. Shanghai/126 (Mar. 1939), 14.

24. The Japanese could get the Shanghai Municipal Police to suppress Chinese-owned newspapers on this score, but, as we shall see below, the use of foreigners as proxy owners defended many patriotic Chinese publishers from this kind of control and infuriated the Japanese community in Shanghai. Ibid., and P.R. Shanghai/127 (Apr. 1939), 11–12.

25. *SB*, 12 Apr. 1939, 10.

26. He was a native of Suzhou. During his period of study at the Tokyo ika daigaku, Dr. Xi had taken a Japanese wife. In Shanghai she became the senior

of his two concubines, the principal wife and other concubine being Chinese. Ibid.; SMP, D9122, 4/11/39.

27. According to *Shen bao*, Dr. Xi's eldest son, Xingzhi, was in charge of a special radio broadcasting station "engaged in spreading strange reports," and acting as an agent on behalf of Japan. *SB*, 12/4/39, 10.

28. *Tairiku shimpo*, 12 Apr. 1939, transl. in SMP, D-9122, 13/4/39.

29. Yuan's native place was either Songjiang or Kunshan. He was described as being about 5'6" tall with "thin build, thin face, pale complexion, long hair brushed back, wears foreign clothes, no hat, speaks Shanghai dialect." SMP, D-9122, 15/4/39.

30. On 21 July 1939 (three days before the Craigie–Arita formula was openly announced), the Japanese Military Police informed the Shanghai Municipal Police, who had handed Zhao over to them, that the prisoner had been sentenced to death on 10 July. Ibid., 22/7/39.

31. Ibid., 11/4/39.

32. Zhao had met Yuan in the first place through a Pudong guerrilla section chief surnamed Zhang, who had defected to the Japanese in January 1939. Ibid., 11/4/39.

33. Ibid. Juntong, which had an excellent telephone and telegraph monitoring section, used Shanghai hotels as listening posts. Shen Zui, *Juntong neimu*, 46–47. The operator in this case, one Pu Fuxin, was interrogated by the Shanghai Municipal Police after the assassination and released. The Japanese consular police later claimed that he was a key figure in the assassination ring, but even with the help of the Shanghai Municipal Police they were unable to run him down. SMP, D-9122, 13/4/39 and 12/5/39.

34. The letter from Zhou Jianhua (see below), later found by the police in Peng Fulin's room at the Nanjing Hotel, referred to an earlier "matter" that Yuan, Peng, and Zhao had successfully carried out, strongly suggesting that Zhao had worked together with the other two Juntong agents in an earlier operation. Ibid., 11/4/39.

35. Zhao was told to remember the agent's appearance but not his name. Ibid., 11/4/39.

36. Ibid.

37. The room at No. 11 Wenxian li, rue Lafayette, was bare, but Yuan supplied some furniture and Zhao provided his own cotton-quilt bedding. Ibid.

38. Peng, who was from Liyang, later claimed on his deathbed that he had met both men earlier at the Wing On (Yongan) Department Store roof garden and that they had become bosom friends. Ibid. Zhao Zhixiang said, however, that he had known Peng before the war broke out in Shanghai, and that Peng (who was then a waiter at the Dadong xin lüguan) and he would often rent a room with a couple of friends to play mahjong. Ibid., 11/4/39. Peng, who most likely was a trained Juntong agent, also later told the police that he had just happened to bump into Yuan Dechang outside a Chinese movie theater on Avenue Edward VII on April 7, and that he had told Yuan that he had no interest in participating in "patriotic activities."

39. Ibid., 11/4/39 and 12/4/39.

40. Ibid., 11/4/39. Peng Fulin claimed that Yuan only produced the revolvers and taught them how to use them on 8 April. Ibid., 12/4/39.
41. Ibid.
42. The envelope had part of a three-cent stamp, which Zhao noticed was not postmarked. This was corroborated later by the police when they found the letter in Peng Fulin's hotel room. Ibid., 15/4/39.
43. The name reads "Zhou [the dynasty] Sword China." The return address on the envelope was the Guansheng yuan shop at 416 rue du Consulat. When Shanghai Municipal Police detectives later visited this store, they were not surprised to find no one named Zhou on the premises. Ibid., 11/4/39 and 15/4/39.
44. Cited in ibid., 11/4/39. See also the testimony dated 14/4/39.
45. Xi Shitai's house was located at No. 12, Lane 127, Lloyd Road, but the backdoor opened onto Lane 139. Ibid., 11/4/39.
46. One of the interrogations suggests there may have been a third look-out, Peng Fulin's younger brother Jinyi, who escaped with Yuan Dechang. Ibid., 13/4/39.
47. The forty-year-old Shandong guard, Song Jiangrong, was Chinese Police Watchman no. 277, licensed to bear firearms. Zhao, the Chinese beat policeman, Chinese Police Constable no. 730, was armed only with his whistle. Ibid., 11/4/39.
48. The initial police report stated that one shot had gone through Xi Shitai's elbow, but the autopsy held on 12 April noted the wounds mentioned here. If the elbow was shot, then the spent bullet might have been one of the two caught in Xi's clothing. Ibid., 13/4/39.
49. The Japanese Residents Corporation later sent a sum of money to Constable Zhao. *Mainichi*, 13 Apr. 1939, transl. in ibid., 13/4/39.
50. SMP, D-9122, 11/4/39.
51. The twenty-three-year-old waiter, a teaboy at the Dadong xin lüguan (94 rue Palikao), was named Li Xinghe. The police initially mistook him to be Peng Jinyi, Peng Fulin's brother; but they soon discovered his real identity. Li Xinghe claimed to have met the wounded man along Lloyd Road, where he had hired two rickshas to take them to the Nanjing Hotel. On the way, however, the two had stopped by Yuan Dechang's place, where Peng Fulin had given him back his pistol. Ibid., 11/4/39, 12/4/39, 15/4/39.
52. Ibid., 11/4/39.
53. Ibid.
54. Ibid., 11/4/39 and 15/4/39.
55. "Wipe Out the Chongqing Government Agents," *TS*, 12 Apr. 1939, clipped and transl. in SMP, D-9122, 13/4/39.
56. "Important Determination of Our Military Authorities over the Assassination of Dr. Xi," *TS*, 12 Apr. 1939, transl. in SMP, D-9122, 13/4/39.
57. "Criticism of Settlement Authorities," *XSB*, 13 Apr. 1939, transl. in SMP, D-9122, 13/4/39.
58. SMP, D-9122, 13/4/39; and Domei, 19 Apr. 1939, transl. in ibid., 21/4/39.
59. SMP, D-9122, 21/4/39.

60. Ibid., 20/4/39. This was two days after the "execution" in the French Concession of Wang Xianming, a section chief (*kezhang*) in the puppet municipal government by a Nationalist assassin, and on the very day that Yang Qiguan, chief of the municipal Department of Statistics and Taxes (Tongshui chu), was repeatedly stabbed by a "heroic Han" (zhuang Han). *SB*, 18 Apr. 1939, 12, and 21 Apr. 1939, 11.

61. *FRUS 1939*, 19 May 1939, 53–56; BFOR, F0371-24682, Memorandum from Major K. M. Bourne to C. Akagi, enclosure in Shanghai despatch to Embassy, Shanghai, 635, 22/11/39, dated 16 Nov. 1939, in F1006, 9/2/40; Michael, "The Significance of Puppet Governments," 409.

62. See the material on the Yellow Way Society in *RDS*, 893.00 P.R. Shanghai/119 (Aug. 1938), 17–18.

63. *XSB*, 30 Mar. 1939, transl. in SMP, D-8116, 31/3/39.

64. *XSB*, 1 May 1939, transl. in ibid., 2/5/39.

65. *FRUS 1939*, 51.

66. Ibid., 42–43.

67. Ibid., 42.

68. Ibid., 52. See also Jones, *Japan's New Order in East Asia*, 141.

69. Langer and Gleason, *The Challenge to Isolation*, 136–147.

70. *FRUS 1939*, 53–56.

71. Langer and Gleason, *The Challenge to Isolation*, 148.

72. *FRUS 1939*, 60.

73. Ibid., 62–63.

74. *RDS*, 00/14387.

75. *RDS*, 893.00 P.R. Shanghai/142 (Feb. 1939), 64.

76. Langer and Gleason, *The Challenge to Isolation*, 157.

77. The U.S. public was also outraged by the Japanese bombing of Chongqing, which almost sank the U.S. gunboat *Tutuila*, and by the indignities inflicted by the Japanese military on British citizens in China. Heinrichs, "Franklin D. Roosevelt and the Risks of War," 149.

78. Taylor, *The Struggle for North China*, 141.

79. Ibid., 147, 157–159.

80. "Political Terrorism Unabated Here," 92.

7. The puppet police and 76 Jessfield Road

1. *RDS*, 893.00 P.R. Shanghai/126 (Mar. 1939), 14. See the article "SMC Assumes Arrogant Attitude in Western District," from *XSB*, 11 July 1939, transl. in SMP, D-8116, 12/7/39.

2. There was a tentative expansion under the Dadao puppet government, which established police and Peace Preservation Corps (Baoandui) offices in Nantong in February 1938. SMA, Wang 1.1.77—Dadao file—"Diaocha Nantong deng liu xian" [Investigation of Six Districts in Nantong], 2 February 1938. See also *Baoshan xianzhi*, 1992, 22:721. Under Mayor Fu's administration, twenty recent graduates of the Nanjing government's police academy were

appointed sub-inspectors at the various Shanghai branch bureaus, and the monthly budget of the Shanghai city government police was increased from $160,000 to $200,000 in May 1939. The mayor also approved the formation of a police band with thirty-three members. SMP, D-8155 (2), 8/6/39.

3. SMA, Wang 1.1.137—Dadao file—"Jiaobu daofei qizei an" [Cases of Exterminating and Arresting Bandits and Thieves], 11 Jan. 1938, 1b; SMA, Wang 18.142, Nov. 1939, 8a; *CP*, 13 Oct. 1939, in SMP, D-8155(1), 13/10/39.

4. One group of guerrillas joined the Nanhuai Anti-Communist Self Defense Corps mentioned below. See SMP, D-8155, 13/10/39.

5. Ibid. Yin was also known as Yin Zhongyu.

6. SMP, D-8155, 13/10/39.

7. This was done to increase the supervision of the Japanese Special Services Section over these areas, using the puppet police it already controlled. SMP, D-8155 (2), 10/8/39.

8. SMP, D-8155, 21/7/39.

9. Ibid., 10/8/39. By February 1940 the roster had increased to 6,843, plus 648 reserves. SMP, D-8155 (1), 7/2/40.

10. Ibid.

11. Mayor Fu did not trust the head of the Special Branch, Wang Wenkui, formerly a detective in the French Concession police, because he was appointed by his predecessor. Ibid., 21/7/39.

12. Ibid., 11/9/39.

13. Wang Zilin was named Guo Shaoyi's deputy. Ibid., 10/10/39.

14. The Nanhuai Corps remained, however, under the direction of the Japanese Special Services Section. Ibid., 1/11/39. See, for the earlier assessment of taxes by local defense corps, SMA, Wang 18.121, "Zhengshou 1938 tianfu" [Tax Receipts for 1938]. The Pudong local defense corps also traded in confiscated and stolen rice, dealing directly with village heads. SMP, D-9070/14, 6/9/39.

15. SMP, D-8155, 13/10/39.

16. Ibid., 4/8/39.

17. Constables wounded in the event of an affray would be given $500 by way of compensation. The families of policemen killed in this line of duty would receive $2,000 to $20,000, depending upon rank and seniority. Ibid., 24/8/39.

18. White, "Non-governmentalism in the Historical Development of Modern Shanghai," 48–49.

19. Each nine-man patrol was armed with rifles and five rounds of ammunition. SMP, D-8155, 11/9/39.

20. Ibid., 13/9/39.

21. Ibid., 15/9/39.

22. Ibid., 14/9/39, 15/9/39.

23. Ibid., 29/9/39.

24. BWOR, Shanghai dispatch 1059, 7/11/39, WO-208-246A.

25. Oakes, *White Man's Folly,* 362–363.

26. "Banditry Rampant in Foreign Settlements," *XSB*, 4 Feb. 1940, transl. in SMP, D-8116, 11/2/40.

27. Wakeman, *Policing Shanghai*, ch. 4.
28. "Banditry Rampant in Foreign Settlements," *XSB*, 4 Feb. 1940, transl. in SMP, D-8116, 11/2/40.
29. The "Outline of Readjustment of Sino-Japanese Relations" (Ri-Zhi xin guanxi tiaozheng yaogang), which was based upon Wang Jingwei and Colonel Kagesa's negotiations in Shanghai in June 1939 and which was formally signed on 30 October, contained many concessions to Japan, including jurisdiction over Inner Mongolia, the virtual independence of North China, the assignment of Japanese advisors to all levels of organizations, and the promise to compensate Japanese civilians for war damages. However, the meeting of the three main puppet leaders—Wang Jingwei, Liang Hongzhi, and Wang Kemin—at Qingdao on 23–24 January 1940 finally led to the formation of a unitary national government. Liu Qikui, "Wang Kemin," 352–353; Huang Meizhen and Zhang Yun, *Wang Jingwei guomin zhengfu chengli*, 92–94, 109–116, 421–427, 662–665; T'ang, *Fundamentals of National Salvation*, 97–101; Kamio Shigero, "Wang Ching-wei vs. Chungking," 380; Lu, *From the Marco Polo Bridge to Pearl Harbor*, 94–96; Wu, "Contending Political Forces during the War of Resistance," 68–70. Wang Kemin narrowly escaped being assassinated by Dai Li's agents, led by Chen Gongshu, on 28 March 1938. A Japanese advisor sitting in Wang's usual car seat was killed instead and the puppet was only lightly wounded. Liu Qikui, "Wang Kemin," 347–348.
30. The Shanghai Municipal Government had proclaimed on 8 January 1940, over Fu Xiaoan's signature, that, with Japanese help, it intended to recover sovereignty over Huxi (Western Shanghai) and once and for all resolve the extra-Settlement roads dispute "long undecided for several decades." *RWSSZ*, 56–57.
31. Note, however, that they were identified as Chinese secret agents by the U.S. consul general. CSDCF, 893.00 P.R. Shanghai 136 (Jan. 1940), 12–13.
32. BFOR, FO371-24682, F312, 13/1/40, and F1534, 4/3/40; SMP, D-8373/12, 28/11/40; Davidson-Houston, *Yellow Creek*, 163–164.
33. *RWSSZ*, 58–60; BFOR, FO371-24682, F226, 10/1/40; F839, 6/2/40; F1209, 18/2/40; CSDCF, 893.00 P.R. Shanghai/137 (Feb. 1940), 9.
34. Transl. in SMP, D-8116, 22/2/40.
35. The government was originally supposed to be inaugurated on New Year's day of 1940, but according to Dai Li's intelligence report to Chiang Kai-shek on 22 December 1939, it had to be postponed by three months because there was not enough time to make all the necessary arrangements. Qin Xiaoyi, *Zhonghua minguo zhongyao shiliao chubian—Dui Ri zhanzheng shiqi. Di liu bian: Kuilei zuzhi*, 162.
36. *CWR*, 16 Nov. 1940, 351; Ch'eng Nai-shan, *The Banker*, 327.
37. He studied economics there, and was strongly influenced by Kawakami Hajime, who translated *Das Kapital* into Japanese. Marsh, "Chou Fo-hai," 323; Boorman, *Biographical Dictionary of Republican China*, 405. For his control of Nanjing intelligence, see "History and Methods of the Nanking Puppet Intelligence Section," passim. "The Shanghai city government Police Bureau

is under the direct control of Mayor Fu Siao En [Fu Xiaoan] as far as police functioning is concerned, but matters relating to organization, training, treatment and personnel etc., are subject to the direction of the Ministry of Police Administration of the new Central Administration at Nanking, the Minister being Chow Fu Hai [Zhou Fohai]." SMP, D-8155(1), 25/6/40. This file also contains a roster of the commanding officers and numbers of the rank and file for the entire Shanghai puppet police system, including the River Police.

38. Marsh, "Chou Fo-hai," 324; Epstein, *The Unfinished Revolution in China*, 307–309; Boyle, *China and Japan at War, 1937–1945*, 168–169.

39. He paid his officials with some of the funds from the Chinese customs receipts deposited in the Yokohama Specie Bank that the Japanese permitted him to use to finance his peace movement. Marsh, "Chou Fo-hai," 318–319.

40. *XSB*, 1 Apr. 1940, transl. in SMP, D-8116, 4/4/40.

41. *XSB*, 10 Apr. 1940, transl. in SMP, D-8116, 15/4/40.

42. "It was the custom to hold wealthy or influential prisoners at '2. 76' and permit them to observe other prisoners being tortured; and after several days of this the victims would be offered their freedom on condition they would agree to join the puppet Nanking Government, or, if they happened to be wealthy or had wealthy relatives, to hand over a large sum of money." Powell, *My Twenty-Five Years in China*, 335.

43. Tao Juyin, *Tianliang qian de gudao*, 1.

44. Yeh, "Dai Li and the Liu Geqing Affair," 552; Haruke Keiin, *Shanghai tero kōsaku 76 gô*, 26–28. For a graphic description of the various tortures rendered within "76," see "History and Methods of the Nanking Puppet Intelligence Section."

45. Yeh, "The Liu Geqing Affair," 27. But see also *CWR*, 16 Nov. 1940, 351. A number of other leading Nationalist intelligence agents also surrendered to the enemy: Chen Junhe, who became deputy chief of Wang Jingwei's *zhengzhi baowei ju*; Jin Jihuan, head of the second section of the Hangzhou office of the *baowei ju*; and Xu Chuqing, head of the first section of the Hangzhou district *tegong zongbu*. Zhang Weihan, "Dai Li yu 'Juntong ju,'" 145.

46. Shi Yuanhua, "Li Shiqun," 433–436.

47. Huang Meizhen and Shi Yuanhua, "Wang wei tegong zongbu shimo," 354–355.

48. These included Yang Jie, Lin Zhijiang, and Su Chengde—all former Zhongtong agents. "History and Methods of the Nanking Puppet Intelligence Section."

49. Yeh, "Dai Li and the Liu Geqing Affair," 553; Chen Gongshu, *Kangzhan houqi fanjian huodong*, 206; Mao Xiaotian and Wang Mengyun, "Wang Wei 'tegong zongbu' qishiliu hao de jianli," 268–272; Pan, *Tracing It Home*, 79–80. Wu Shibao, who was more commonly called Wu Sibao, was once employed by Sterling Fessenden, former secretary general of the International Settlement, as a chauffeur. His grandfather was a horse groom at the Shanghai Race Track and his father was a hot water huckster on Chengdu Road. For a chilling portrait of this gangster, who specialized in kidnapping, see Yang Yang, "Wu Sibao," 485–495; and for a description of his wife, Yu Aizhen,

"her face caked with makeup, her hair done up in curls, the perfect image of some hoodlum's moll . . . the side slits in her Mandarin-style dress [running] all the way up to her thighs," see Ch'eng Nai-shan, *The Banker*, 338–339. See also *CWR*, 16 Nov. 1940, 351. "It was [Wu Shibao's] custom to take the prisoners out for a walk in the evenings, the stroll ending up at a corner of the walled compound, where there were several freshly filled graves. Wu would then throw his arm affectionately over the victim's shoulder and tell him of the benefits to be derived from joining the puppet régime or contributing a liberal sum to its support." Powell, *My Twenty-Five Years in China*, 336.

50. Pan Ling, *Old Shanghai*, 147–149.

51. Section One, which became Zhongtong, was directed by Xu Enzeng. Section Two, which absorbed Section Three and became Juntong in August 1938, was directed by Dai Li.

52. Yeh, "The Liu Geqing Affair," 27–28; Zhang Weihan, "Dai Li yu 'Juntong ju,'" 145; Mao Xiaotian and Wang Mengyun, "Wang Wei 'tegong zongbu' qishiliu hao de jianli," 259–262. See also Pan Ling, *Old Shanghai*, 120.

53. Ch'en Li-fu Materials, "Ting Mo-ts'un File," 1.

54. Nanjing shi dang'an guan, *Shenxun Wang wei hanjian bilu*, 671.

55. Ch'en Li–fu Materials, "Ting Mo-ts'un File," 2–3.

56. Yeh, "Dai Li and the Liu Geqing Affair," 551.

57. Boyle reads his name as Haruke Keiin. Lieutenant Colonel Haruke eventually became chief of the China Section of the Intelligence Division of the General Staff, and in 1944 proposed negotiating a separate peace settlement with the Communists in Yan'an. Boyle, *China and Japan at War, 1937–1945*, 282, 312. The intelligence chiefs of the ingrown China Section were not the cream of the General Staff. Kitaoka Shin'ichi, "China Experts in the Army," 343.

58. Yeh, "Dai Li and the Liu Geqing Affair," 552. See also Shi Yuanhua, "Li Shiqun," 436–441.

59. The Li–Ding counterintelligence group moved first to 67 Daxi Road (today 665 West Yan'an Road), and then, as its numbers expanded, to a Western-style residence off of what is now Jiangsu Road. After Li and Ding moved to 76 Jessfield Road, which was the former mansion of General Chen Tiaoyuan (head of the Nationalist Military Advisors Council), "76" became a metonym for the puppet secret service. Shanghai shi difangzhi bangongshi, *Shanghai cidian*, 212.

60. Yeh, "Dai Li and the Liu Geqing Affair," 555.

61. Or so both men claimed. "Deposition of Dan Pau Nyi," 4; "Deposition of Ping Foh Chang," 4–5; "Statement of Dan Pao Yee," 5–6; "Further Statement of Ping Foo Chang," 5–8; "How the Foreign Minister Was Assassinated"; Qiao Jiacai, *Dai Li jiangjun he tade tongzhi*, 1:14–17.

62. "Further Statement of Dan Pao Yee," 1–2; "Further Statement of Ping Foo Chang," 7; "Deposition of Dan Pau Nyi," 4.

63. "Deposition of Ping Foh Chang," 5–6; "Deposition of Dan Pau Nyi," 4–5; "Japanese Arrest Nine Men Detailed by Chungking [Chongqing] for Assassination Work," *ZR*, 9 Nov. 1939, transl. in SMP, D-9037, 9/11/39.

64. Shanghai Municipal Police, D-9037, 1/7/39; *XSB*, 9 Nov. 1939, clipped in

SMP, D-9037, 9/11/39; and *ST,* 10 Nov. 1939, clipped in SMP, D-9037, 10/11/39.

65. The Shanghai Municipal Police also took a third man, Tan Baocheng, into custody. He turned out to be Tan Baoyi's brother, but he was only a visitor, had nothing to do with Juntong, and was quickly released. "Deposition of Dan Pau Nyi," 5; "Deposition of Ping Foh Chang," 6.

66. See depositions in SMP, D-9037, 30/6/39. Ping Fuchang was using an alias, Wang Yanbin, but his true identity was quickly uncovered.

67. SMP, D-9037, 3/7/39.

68. For a chilling personal account of the routineness of torture and murder by the Kempeitai, see Cook and Cook, *Japan at War,* 152–157.

69. "Deposition of Guo Zhiliang (Koh Tszu Liang)," SMP, D-9037, 26/3/39, 1–5.

70. SMP, D-9037, 17/3/39; NCDN, 18 March 1939, clipped in ibid., 30/3/39.

71. SMP, D-9037, 17/3/39.

72. Ibid., 18/3/39.

73. Ibid., 22/3/39.

74. "Deposition of Shao Fusheng (Zau Foo Sung)," SMP, D-9037, 26/3/39, 1.

75. Ibid., 2.

76. The Chinese detective said his name was May Yeu Vung (Mao Youwen). Mao was obviously working for the Japanese on the side, and it is surprising that he identified himself to Shao since he must have known that the Chinese prisoner was only in Japanese custody "under receipt" from the Shanghai Municipal Police, and would have to be returned alive by 25 March 1939. When Shao later told Detective Sub-Inspector John Crighton about Mao's presence during the interrogation, Crighton identified him as Mao Youwen, the DSI in charge of Chinese detectives at the Sinza Station. SMP, D-9037, 26/3/39.

77. "Deposition of Shao Fusheng (Zau Foo Sung)," 3.

78. Ibid., 4.

79. SMP, D-9037, 26/3/39.

80. On 12 May, Shao Fusheng tried to hang himself in his cell at Central Station, but the cloth strip he had fashioned into a noose broke. Deemed "mentally unbalanced" and subsequently hospitalized, he was released from SMP custody on 21 July 1939. Ibid., D-9037, 26/3/39, 15/5/39, and 22/7/39.

81. "It now transpires that the Japanese Gendarmerie do not want these men under those conditions." Ibid., 17/7/39.

82. Whether this was close to the piece goods shop on rue Frélupt where Tan Baoyi stayed with his cousin, I do not know.

83. Ibid., 11/10/39. According to Wen-hsin Yeh, Wang Luzhao was captured by the Japanese around this same time, prompting Dai Li to think that Wang Tianmu had turned coat. Wang Luzhao somehow managed to keep his captors from knowing who he really was, and he later ended up as chief of police in Hong Kong.

84. For some of these rumors, see NCH, 9 Sept. 1939, 1. The Japanese attributed leadership of the terrorists to the Communist leader Pan Hannian and to Dai Li. Pan was either supposed to be in Jinhua, Zhejiang, the base of the cultural

operations of the Eighth Route Army; or hiding in the foreign concessions along with Dai Li and Liu Zhe of the CC Clique. *XSB*, 25 Sept. 1939, transl. in SMP, D-8615, 31/1/40; see also 22/9/39, 1. The Shanghai Municipal Police discounted all claims by the Japanese and puppets that the Chinese Communist Party, the Blue Shirts, and the CC Clique were linked in a terrorist conspiracy. SMP, D-8615, 22/9/39, 1.

85. SMP, D-9037, 30/10/39. The rue Frélupt document was cited in the letter from the Japanese Military Police to Major K. M. Bourne, commissioner of the Shanghai Municipal Police, in the formal request dated 6 October 1939, in ibid., 7/10/39.

86. Ibid., 19/10/39.

87. "How the Foreign Minister Was Assassinated."

88. "Further Statement of Dan Pao Yee," 3–4.

89. "Further Statement of Ping Foh Chong (II)," 3.

90. Ibid.

91. "Further Statement of Ping Foh Chong (III)," 1.

92. Ibid.

93. "Further Statement of Dan Pao Yee," 4.

94. "Further Statement of Ping Foh Chong (III)," 2.

95. "Further Statement of Dan Pao Yee," 2.

96. Ibid., 4.

97. Ibid.; "Further Statement of Ping Foh Chong (III)," 2.

98. "How the Foreign Minister Was Assassinated."

99. "Further Statement of Ping Foo Chang," 7.

100. Ibid., D-9037, 8/11/39.

101. Ibid., 26/10/39.

102. SMP, D-9037, 30/10/39.

103. Ibid., 10/11/39.

104. Ibid., 21/6/40. On 12 December 1939, a party of Shanghai Municipal Police, acting at the request of the Japanese Military Police, raided Room 33 of a lodging house at 85 Lane 510, Elgin Road. Among others seized was Xu Zhihao, age thirty-six. At Crime Branch headquarters, Xu identified his own photograph in a book produced by Sub-Lieutenant Katoda and admitted to being a lookout during the murder of Chen Lu. Xu Zhihao was later handed over to the Japanese for sentencing. Ibid., 13/12/39 and 14/12/29.

105. *NCH*, 11 Oct. 1939, 1.

106. It should be noted, however, that two prominent collaborators, Yang Jinhai and Luo Zhibin, were assassinated on 9 November; and a Japanese textile mill manager was killed on 19 November. *SB*, 10 Nov. 1939, 9, and 21 Nov. 1939, 7.

8. Terrorism and crime

1. Yeh, "Dai Li and the Liu Geqing Affair," 553. A few Western journalists, such as Jack Belden, had vague inklings of these developments, including attacks

on underground Communists. Epstein, *The Unfinished Revolution in China,*
135.

2. BFOR, FO371-24663, 3/4/40; *SB,* 13 Dec. 1939, 8.

3. There is a roster of two such units, plus the Zhoujiacun branch police station,
   in the Shanghai Municipal Archives. It contains seventy-eight certificates
   (*baozhengshu*) for officers and members of these units in June 1940, including
   the names of guarantors (with store chops when possible) and photographs of
   the individual plainclothesmen. SMA, Wang 18.286—Wang wei Shanghai
   tebie shi Huxi qu gongshu—"Zhoujiacun fensuo guanyu ziweituan fen dui
   zhong renmian" [Personnel changes in the two self-defense guards units and
   the Zhoujiacun Precinct Station], June 1940, 1–76. At that time, the other
   nonheadquarters Special Services Group consisted of 250 members, mainly
   armed with Mauser pistols, stationed at 55 Jessfield Road, 35 Edinburgh
   Road, 17 Meihuali off of Edinburgh Road, 818 Yuyuan Road, and 1
   Zongyueli off of Jessfield Road. SMP, D-8155(1), 31/1/41.

4. BFOR, FO37124663, enclosure no. 2 in dispatch no. 268, 2/5/40. Earlier, on
   16 April the British and U.S. diplomatic authorities brought to the attention of
   the Japanese consul a confidential police report indicating that there would be
   attempts instigated by the Japanese to assassinate newly elected members of
   the Shanghai Municipal Council. *FRUS 1940, 735.*

5. This particular case concerned the killing of the director of the Central China
   Marine Products Industrial Company on Gordon Road on 6 May. BFOR,
   FO371-24663, enclosure no. 3. Perhaps more troubling to the Japanese was
   the assassination of one of their top agents, Shanghai Municipal Police Superintendent Tan Shaoliang, on 14 April 1940, by a member of a Chinese Nationalist guerrilla unit. Ibid., 3502/31/10 (1 May 1940).

6. See, for the Yokohama Specie Bank and customs funds, Michael, "The Significance of Puppet Governments," 408–409. "In protracted negotiations with
   Britain during 1938 and 1939 Japan represented her client régime's in arguing
   for [the puppets' gaining access to these funds]. . . . But at the same time she
   had her own interests to look out for: early in the war Britain's Sir Frederick
   Maze, Inspector General of Customs, had taken steps to freeze the payment of
   . . . Chinese debts to Japan and these funds were sorely needed as Japan's war
   costs rose in 1938. When it came to an application of force to overcome
   British opposition, Japan picked the issue closest to home—unfreezing the
   blocked debt payments. By May 1938 funds from the Chinese customs were
   flowing into the Yokohama Specie Bank. . . . Japan was not prepared to
   apply similar force on behalf of her puppets . . . [who] continued to be denied
   the customs revenue that alone could have eased their financial plight." Boyle,
   China and Japan at War, 1937–1945, 114–115. See also Clifford, *Retreat
   from China,* 56–61.

7. NCDN, 11 May 1940, clipped in BFOR, FO371-24663.

8. BFOR, FO371-24663. See also *FRUS 1940, 736–737.*

9. *FRUS 1940, 737–738.* Cordell Hull radioed the U.S. Embassy in Tokyo on 18
   May, and on 4 June 1940 Ambassador Grew and Sir Robert L. Craigie made
   representations to the Japanese Foreign Office in this regard. Ibid., 738–739.

10. Ibid., 740–741.
11. Some of the reasons given for this drop were the drain on Chongqing's special service funds, the movement of anti-Japanese elements to Nanjing, increased action of the Special Services Corps at "76," and the effectiveness of the Japanese Military Police Special Services Section. Domei statement in BFOR, FO371-24663. There had been unconfirmed hints of a covert momentary truce between Dai Li and Zhou Fohai or Li Shiqun. Xu Zongyao, "Zuzhi Juntong Beiping zhan heping qiyi de qianqian houhou," 132.
12. Mu was general manager of the newspaper *Guomin xinwen* and a special deputy in Shanghai of Wang Jingwei's Ministry of Propaganda, which sponsored a campaign to "expound and propagate theories of peace" among the city's residents by handing out illustrated pamphlets and cartoon books (*lianhuan hua*). Qin Xiaoyi, *Zhonghua minguo zhongyao shiliao chubian—Dui Ri zhanzheng shiqi. Di liu bian: Kuilei zuzhi*, 852. Li Shiqun offered a reward of $10,000 for help in solving the case. Shao was the manager of the Daguangshe (Great Illumination Society). BFOR, FO371-24663, F3938 (20/8/40).
13. Davidson-Houston, *Yellow Creek*, 164.
14. BFOR, letter from Consul General A. H. George to the Ambassador, in FO371-24663 (16/9/40). Another factor was the dispute in August 1940 between Japan and the United States over which forces should replace the British troops then evacuating Shanghai. The argument led the United States to ban the export of all scrap metal to Japan on 24 September, which was followed three days later by the signing of the Tripartite Pact between Japan, Germany, and Italy. Heinrichs, "Franklin D. Roosevelt and the Risks of War," 154.
15. CSDCF, 893.00 P.R. Shanghai/144 (Sept. 1940), 18.
16. BFOR, letter from Consul General A. H. George to the Ambassador, in FO371-24663 (16/9/40).
17. Ibid.
18. Ibid.; *CWR*, 8 Feb. 1941, 330.
19. *CWR*, 21 Sept. 1940, 92–93.
20. SMP, D-420, 10/10/40. See also Heppner, *Shanghai Refuge*, 73–76.
21. CSDCF, 893.00 P.R. Shanghai/144 (Sept. 1940), 17.
22. Ibid. The Shanghai Municipal Police's Special Branch by then had developed a system of distinctive forms listing pertinent details of handbill distribution and relevant sections of the criminal code. SMP, D-420, 12/10/40.
23. *RWSSZ*, 63–64.
24. BFOR, FO371-24663; Zhang Weihan, "Dai Li yu 'Juntong ju,'" 138–139; CSDCF, 893.00 P.R. Shanghai/145 (Oct. 1940), 15; *CWR*, 11 Oct. 1940, 168. A $50,000 reward was put on Zhu's head and the Japanese launched a manhunt throughout all of occupied China, but Zhu was never caught. *RWSSZ*, 64–65; Cheng Shuwei and Liu Fuxiang, *Daoguang jianying*, 168–174.
25. *CWR*, 16 Nov. 1940.
26. *CWR*, 18 Jan. 1941, 229; Shi Yuanhua, "Chen Gongbo," 176. After Wang

Jingwei died on 10 November 1944 Zhou finally became mayor of Shanghai. Boorman, *Biographical Dictionary of Republican China*, 408.

27. Ibid., 16 Nov. 1940, 352. Zhou Fohai much later, in early 1945 after Wang Jingwei's death, took over the Shanghai police with the full knowledge of Dai Li in Chongqing. Zhang Yun, "Zhou Fohai," 252–253.

28. CWR, 11 Jan. 1941, 198, and 18 Jan. 1941, 229.

29. CWR, 11 Jan. 1941, 199.

30. Oakes, *White Man's Folly*, 357–358.

31. CWR, 25 Jan. 1941, 272.

32. Finch, *Shanghai and Beyond*, 310. On 8 January 1941, a typical Shanghai kidnapping occurred. Three hoodlums—one of them dressed in a police uniform without a badge number—stopped the automobile of a Mr. Wang, owner of the Fuxing Dyestuff Company, on Avenue Foch. They ejected the chauffeur and two of Wang's relatives, and drove Wang off to Fahua village, a "famous hoodlum hangout," where he was held for ransom. CWR, 22 Mar. 1941, 90. The gangster in uniform could easily have been a policeman. Captain Chen Yawen of the Huxi district police was convicted of committing numerous kidnappings and robberies in the First Special Court one week after the kidnapping described just above. CWR, 25 Jan. 1941, 272. Nine days after this trial, a Chinese police constable attached to the Bubbling Well Police Station was charged with renting guns to robbers for $47 apiece. They returned the guns to him when they were done. CWR, 15 Feb. 1941, 387.

33. One letter to the editor read, "Since the occupation of the Shanghai outskirts by the Japanese invaders and their 'running dogs,' headed by Wang Ching-wei [Jingwei], this city which was formerly known as a metropolis of peace and order has now become a place of horror." CWR, 29 Mar. 1941, 109.

34. CWR, 25 Jan. 1941, 273. Homes were frequently ransacked by gangs of five to six men.

35. Ibid., 272; NCH, 19 Feb. 1941, 285.

36. BWOR, Shanghai summary no. 74, 18/7/41, WO208-246A.

37. CWR, 8 Feb. 1941, 342; and see also 25 Jan. 1941, 273.

38. CWR, 11 Jan. 1941, 198.

39. The strength of the Shanghai municipal government Police Bureau under the Wang Jingwei régime in January 1941 was 7,501. This was a slight decline from the preceding roster of 7,801. Of the total, 6,381 were constables. SMP, D-8115(1), 24/1/41. For a complete roster of department and station commanders, see ibid., 3/10/40. For the organization and regulations of the Shanghai municipal government's Western Shanghai (Huxi) police, see SMA, Wang 18.16, "Wang wei guomin zhengfu neizhengbu deng danwei fenbu geji jingcha jiguan zuzhi fagui" [Organization and regulations of each police organ under the Wang puppet government's Ministry of the Interior], Jan. 1940 to Dec. 1942, 11–12, 24–25.

40. CWR, 11 Jan. 1941, 198–199.

41. Shanghai Municipal Council, *Report for the Year 1937*, 85; CWR, 28 Nov. 1936, 437.

42. *CWR,* 28 Nov. 1936, 437, and 12 Dec. 1936, 68.

43. *CWR,* 5 July 1941, 155. The total number of Japanese subjects living in Shanghai and its environs on 1 June 1941 was 138,020. Of these, 87,277 lived in Shanghai proper: 79,192 Japanese, 5,144 Koreans, and 2,941 Formosans. *CWR,* 5 July 1941, 155. Once full-scale war broke out, Japanese adventurers—including vagabond soldiers of fortune (*rônin*)—rushed to China. Between 1 June 1938 and 1 June 1939, 220,000 people embarked at Kobe "to seek prosperity on the continent." *Japan Chronicle,* 1 June 1939, cited in Taylor, *The Struggle for North China,* 149. See also Boyle, *China and Japan at War, 1937–1945,* 40.

44. The Shanghai Municipal Council consisted of fourteen members: seven Anglo-Saxon men, five Chinese, and two Japanese. The latter tried to increase their representatives to three in 1935, but the British taipans dissuaded them. A year later the Japanese simply nominated three councilors, planning to vote one of the seven white members out. This would have created a majority of Chinese and Japanese councilors. "It was the yellow peril—Asia for the Asiatics. And the British and American communities decided to fight for an 'international front' of seven white men while the fighting was good." British and U.S. ratepayers voted en bloc for the white race, and the status quo was temporarily preserved. The election was declared invalid, because the British officers in charge of the election had overlooked one ballot box of 323 votes, mostly representing Japanese residents' responses. But the Japanese still did not have the numbers to win, and so withdrew their third candidate. At an ensuing banquet Mr. Hayashi, head of the Japanese street unions, cut his finger and wrote in blood on a piece of paper: "I assume full responsibility for what has happened." Hauser, *Shanghai: City for Sale,* 287–290.

45. *CWR,* 1 Feb. 1941, 291.

46. Japanese landlords paid the municipal taxes themselves, passing on prorated costs to their tenants. Because the British and Americans' voting power resulted from numerous ownerships, the Japanese arranged for tenants to pay rates themselves and thus qualify for voting rights. "In the greatest secrecy, British and American properties were subdivided in a similar way, and even in ways that the Japanese had not dreamed of. These new voting powers were, by arrangement, dumped on the Registrar at the latest possible moment before the 1938 municipal elections, so that the Japanese were confronted with a *fait accompli,* with no time for a counter attack, just when they thought they were going to have everything their own way. To say that they were enraged would be putting it mildly." Collar, *Captive in Shanghai,* 2–3.

47. *CWR,* 1 Feb. 1941, 294–295.

48. CSDCF, 893.00 P.R. Shanghai/182 (July 1940), 22; *CWR,* 16 Nov. 1940, 352. The puppet government had been pressing the Shanghai Municipal for the Chinese land records since March 1939. Clifford, *Retreat from China,* 109.

49. The Japanese invasion had restricted Jardine's shipping along the China coast (although some claimed that Jardine's was making huge profits by ferrying Japanese troops between Japan and the mainland), and shipments of raw silk and cotton did not always get through to Jardine mills. The British and

Chinese Corporation (one of Jardine's financial subsidiaries) had a monopoly selling supplies to China's longest railway line from Shanghai's North Station to Mukden. Sales of railway equipment had languished since the Japanese seized the Chinese line in 1937. *CWR*, 16 Nov. 1940, 351.

50. The only possible bank lenders were either the Yokohama Specie Bank (which sequestered customs funds) or Wang Jingwei's central bank (which was flooding the countryside with worthless paper currency).

51. *CWR*, 1 Feb. 1941, 292.

52. Ibid., 292–293.

53. He was referred to in the Japanese press as a man "compelled to take desperate action for a noble cause against the self-complacent attitude of British and American Council officials." Ibid., 295.

54. Ibid., 294.

55. "It was a striking victory for Shanghai's old guard vested interests; a striking victory for Western susceptibilities outraged by the shooting affray on January 28; and, most of all, it was a victory for the senseless system of race and nationalism by which the Shanghai Municipal Council's 'pivot boys' have managed to retain their well-paid posts at the cost of those who can afford them least at a time when they are hardest hit." *CWR*, 8 Feb. 1941, 333. See also *CWR*, 10 May 1941, 324.

9. Rackets

1. *CWR*, 8 Feb. 1941, 330; *MG*, 12 Feb. 1941, 32.

2. *MG*, 12 Feb. 1941, 29.

3. The official language of the WASP was Chinese.

4. However, there were two additions planned: a reserve unit of 78 riot police plus another group of 131 seconded from the city police. Thereafter the strength of WASP was not to be altered without the agreement of the Shanghai Municipal Government and the Shanghai Municipal Council. Ibid., 29, 34. For the jurisdiction of each of the five divisions, see *CWR*, 8 Feb. 1941, 331.

5. *MG*, 12 Feb. 1941, 30; *CWR*, 8 Feb. 1941, 331.

6. CSDCF, 893.00 P.R. Shanghai/149 (Feb. 1941), 13–14.

7. *MG*, 12 Feb. 1941, 31–34; *CWR*, 8 Feb., 1941, 330–333.

8. *MG*, 12 Feb. 1941, 35.

9. *CWR*, 1 Mar. 1941, 462; Oakes, *White Man's Folly*, 357. Earlier in February, the puppet police had opened an Anti-Opium Section to license addicts and conduct the public sale of opium. Shanghai Municipal Police, D-8155(1), 13/2/41.

10. *CWR*, 8 Feb. 1941, 331, and 8 Mar. 1941, 22; *MG*, 12 Feb. 1941, 29; "Shanghai Mayor Keeps His Promise to the Public," 2.

11. Superintendents R. C. Hall and J. B. Clissold were nominated by the Shanghai Municipal Police to be deputy commissioners; A. H. Chamberlain was named the liaison officer. *CWR*, 8 Feb. 1941, 330; *NCH*, 19 Mar. 1941, 444.

12. *CWR*, 22 Mar. 1941, 87, and 29 Mar. 1941, 112; *Annual Report of the Shanghai Municipal Council, 1939*, 100. Shanghai Municipal Police Com-

missioner K. M. Bourne and Deputy Commissioner J. B. Clissold be-
grudgingly permitted Chief Inspector Blenkinsop and Detective Inspector
Tilton to resign from the WASP after they requested transfers because of the
bribes paid by gamblers into a police slush fund controlled by C. C. Pan. SMP,
file #F5000/5/11, 22 May 1941, in SMA, U-102-5-15/7. I am grateful to Dr.
Robert Bickers of Nuffield College, Oxford, for sharing photocopies of this
valuable file with me.

13. The French Concession authorities, meanwhile, permitted gangsters close to
"76" to open a gambling casino and opium den at 43 route Courbet in
November. Ibid., 16 Nov. 1940, 352.

14. *CWR,* 12 Apr. 1941, 186.

15. Ibid., 187.

16. Ibid.

17. Ibid.

18. *CWR,* 18 Jan. 1941, 238.

19. The Silver Palace casino was operated by a foreign syndicate under the name
of the Portuguese Commercial Enterprise, registered by Jose Maria Botelho.
The casino had six rooms, four outfitted for gambling and two for opium
smoking. The casino was raided on 2 February 1941. *CWR,* 15 Feb. 1941,
386, and see also 18 Jan. 1941, 238.

20. *CWR,* 29 Mar. 1941, 121.

21. CSDCF, 893.00 P.R. Shanghai/150 (Mar. 1941), 138.

22. "Shanghai Mayor Keeps His Promise to the Public," 2–4. One of the grandest
of these earlier casinos was the Asia Club, which had been opened under
Sterling Fessenden and then was closed when Consul General Gauss complained to the Japanese consul general about the club's alleged Japanese connections. The Asia Club was reopened under the protection of the same
puppet officials who operated the China Club on Great Western Road. *CWR,*
16 Nov., 1940, 352.

23. "Within a few weeks more than a dozen gambling houses and opium smoking
divans were opened. Each had its own armed guards, one house boasting of
four hundred, each armed with a Mauser." Ibid., 351.

24. Through Formosan connections close to General Doihara, Du Yuesheng was
able to obtain gambling licenses as well. Marshall, "Opium and Gangsterism
in Nationalist China," 39.

25. *CWR,* 16 Nov. 1940, 351; see 18 Jan. 1941, 228.

26. *CWR,* 18 Jan. 1941, 229.

27. *CWR,* 8 Feb. 1941, 330. See, for the income of the special organ at "76,"
Haruke Keiin, *Shanghai tero kôsaku 76 gô,* 76–78.

28. *CWR,* 18 Jan. 1941, 229; Madancy, "Propaganda versus Practice," 27; Boyle,
China and Japan at War, 1937–1945, 115.

29. *CWR,* 11 Jan. 1941, 198, and 18 Jan. 1941, 229 and 238. The Russians who
ran this club were also connected with a new gambling house on the seven-
teenth floor of the Broadway Mansions.

30. *CWR,* 11 Jan. 1941.

31. *CWR*, 18 Jan. 228. A photograph of the entrance to the club notes that parents are welcome to bring their infants to the casino. The club's daily expenses came to more than $70,000, which was an indirect indication of the casino's vast profits.

32. *CWR*, 15 Feb. 1941, 386–387; 22 Feb. 1941, 414–415; 12 Apr. 1941, 187.

33. *CWR*, 22 Feb. 1941, 414. There had been another spectacular shoot-out on 4 February at a gambling casino just a block beyond the Settlement boundary on Yuyuan Road in the badlands. Japanese gamblers, who believed they had been cheated, called in puppet police who engaged the casino's guards in a gun battle. Thirty-odd gamblers stampeded for the door, breaking it down. Bullets left three of them dying on the floor and wounded a number of others. *CWR*, 8 Feb. 1941, 342, and 22 Feb. 1941, 415; CSDCF, 893.00 P.R. Shanghai/149 (Feb. 1941), 14.

34. *CWR*, 12 Apr. 1941, 186, 208.

35. *CWR*, 22 Feb. 1941, 414.

36. *CWR*, 28 June 1941, 108–109.

37. However, crime rates were down in the French Concession in March 1941. The decline was attributed to the installation of new movable barbed wire barricades that were placed across strategic roads into the International Settlement whenever crimes were committed in the Concession. *CWR*, 22 Mar. 1941, 90.

38. *CWR*, 8 Feb. 1941, 342; 15 Feb. 1941, 387; 22 Feb. 1941, 416; 8 Mar. 1941, 22; 22 Mar. 1941, 90.

39. Oakes, *White Man's Folly*, 380–381.

40. *CWR*, 15 Feb. 1941, 387; 22 Mar. 1941, 90; 5 Apr. 1941, 162. "We have often heard of terroristic organs set up by the Wang gang known as '76' '75' '82' and '13' (branches of the latter organ are known to all the people in Japanese occupied areas as headquarters from which agents have been dispatched to kidnap rich men and murder the innocent), from which places deadly claws have been stretched to take away lives of the innocent for purposes of extortion or those of their rivals in order to seize more power." Letter from Fan Jih-tse, in *CWR*, 29 Mar. 1941, 109. The Gold Stock Exchange was a Nanjing-sponsored establishment. *NCH*, 28 May 1941, 332.

41. "'Gestapo-Style' Terror," 111. According to Domei, more than forty Chongqing agents had been infiltrated into Shanghai in February 1941, many slipping in from Hong Kong. *NCH*, 26 Feb. 1941, 327.

42. See, for example, the kidnapping of Pan Tse-chuen, the forty-two-year-old comprador of Jardine, Matheson & Co., who was seized by armed men from "76" on 11 January 1941. Jardine officials—perhaps responding to Keswick's desire not to anger the Japanese—said no political motives were involved and that money (perhaps as much as $3 million ransom) was the only motive. *NCH*, 12 Jan. 1941, 294.

43. *NCH*, 8 Feb. 1941, 342.

44. BFOR, enclosure no. 4 in FO 371-24663.

45. "[Li Shiqun] last week washed his hands of the unlovely thing he fathered at

76 Jessfield Road, headquarters of Nanking's 'Gestapo,' and hideout for the foulest collection of desperadoes and cutthroats ever assembled in China outside of Ward Road Jail." *CWR*, 18 Jan. 1941, 228.

46. SMP, D-8155(1), 24/1/41. The Japanese-controlled *Xin shenbao* reported that there had been plans to move the nucleus of "76" to Nanjing, which would have kept Li Shiqun in a stronger position; but not until August 1941, when Li was pushed aside, did any major reorganization of "76" occur. *NCH*, 22 Jan. 1941, 128.

47. These were the Loh Kuo Hotel at 346 Avenue Haig, the China Club at 29 Tifeng Road, the Hwa Loh Hotel at 792 Yuyuan Road, and the Union Club at 6 Tifeng Road. SMP, D-8039A, 15/3/41.

48. Lu Ying had been promoted from colonel to general in September 1940. In December he had nearly lost his job, partly because of his rivalry with Li Shiqun and partly because Chen Gongbo was unhappy with his reluctance to curb gambling. A timely gift of several armored cars to Zhou Fohai and Ding Mocun among others helped keep him at his Shanghai post instead of being transferred to the civil governorship of Zhejiang province. SMP, D-8155(1), 15/9/40, 30/12/40.

49. Ibid.

50. Sun Guoqun, "Lun jiu Shanghai changji zhidu de fazhan he tedian," 4. The venue of prostitution changed slightly, however. The activities of "travel agencies" or "guide services" (*xiangdao she*), which supplied female escorts, "took over" the hotels. *SS*, 17 May 1939, 23.

51. "During the last half of 1938, more than 35 per cent of all capital invested in new business in Tientsin [Tianjin] was invested in new opium shops and dens." "Opium Profits in North China," 552.

52. This is based on reports from U.S. Treasury Agent Nicholson, who was sent to China, Taiwan, and the Philippines by Harry Anslinger. McWilliams, "Covert Connections," 660; Parssinen and Meyer, "International Narcotics Trafficking in the Early Twentieth Century," 49.

53. SMP, D-8039A, 15/3/41.

54. *CWR*, 28 June 1941, 108.

55. *CWR*, 23 Aug. 1941, 361.

56. *CWR*, 28 June 1941, 108.

57. *CWR*, 108–109. In July 1941 the manager of the Argentine at 625 Avenue Haig, where gambling had gone on for several weeks in the second-story rooms, published a notice in the newspaper that declared his establishment had no connection with the gambling den upstairs. *CWR*, 12 July 1941, 173. For Deng Zuyou's earlier position in the Reform Government as a department director (*sizhang*) in the Ministry of Interior, see Qin Xiaoyi, *Zhonghua minguo zhongyao shiliao chubian—Dui Ri zhanzheng shiqi. Di liu bian: Kuilei zuzhi*, 134.

58. *CWR*, 12 July 1941, 109.

59. *CWR*, 28 June 1941, 2 Aug. 1941, 269.

60. *CWR*, 26 July 1941, 234.

61. "Shanghai Mayor Keeps His Promise to the Public," 2.

62. *CWR*, 12 July 1941, 173.
63. *CWR*, 2 Aug. 1941, 269; 6 Sept. 1941, 11.
64. *CWR*, 25 Jan. 1941, 272.
65. Ibid.
66. *CWR*, 22 Feb. 1941, 416.
67. "It is rumored locally that a considerable number of Chungking [Chongqing] agents have recently arrived here." CSDCF, 893.108, 26 Feb. 1941, 292.
68. *CWR*, 1 Mar. 1941, 462.
69. *CWR*, 15 Mar. 1941, 62.
70. CSDCF, 893.108, 15 Mar. 1941, 294.
71. *CWR*, 22 Mar. 1941, 90.
72. Ibid.
73. *CWR*, 5 Apr. 1941, 162.
74. CSDCF, 893.108, 10 Apr. 1941, 307. On the night of 4 April, the Shanghai Municipal Police raided an address in the Central district and arrested sixteen Chinese, several of whom admitted to being Chongqing agents. Revolvers and hand grenades were also seized. *CWR*, 5 Apr. 1941, 306.
75. *CWR*, 19 Apr. 1941, 230.
76. Ibid., 231; *NCH*, 16 Apr. 1941, 92.
77. *CWR*, 3 May 1941, 289; *NCH*, 30 Apr. 1941, 171.
78. *CWR*, 3 May 1941, 289.
79. Coble, "Chinese Capitalists," 6. As Coble points out, many Shanghai capitalists had no choice but to collaborate, having been abducted by the Japanese Military Police or taken into 76 Jessfield Road. See, for example, the cases of Woo Ching-yu [Wu Jingyu] and Yu Shao-yin [Yu Shaoyin]. *CWR*, 2 Aug. 1941, 280; *CP*, 19 Apr. 1946, 1.

10. Terrorist wars

1. Ma Guangren, "Ri wei zai Shanghai de xinwen huodong gaishu," 171–173. The Shanghai Municipal Police continued to censor movies. During 1939 the police of the International Settlement censored 1,275 films, including documentaries and newsreels. Most of these were from the United States. *Annual Report of the Shanghai Municipal Council, 1939*, 104–105.
2. Fu, "Intellectual Resistance in Shanghai," 4–5; *CWR*, 11 Jan. 1941, 198.
3. Fu, *Passivity, Resistance, and Collaboration*, 114–115; Gunn, *Unwelcome Muse*, 21.
4. Ma Guangren, "Ri wei zai Shanghai de xinwen huodong gaishu," 176; Fu, "Intellectual Resistance in Shanghai," 5; *CWR*, 17 Feb. 1938, 80–81; 26 Feb. 1938, 345; 5 Mar. 1938, 18. The letters were signed "Zhongyi tuan" (Loyal and Patriotic League). *CWR*, 19 Feb. 1938, 320. Samuel H. Chang, a native of Chaozhou married to the daughter of a well-known family living in Salt Lake City, had graduated from Haverford. Powell, *My Twenty-Five Years in China*, 337.
5. CSDCF, 893.00 P.R. Shanghai/142 (July 1940), 16. His death deeply shocked foreign newspapermen in Shanghai. Powell, *My Twenty-Five Years in China*,

337. On 22 July 1939, for example, a gang of gunmen from the badlands entered the offices of *Dawan bao* (Evening News) and of *Zhongmei ribao* (Chinese American Daily) and opened fire, wounding a dozen workers and killing one foreigner. *SB,* 23 July 1939, 9. Samuel Chang's close friend, T. Y. Lee, who was the assistant manager of the *Damei wanbao,* slept in the *Evening Post and Mercury* offices for a year after Chang's death, but in the end was shot in the back of the neck in broad daylight by a pro-Nanjing gunman on Avenue Edward VII on 23 June 1941. *CWR,* 28 June 1941, 125; *NCH,* 25 June 1941, 490. The night and literary editor of that same newspaper, Zhu Xinggong, had been shot and killed two years earlier by a pro-Nanjing assassin. *SB,* 31 Aug. 1939, 9; Gunn, *Unwelcome Muse,* 21–22.

6. Oakes, *White Man's Folly,* 363.
7. The foreigners included John Powell of the *China Weekly Review,* C. V. Starr and Randall Gould of the *Shanghai Evening Post and Mercury,* Carroll Alcott of the *China Press,* Hal Mills of *Huamei wanbao,* and J. A. E. Sanders-Bates of the University Press. Powell, *My Twenty-Five Years in China,* 338.
8. CSDCF, 893.00 P.R. Shanghai/142 (July 1940), 6–7.
9. *CWR,* 11 Jan. 1941, 198, and 15 Mar. 1941, 62; Jing Shenghong, *Minguo ansha yaoan,* 364.
10. Tao Juyin, *Tianliang qian de gudao,* 3. The Chinese translation of "badlands," *dai3tu3,* was derived from the word for scoundrel, ruffian, or thug, *dai3tu2,* For the steel doors, see Finch, *Shanghai and Beyond,* 311.
11. *NCH,* 4 June 1941, 371.
12. *CWR,* 11 Jan. 1941, 198; Zhang Weihan, "Dai Li yu 'Juntong ju,'" 145.
13. On the evening of September 13, a worker in the library of *Shen bao* took a book down from a shelf only to discover that it was a bomb, though thankfully a dud. A heavy charge of TNT had been concealed within the hollowed covers of three books pasted together into a single block. When the book was opened, the bomb failed to go off because the batteries wired to the charge had run down. "Political Terrorism Unabated Here," 93.
14. *NCH,* 8 Jan. 1941, 56.
15. *CWR,* 11 Jan. 1941, 198; *NCH,* 8 Jan. 1941, 56.
16. *CWR,* 11 Jan. 1941, 198, and 11 Oct. 1941, 168. The Shanghai Municipal Police hoped to use Tian's confession to close down 76 Jessfield Road. The murder of a Japanese sanatorium worker, Iwao Nishi, on 11 January on Nanking Road led the local Japanese newspapers to carry the usual bitter condemnation of the Settlement police and had the effect of neutralizing the diplomatic advantage secured by the Shanghai Municipal Police through the confession of the *Shen bao* terrorist. There was some suspicion on the part of the Shanghai Municipal Police that Japanese special services had set up the Iwao Nishi assassination as a diversion. *CWR,* 18 Jan. 1941, 229.
17. *CWR,* 8 Feb. 1941, 342, and 11 Oct. 1941, 168. Jin Huating was survived by a wife and seven children.
18. Zhang Weihan, "Dai Li yu 'Juntong ju,'" 145. See also *CWR,* 3 May 1941, 289; CSDCF, 893.108, 29 Apr. 1941, 315.
19. *CWR,* 19 Apr. 1941, 230.

20. The puppet press, and especially *Xin shenbao,* made much of the allegations that Yang Qi, the president of the First Special District Court, was selling confiscated opium until apprehended by the French police. *XSB,* 3 Sept. 1939, transl. in SMP, D-8826, 4/9/39.
21. BFOR, F-4387, 25/9/40, FO-371-24663. This coincided with the assassination of K. A. (Charles) Metzler, chairman of the Russian Emigrant Committee, who had been doing all he could to stiffen the French Concession and French consular authorities against turning the municipality lock, stock, and barrel over to the Japanese. The puppet régime was said to be "furiously drilling a new police force" to take over the French Concession at this time. "The Ivanov Murder," 97. See also CSDCF, 893.00 P.R. Shanghai/143 (Aug. 1940), 17–18; *CWR,* 11 Oct. 1941, 157; Ristaino, "White Russian and Jewish Refugees in Shanghai," 56–61; Ristaino, "Russian Emigration in Shanghai," 14–15.
22. Transl. in "Political Terrorism Unabated Here," 92.
23. Ibid.
24. In April 1941 the French municipal police and Nanjing, as represented by Sun Shao-kang [Sun Shaokang], president of the court, agreed that all gambling and opium smoking cases would be handled by the Second Special District Court. *CWR,* 19 Apr. 1941, 230.
25. *CWR,* 11 Oct. 1941, 168.
26. "'Gestapo-Style' Terror," 112.
27. *CWR,* 8 Feb. 1941, 342; *NCH,* 5 Feb. 1941, 210.
28. *CWR,* 8 Mar. 1941, 22.
29. *CWR,* 26 Apr. 1941, 267; *NCH,* 23 Apr. 1941, 140.
30. CSDCF, 893.108, Apr. 1941, 311–313.
31. *NCH,* 7 May 1941, 212; see also 14 May 1941, 251.
32. BWOR, Extract from Shanghai Intelligence Dispatch 258, 4/6/41, WO-208-246A. Up to then Judge Xu Weizeng had not yet been released by his kidnappers.
33. *CWR,* 3 May 1941, 289.
34. Lieu, "The Sino-Japanese Currency War," passim. The battle began in North China in March 1938 with the founding of the Federal Reserve Bank of China. Boyle, *China and Japan at War, 1937–1945,* 97–98 and 115.
35. Many observers viewed the attacks on Chongqing-controlled banks as a "frantic effort of Nanking to get recognition of their Central Reserve banknotes." *CWR,* 29 Mar. 1941, 121; Ch'eng Nai-shan, *The Banker,* 328.
36. "'Gestapo-Style' Terror," 111–112.
37. On 30 January 1941, unidentified gunmen killed Ki Ming-dah [Qi Mingda], manager of the Wei Nyeu Native Bank, which was believed to be connected with the Nanjing Central Reserve Bank, the currency-issuing organ of Wang Jingwei's government. *CWR,* 8 Feb. 1941, 342.
38. CSDCF, 893.108, 20 Feb. 1941, 291.
39. On 6 January 1941, the Shanghai branch of the Central Reserve Bank was established at Number 15 on the Bund, the address of the former Central Bank of China. Ch'eng Nai-shan, *The Banker,* 327.

40. The building was packed with Japanese and puppet guards, but most of those were concentrated in the part of the building housing officials. *CWR,* 22 Feb. 1941, 415, and 1 Mar. 1941, 462.
41. *NCH,* 26 Feb. 1941, 327.
42. Ibid.
43. *CWR,* 8 Mar. 1941, 22; CSDCF, 893.108, 22 Mar. 1941, 295.
44. *NCH,* 26 Mar. 1941, 483.
45. CSDCF, 893.108, 22 Mar. 1941, 295; " 'Gestapo-Style' Terror," 111; BWOR, Extract from Shanghai Naval and Military Intelligence Summary No. 7, 9/4/41, in WO-208-246A; *CWR,* 29 Mar. 1941, 121.
46. Quoted in CSDCF, 893.108, 24 Mar. 1941, 296.
47. CSDCF, 893.108, 25 Mar. 1941, 299; *CWR,* 29 Mar. 1941, 121.
48. *CWR,* 29 Mar. 1941, 121.
49. Ibid.
50. CSDCF, 893.108, 25 Mar. 1941, 299.
51. Ibid., 298.
52. Ibid., 27 Mar. 1941, 300.
53. Ibid., 29 Mar. 1941, 309.
54. *CWR,* 5 Apr. 1941, 162.
55. Ibid., 151.
56. Anonymous letter signed "A Banker," dated 22 Apr. 1941, in *CWR,* 26 Apr. 1941, 242. See also Ch'eng Nai-shan, *The Banker,* 333.
57. *CWR,* 26 Apr. 1941, 267; *NCH,* 23 Apr. 1941.
58. CSDCF, 893.108, 17 Apr. 1941, 308.
59. Anonymous letter signed "A Banker," dated 22 Apr. 1941, in *CWR,* 26 Apr. 1941, 242 and 267.
60. *CWR,* 26 Apr. 1941, 267.
61. Ibid.; CSDCF, 893.108, 22 Apr. 1941, 310; *NCH,* 23 Apr. 1941.
62. The owner of the bank, S. S. Pan, had been named a standing member of the Shanghai Municipal Council by the Nanjing government. *CWR,* 3 May 1941, 289.
63. CSDCF, 893.00 P.R. Shanghai/151 (Apr. 1941), 16.
64. Ibid., 108 30 (Apr. 1941), 316.
65. On 2 and 3 April 1941, members of the Loyal and Patriotic National Salvation Army (Zhongyi jiuguo jun) in Nanjing set off bombs in the Nanjing Theater and the Lidu Garden, causing twenty casualties. The Japanese army closed Nanjing's city gates on 5 April to all Chinese and sent out patrols that arrested eight members of Dai Li's group. BFOR, Dispatch no. 30, 8/4/41, from His Majesty's Consul at Nanjing, in FO-371-27735.
66. The bombs were exploded in the Ritz Theater on Haining Road and in the Tôa Theater on Chapoo Road. The Japanese thereafter stationed guards at movie entrances, and began to organize a vigilante group to help the military search houses north of Suzhou Creek. CSDCF, 893.108, 28 Apr. 1941, 314; *CWR,* 3 May 1941, 289; *NCH,* 30 Apr. 1941, 171.
67. " 'Gestapo-Style' Terror," 111.
68. *CWR,* 26 Apr. 1941, 267. French Concession Police at the Poste Foch

detected several armed individuals in a lane off route de Grochy. They ordered them to surrender and when the Chinese refused, the police opened fire, wounding two men and killing a third, who turned out to be General Lu Ying's bodyguard. *NCH,* 23 Apr. 1941.

69. *CWR,* 26 Apr. 1941, 267.
70. White, "Non-governmentalism in the Historical Development of Modern Shanghai," 49.
71. "Terrorism Again Hits Shanghai," 5.
72. Ibid.
73. Ibid., 6–7.
74. BWOR, Extract from Shanghai Summary no. 74, 18/7/41, WO-208-246A; CSDCF, 893.00 P.R. Shanghai/153 (June 1941), 15.
75. "Terrorism Again Hits Shanghai," 6–7.
76. Sam Sharrock, the acting chief inspector of the WASP pursued one of the assassins by motorcycle, and with the help of a Chinese constable, Liu Chuanyi, captured him. The Mauser pistol the murderer held was still hot. Ibid., 8. Sharrock and Liu were later awarded citations and silver cups by Deputy Commissioner J. B. Clissold and Commissioner C. C. Pan, chief of the WASP. For a picture of the awards ceremony, see the illustrated matter in *CWR,* 30 Aug. 1941.
77. *NCH,* 25 June 1941, 479.
78. "Terrorism Again Hits Shanghai," 9–10; BWOR, Extract from Shanghai Summary no. 74, 28/7/41, WO-208-246A.
79. The collaborationist periodical *Shanghai* once again claimed, in the wake of the Akagi killing, that the success of the WASP in "cleaning up" the badlands proved the efficacy of a joint multinational force of Chinese, Japanese, and Western police arrayed against pro-Chongqing terrorists. It noted that the Japanese and Chinese municipal authorities had repeatedly asked the foreign police to act in collaboration with them, "but for some reason or other" the foreign police failed to take advantage of "this offer of collaboration" and "with very sad results." "Terrorism Again Hits Shanghai," 10.
80. *CWR,* 22 Feb. 1941, 415, and 1 Mar. 1941, 462.
81. Yeh, "Dai Li and the Liu Geqing Affair," passim.
82. Cheng Yiming, "Juntong tewu zuzhi de zhenxiang," 231–233; Shen Zui, *Juntong neimu,* 83. Emily Hahn poked fun at the public rumors in the 1940s that Chiang Kai-shek was "in constant secret communication with Wang Ching-wei [Jingwei]," as an emblem of the Chinese obsession with espionage, but the truth was not far removed insofar as Dai Li was concerned. Hahn, *China to Me,* 96.
83. Zhang Weihan, "Dai Li yu 'Juntong ju,'" 146.
84. Liu Gong, "Wo suo zhidao de Zhongtong," 79; Zhu Zijia, *Wang Zhengquan de kaichang yu shouchang,* vol. 2, 68–74.
85. Xu Zongyao, "Zuzhi Juntong Beiping zhan heping qiyi de qianqian houhou," 206; Xu Zhaoming. "Hanjian Zhou Fohai goujie Juntong ji qi xiachang," 204–208; Fu, *Passivity, Resistance, and Collaboration,* 152–153.
86. Mao Dun, *Fushi,* passim; Nettelbeck, "Getting the Story Right," 261–265.

"*The Sorrow and the Pity* thus disclosed a structural tension: the transmission of a history so full of conflict depends on an alchemy whose secret no one possesses—not the actors, not the historians, not the filmmakers. Nor can anyone claim exclusive possession of the truth. The truth is partial in both senses. History is not the mortar out of which an artificial unity can be created—unless the mortar is mixed with that express purpose in mind." Rousso, *The Vichy Syndrome*, 114.

87. The series, based upon a work by Lao She, was called "Four Generations under the Same Roof" (Sishi tongtang). One major exception is the research group under Professor Huang Meizhen at Fudan University. See, e.g., Huang Meizhen and Zhang Yun, *Wang Jingwei guomin zhengfu chengli*, passim.

88. This discussion owes much to Fu Poshek's subtle analysis in *Passivity, Resistance, and Collaboration*, 162–165.

89. "Feeling guilty for not following the government into the materially backward interior to carry on the national resistance, Chinese writers in Shanghai identified human dignity with patriotic duty. How, they have appeared to have wondered, could they survive the occupation without betraying their country and thus themselves?" Fu, "Intellectual Resistance in Shanghai," 7.

11. Dimout

1. See, for example, the eleven-page "List of murder and attempted murder cases committed by the members of the Shanghai Blue Shirts Society" during 1939–1941 in SMP, D-4685(B), 1941.

2. "'Blue Shirts' to Suspend Anti-Japan Activities," 1.

3. Wakeman, "Confucian Fascism," passim; Snow, *The Battle for Asia*, 354.

4. The newspapers included *Zhongyang ribao* (Central China Daily News), *Guomin ribao* (Citizens Daily), *Bing bao* (Soldiers News), *Xin Zhongguo ribao* (New China Daily), and *Guo bao* (National News). The stories were published on 17 November 1941, and there are clippings and translations, including several pages of membership lists, in SMP, D-4685B, 29/11/41.

5. *CWR*, 19 Apr. 1941, 230. For the "model peace zone" plan, see Chen, *Making Revolution*, 81.

6. *CWR*, 10 May 1941, 324. In July 1941 Japanese naval spokesmen announced that three bands of Blue Shirts terrorists had slipped past Japanese patrols into the Japanese-occupied section of Shanghai. *CWR*, 5 July 1941, 155. See also, e.g., *NCH*, 22 Oct. 1941, 140.

7. *CWR*, 28 June 1941, 125.

8. Ibid.

9. *CWR*, 5 July 1941, 155.

10. *CWR*, 12 July 1941, 184.

11. Ibid.

12. Ibid.

13. Hua was shot on 13 July. *CWR*, 19 July 1941, 221.

14. *CWR*, 26 July 1941, 233.

15. This was probably done in revenge for the shooting of two of Wu Shibao's bodyguards by a U.S. policeman on duty at the barricade between the International Settlement and the badlands. Ibid., 233–234.
16. Ibid. *NCH,* 23 July 1941, 134.
17. *CWR,* 2 Aug. 1941, 280. See also *NCH,* 2 July 1941, 15.
18. *CWR,* 2 Aug. 1941, 280.
19. *NCH,* 13 Aug. 1941, 258.
20. *CWR,* 16 Aug. 1941, 332.
21. Ibid.
22. Ji's bank, the Ho cheng, mainly dealt in remittances between Shanghai and the interior of "Free China." *CWR,* 23 August 1941, 369; CSDCF, 893.00 P.R. Shanghai/154 (Aug. 1941), 13.
23. The article was republished after his death. See "Effect of Freezing on Interior Remittances," 369.
24. CSDCF, 893.00 P.R. Shanghai/108 (15 August 1941), 319; "Wave of Local Terror Rises," 361, 369.
25. "Wave of Local Terror Rises," 361, 373.
26. Ibid., 361; "Terrorist Killings," 393; CSDCF, 893.00 P.R. Shanghai/108 (26 Aug. 1941), 320.
27. "Wave of Local Terror Rises," 361. The old barbed wire barricades, in use by the Japanese Military Police at least since January, only blocked street intersections. CSDCF, 893.00 P.R. Shanghai/148 (Jan. 1941), 16.
28. After 28 August, Chinese delivery boys were not allowed to take groceries to foreign residents in Hongqiao. *CWR,* 6 Sept. 1941, 16.
29. A Chinese crossing the bridge with a smoking cigarette in his mouth was liable to be stopped by a Japanese sentry and burned on the lips. Brandt, "Shedding a Tear," 40.
30. "Terrorist Killings," 393.
31. Ibid.
32. Thereafter, members of the Political Defense Bureau (Zhengzhi baowei ju), under the Wang Jingwei Military Affairs Commission, were given the right, during emergencies, to command and direct local special services police in cases of bombing, assassination, and other political crimes. *Jingcha faling,* 145–146.
33. In April 1942 the regular Police Headquarters Bureau was downgraded yet again by being named a Police Department (Jingzheng si) within the Ministry of Interior. Ibid., 3–4, 12.
34. Argus, "Motives Behind the Reorganization of the Puppet Government," 11.
35. In his intelligence report of 21 August 1941 to Chiang Kai-shek, General Dai Li attributed the reorganization primarily to Wang Jingwei's desire to regain control over his special services organizations and reduce Li Shiqun's power. Qin Xiaoyi, *Zhonghua minguo zhongyao shiliao chubian—Dui Ri zhanzheng shiqi. Di liu bian: Kuilei zuzhi,* 219.
36. Ibid.
37. Chen Qun was minister of the interior in Liang Hongzhi's Reform Government. *Zhonghua minguo weixin zhengfu zhenggang,* "Weixin zhengfu zuzhi

xitong ji zhongyao zhiyuan biao" [Table of organization and important personnel of the Reform Government] (10 Sept. 1939), attachment to p. 311.

38. Huang Meizhen, "Wang Jingwei," 116–118; Liu Feng, "Zai wei jingchaju li de douzheng," 178; Yu Zidao, "Wang Jingwei guomin zhengfu de 'qing xiang' yundong," 323; Argus, "Motives Behind the Reorganization of the Puppet Government," 11, 28; SMA, "Riwei suijing bu zhiding de 'Xiang qu fanggong ziwei tuanjie zuzhi tiaoli,'" Microfilm R18-1-141, 5 Dec. 1938. Li was eventually poisoned by the Japanese, either at the request of Zhou Fohai (whom Li had publicly accused of corruption) or because of certain connections that Li Shiqun had clandestinely developed with the Communist New Fourth Army outside of Yangzhou. Zhang Weihan, "Dai Li yu 'Juntong ju,'" 145; Chen Gongshu, *Kangzhan houqi fanjian huodong*, 370–371; "History and Methods of the Nanking Puppet Intelligence Section," p. 1; Haruke Keiin, *Shanghai tero kôsaku 76 gô*, 148–157; Fu, *Passivity, Resistance, and Collaboration*, 132–133; Pan Ling, *Old Shanghai*, 162–163. Ding Mocun was nearly led into a fatal ambush by his teenage mistress, a schoolgirl who was the daughter of a Chinese father and a Japanese mother. When Ding ordered his men to shoot her, she asked simply that the executioner not mutilate her face. Ibid., 146; Boyle, *China and Japan at War, 1937–1945*, 285.

39. The director of intelligence in Nanjing was Huang Ziqiang, an inexperienced military man who replaced Ma Xiaotian, deputy head of the puppet gendarmerie. "History and Methods of the Nanking Puppet Intelligence Section." OSS report XL-20586, Kunming, 24/8/45.

40. Argus, "Motives Behind the Reorganization of the Puppet Government," 11; *CWR*, 30 Aug. 1941. 391.

41. The Shanghai City Government Police Bureau was moved from the civic center at Jiangwan to the former Shanghai Second Middle School downtown in Nandao between 17 and 19 July 1941. General Lu Ying planned to move again in September after the Japanese Military Police withdrew from the regular Public Safety Bureau on Penglai Road. SMP, D8115(1), 24/7/41.

42. Earlier, in August 1940, there were thirty gambling dens operating in Nandao. CSDCF, 893.00 P.R. Shanghai/143 (Aug. 1940), 20.

43. Eskelund is quoted in *CWR*, 11 Oct. 1941.

44. Tao Juyin, *Gudao jianwen*, 90–92; *CWR*, 11 Oct. 1941, 168; "Japanese Demand Changes in Settlement Police," 108; CSDCF, 893.00 P.R. Shanghai/108 (16 Oct. 1941), 322.

45. "Japanese Demand Changes in Settlement Police," 108. For examples of joint raids against Blue Shirts after the 23–28 August "high tide" of terrorism, see the lengthy file in SMP, D-8299, 29/8/41.

46. The concessions were not turned over until 1 August 1943, more than seventeen months after sovereignty over the Tianjin and Guangzhou foreign concessions was given to the Reform Government. For some of the strategic reasons for this delay, see the excellent discussion in Tang Zhenchang and Shen Hengchun, eds., *Shanghai shi*, 829–830. For the sense of the inevitability of war, see Collar, *Captive in Shanghai*, 13.

47. Protesting low wages and high rice prices in the wake of a strike by French Concession Tram Company Employees, 100 Shanghai Municipal Police Chinese constables went on a one-day strike themselves on 29 November 1940. Their wages, plus allowances, were about 60% of the minimum subsistence cost of living for a family of four. CSDCF, 893.00 P.R. Shanghai/146 (Nov. 1940), 17.
48. Tao Juyin, *Tianliang qian de gudao,* 5, 7–8.
49. Oakes, *White Man's Folly,* 358.
50. *CWR,* 4 Oct. 1941, 186.
51. "Japanese Demand Changes in Settlement Police," 108.
52. Liu Feng, "Zai wei jingchaju li de douzheng," 178; Tsai, "One Kind of Control," 54, 69; Tao Juyin, *Tianliang qian de gudao,* 15–16; Zhang Jishun, "Shi kong yi wei," 4–5. See, for colonial Taiwan as an "island of policemen," Kublin, "The Evolution of Japanese Colonialism," 77.
53. Many intellectuals, of course, saw the ideological vacuity of this concept, e.g., Zhong Wu, "Jianshe Dongya xin zhixu de fangong," A-4.
54. As adapted from Fu, "Intellectual Resistance in Shanghai," 4.

Epilogue: Outcomes

1. Eskelund and Schiff, *Squeezing Through!* n.p.
2. Finch, *Shanghai and Beyond,* 339.
3. *Jiefang ribao,* Shanghai, 3 June 1949, in Chinese Press Review, #904, 3 June 1949, 1.

Bibliography

Adams, Leonard P., II. "China: The Historical Setting of Asia's Profitable Plague," in Alfred W. McCoy et al., eds., *Politics of Heroin in Southeast Asia.* New York: Harper & Row, 1972, 363–383.

"Alleged Puppet Claims Credit for Activities." *CP,* 16 Mar. 1946, 1.

Annual Report of the Shanghai Municipal Council, 1939. Shanghai: North China Herald, 1940.

Argus. "Motives Behind the Reorganization of the Puppet Government," *China Weekly Review,* 6 Sept. 1941, 11, 28.

"Assassination of Reformed Government Official." Miscellaneous report no. 89/39, dated 19 Feb. 1939, in Shanghai Municipal Police (International Settlement) Files, D-9037, 21/2/39.

Baoshan xianzhi [Baoshan county gazetteer]. Compiled by Shanghai shi Baoshan qu difangzhi bianzuan weiyuanhui. Shanghai: Shanghai renmin chubanshe, 1992.

Bari, Martha Ann. "Helen D. Ling: Dealer, Collector, and Connoisseur," in Jason Kuo, ed., *The Helen D. Ling Collection of Chinese Ceramics.* Seattle: University of Washington Press, 1995, 1–19.

Barnett, Robert W. *Economic Shanghai: Hostage to Politics, 1937–1941.* New York: Institute of Pacific Relations, 1941.

Bates, M. S. "The Narcotics Situation in Nanking and Other Occupied Areas." *Amerasia,* 3 (January 1940):525–527.

" 'Black Hole of Shanghai' Described to Rotarians," *CP* 19 Apr. 1946, 1.

"Blue Shirts Organization." OSS, report XL-47361, 20/3/46 (Source: "Yonkers, N.Y.").

"Blueshirts Organization." Report from Nelson Trusler Johnson, Nanking Legation, to Secretary of State, May 8, 1937, in *RDS China,* no. 00/14121 (10 June 1937).

" 'Blue Shirts' to Suspend Anti-Japan Activities." *ST,* 21 Jan. 1936, 1.

Boorman, Howard L., et al., eds. *Biographical Dictionary of Republican China.* 5 vols. New York: Columbia University Press, 1967–1971, 1979.

Borg, Dorothy. *The United States and the Far Eastern Crisis of 1933–1938: From the Manchurian Incident through the Initial Stage of the Undeclared Sino-Japanese War.* Cambridge, Mass.: Harvard University Press, 1964.

Boyle, John Hunter. *China and Japan at War, 1937–1945: The Politics of Collaboration.* Stanford: Stanford University Press, 1972.

Brandt, Hans. "Shedding a Tear at Memories of Shanghai." *San Francisco Chronicle,* 12 Jan. 1983, 40.

British Foreign Office Records. London: Her Majesty's Public Record Office.

British War Office Records. London: Her Majesty's Public Record Office.

Bunker, Gerald E. *The Peace Conspiracy: Wang Ching-wei and the China War, 1937–1941.* Cambridge, Mass.: Harvard University Press, 1972.

Byron, John, and Robert Pack. *The Claws of the Dragon: The Evil Genius behind Mao: Kang Sheng and His Legacy of Terror in People's China.* New York: Simon & Schuster, 1992.

Candlin, Enid Saunders. *The Breach in the Wall: A Memoir of the Old China.* New York: Macmillan Publishing, 1973.

Cao Zhenwei. "Liang Hongzhi," in Huang Meizhen, ed., *Wang wei shi hanjian* [Ten Wang puppet traitors]. Shanghai: Shanghai renmin chubanshe, 1986, 396–428.

Chang, Maria Hsia. "'Fascism' and Modern China," *China Quarterly,* 79 (Aug. 1979):553–567.

The Chinese Blue Shirt Society: Fascism and Developmental Nationalism. Berkeley: Institute of East Asian Studies, University of California, 1985.

Chang, Sidney H., and Ramon H. Meyers. "The Storm Clouds Clear over China: The Memoir of Ch'en Li-fu, 1925–1992," manuscript, 20 Nov. 1992.

Chen Gongshu. *Kangzhan houqi fanjian huodong* [Counterespionage activities during the later phase of the War of Resistance]. Taibei: Zhuanji wenxue chubanshe, 1986.

Yingxiong wuming: Beiguo chujian [Anonymous heroes: weeding out traitors in north China]. Taibei: Zhuanji wenxue chubanshe, 1941.

Ch'en Li-fu Materials. Materials relating to the oral history of Mr. Ch'en Li-fu, done with Miss Julie Lien-ying How as part of the Chinese Oral History Project of the East Asian Institute of Columbia University between December 1958 and 2 July 1968.

Chen, Yung-fa. *Making Revolution: The Communist Movement in Eastern and Central China, 1937–1945.* Berkeley, Los Angeles, London: University of California Press, 1986.

Ch'eng, Nai-shan. *The Banker.* Trans. by Britten Dean. San Francisco: China Books & Periodicals, 1992.

Cheng Shuwei and Liu Fuxiang. *Daoguang jianying: Minguo ansha jishi* [The glint and flash of cold steel: An actual record of assassinations during the Republic]. Beijing: Tuanjie chubanshe, 1989.

Cheng Yiming. "Juntong tewu zuzhi de zhenxiang" [The truth about the special services organization of Juntong], in *Guangdong ziliao,* vol. 29. Guangzhou, 1980, 186–281.

Ch'i, Hsi-sheng. *Nationalist China at War: Military Defeats and Political Collapse, 1937–1945.* Ann Arbor: University of Michigan Press, 1982.

Ch'ien, Chung-shu. *Fortress Besieged.* Translated by Jeanne Kelly and Nathan K. Mao. Bloomington and London: Indiana University Press, 1979.

China Critic.

China Press.

China Weekly Review.

Clifford, Nicholas R. *Retreat from China: British Policy in the Far East, 1937–1941.* Seattle: University of Washington Press, 1967.

Coble, Parks M. "Chinese Capitalists and the Japanese: Collaboration and Resistance in the Shanghai Area, 1937–1945." Paper submitted to *China Quarterly,* November 1993.

Facing Japan: Chinese Politics and Japanese Imperialism, 1931–1937. Cambridge, Mass.: Council on East Asian Studies, Harvard University, 1991.

"Superpatriots and Secret Agents: The Blue Shirts and Japanese Secret Services in North China." Paper presented at the Center for Chinese Studies Regional Seminar, Berkeley, 21 March 1987.

Collar, Hugh. *Captive in Shanghai.* Hong Kong: Oxford University Press, 1990.

Confidential U.S. State Department Central Files. China: Internal Affairs, 1940–1944. 893.00 P.R. (Political Reports)/Shanghai. Microfilm.

Cook, Haruko Taya, and Theodore F. Cook. *Japan at War: An Oral History.* New York: New Press, 1992.

Coox, Alvin D. "Effects of Attrition on National War Effort: The Japanese Army Experience in China, 1937–1938," *Military Affairs: Journal of the American Military Institute,* 32 (1968):57–62.

Year of the Tiger. Tokyo: Orient/West Incorporated, 1964.

Crichton, Tom. "Unsung Heroes of China's Ordeal of Japanese Invasion." *Free China Review,* December 1986, pp. 56–60.

Davidson-Houston, J. V. *Yellow Creek: The Story of Shanghai.* Philadelphia: Defour Editions, 1964.

"Deposition of Sung Yah Shing," in Shanghai Municipal Police (International Settlement) Files, D-8635, 24/7/38.

"Deposition of Tsou Sue Kong," in Shanghai Municipal Police (International Settlement) Files, D-8635, 26/7/38.

"Deposition of Tsu Zung Foo," in Shanghai Municipal Police (International Settlement) Files, D-8635, 26/7/38.

"Deposition of Wong Tz Koo," in Shanghai Municipal Police (International Settlement) Files, D-8635, 27/7/38.

"Deposition of Zau Liang," in Shanghai Municipal Police (International Settlement) Files, D-8635, 26/7/38.

"Deposition of Zong Kwei Kong," in Shanghai Municipal Police (International Settlement) Files, D-8635, 25/7/38.

Dorn, Frank. *The Sino-Japanese War, 1937–41: From Marco Polo Bridge to Pearl Harbor.* New York: Macmillan Publishing, 1974.

Dower, John W. *War without Mercy: Race and Power in the Pacific War.* New York: Pantheon Books, 1986.

Eastman, Lloyd E. "Facets of an Ambivalent Relationship: Smuggling, Puppets, and Atrocities during the War, 1937–1945," in Akira Iriye, ed., *The Chinese and the Japanese: Essays in Political and Cultural Interactions.* Princeton: Princeton University Press, 1980, 277–303.

"Fascism and Modern China: A Rejoinder," *China Quarterly*, 80 (Dec. 1979):838–842.

Elkins, W. F. "'Fascism' in China: The Blue Shirts Society, 1932–37." *Science and Society*, 33, 4 (1969):426–33.

"Emergency Period Service Group Report." Report of 23 September 1937, in Shanghai Municipal Police (International Settlement) Files, D-8039a, 25/9/37.

Epstein, Israel. *The Unfinished Revolution in China*. Boston: Little, Brown, 1947.

Eskelund, Paula, and Schiff. *Squeezing Through! Shanghai Sketches 1941–1945*. N.p. 1945.

Feng Yi. "Le problème des réfugiés à Shanghai (1937–1940)." Institut d'Asie Orientale, Université Jean Moulin-Lyon 3. Working Paper no. 8. Lyon: Maison Rhône-Alpes des Sciences de l'Homme, 1995.

Finch, Percy. *Shanghai and Beyond*. New York: Charles Scribner's Sons, 1953.

Foreign Relations of the United States: Diplomatic Papers, 1939, vol. 4, The Far East, the Near East, and Africa. U.S. Department of State. Washington: U.S. Government Printing Office, 1955.

Foreign Relations of the United States: Diplomatic Papers, 1940, vol. 4, The Far East. U.S. Department of State. Washington: U.S. Government Printing Office, 1955.

Fu, Poshek. "Intellectual Resistance in Shanghai: Wang Tongzhao and a Concept of Resistance Enlightenment, 1937–1939." Paper delivered at the Association for Asian Studies meetings, San Francisco, 24 March 1988.

Passivity, Resistance, and Collaboration: Intellectual Choices in Occupied Shanghai, 1937–1945. Stanford: Stanford University Press, 1993.

"Struggle to Entertain: The Political Ambivalence of Shanghai Film Industry under the Japanese Occupation, 1941–1945," in Law Kar, ed., *Cinema of Two Cities: Hong Kong–Shanghai*. Hong Kong: Urban Council, 1994, 39–62.

"Further Assistance to Japanese Military Police." Report by Detective Sub-Inspector Crighton in SMP (International Settlement) Files. Microfilms from the U.S. National Archives, D-9037, 18/3/39.

Garver, John W. "China's Wartime Diplomacy," in James C. Hsiung and Steven I. Levine, eds., *China's Bitter Victory: The War with Japan 1937–1945*. Armonk: M. E. Sharpe, 1992, 3–32.

Gee, Kennson. "Effect of Freezing on Interior Remittances," *CWR*, 23 Aug. 1941, 369.

"'Gestapo-Style' Terror Is the Order-of-the-Day Here," *CWR*, 29 Mar. 1941, 111–112.

Gordon, Bertram M. *Collaborationism in France during the Second World War*. Ithaca: Cornell University Press, 1980.

Gray, Adeline. "The Loyal Patriotic Army: A Guerilla Organization Under Tai Li." RG226, entry 139, box 183, folder 2449, O.S.S. Files, National Archives, Washington, D.C., 18–29.

Gunn, Edward M. *Unwelcome Muse: Chinese Literature in Shanghai and Peking, 1937–45*. New York: Columbia University Press, 1980.

Hahn, Emily. *China to Me: A Partial Autobiography*. Philadelphia: Blakiston, 1944.

Han Qitong. *Zhongguo dui Ri zhanshi juanshi zhi guji (1937–1943)* [An estimate of China's losses in the war against Japan (1937–1943)]. Shanghai: Zhonghua shuju, 1946.

Haruke Keiin (Yasutane). *Shanghai tero kôsaku 76 gô* [Working it out in Shanghai's Number 76]. Tokyo: Mainichi shimbun sha, 1980.

Hata Ikuhito. *Nitchû sensô shi* [History of the Sino-Japanese War]. Tokyo: Kasui shobô shinsha, 1961.

Hauser, Ernest O. *Shanghai: City for Sale*. New York: Harcourt, Brace, 1940.

He Li. *Kangri zhanzheng shi* [History of the War of Resistance against Japan]. Shanghai: Shanghai renmin chubanshe, 1985.

Heinrichs, Waldo. "Franklin D. Roosevelt and the Risks of War, 1939–1941," in Akira Iriye and Warren Cohen, eds., *American, Chinese, and Japanese Perspectives on Wartime Asia, 1931–1949*. Wilmington: Scholarly Resources Books, 1990, 147–178.

Henriot, Christian. "Le gouvernement municipal de Shanghai, 1927–1937." Thèse pour le doctorat de 3ème cycle présenté à l'Université de la Sorbonne Nouvelle (Paris III), Juin 1983.

Shanghai, 1927–1937: Municipal Power, Locality, and Modernization. Transl. Noël Castelino. Berkeley: University of California Press, 1993.

Heppner, Ernest G. *Shanghai Refuge: A Memoir of the World War II Jewish Ghetto*. Lincoln: University of Nebraska Press, 1993.

Hewins, Ralph. *Quisling: Prophet without Honor*. London: W. H. Allen, 1965.

"History and Methods of the Nanking Puppet Intelligence Section." OSS report XL-20586, Kunming, 24/8/45. Office of Strategic Services Archives, War Department. U.S. National Archives, Military Reference Division.

Honig, Emily. *Creating Chinese Ethnicity: Subei People in Shanghai, 1850–1980*. New Haven: Yale University Press, 1992.

Sisters and Strangers: Women in the Shanghai Cotton Mills, 1919–1949. Stanford: Stanford University Press, 1986.

Honig, Emily. "Women Cotton Mill Workers in Shanghai, 1919–1949." Ph.D. dissertation, Stanford University, 1982.

"How the Foreign Minister Was Assassinated," *XSB*, 9 Nov. 1939, transl. in SMP, D-9037, 9/11/39.

Hsü, Shuhsi. *The War Conduct of the Japanese*. Shanghai: Kelly & Walsh, 1938.

Hu Zhusheng. "Qingbang shi chutan" [A preliminary exploration of the Green Gang], *Lishi xue jikan*, 3. (1979):102–120.

Huang Meizhen. "Shanghai lunxian shiqi de shehui maodun yu gongyun xingshi" [Social contradictions and the situation of the labor movement during Shanghai's Occupation period]. *"Chengshi wenhua yu ershi shiji Shanghai shehui fazhan" xueshu taolunhui lunwen* [Paper presented at the symposium "Urban Culture and the Development of Shanghai's Society During the Twentieth Century"]. Shanghai: Shanghai Academy of Social Sciences, March 1993.

"Wang Jingwei," in Huang Meizhen, ed., *Wang wei shi hanjian* [Ten Wang puppet traitors]. Shanghai: Shanghai renmin chubanshe, 1986, 1–128.

ed. *Wei ting yin ying lu—Dui Wang wei zhengquan de huiyi jishi* [Chronicles of the secret shadows of the puppet court—Records of the memoirs of the puppet Wang régime]. Beijing: Zhongguo wenshi chubanshe, 1991.

Huang Meizhen and Shi Yuanhua. "Wang wei tegong zongbu shimo" [The whole story of the Wang Puppet Special Work Headquarters], in Fudan daxue lishi xi, ed., *Wang Jingwei hanjian zhengquan de xingwang* [The rise and fall of Wang Jingwei's traitor régime]. Shanghai: Fudan daxue chubanshe, 1987, 350–392.

Huang Meizhen and Zhang Yun, comps. *Wang Jingwei guomin zhengfu chengli* [The establishment of the Wang Jingwei National Government]. Shanghai: Shanghai renmin chubanshe, 1984.

Wang Jingwei jituan toudi [The Wang Jingwei clique defects to the enemy]. Shanghai: Shanghai renmin chubanshe, 1984.

Imai Takeo. *Shina jihen no kaisô* [Reminiscences of the China incident]. Tokyo: Misuzu shobo, 1964.

Inukai Ken. *Yôsukô wa ima mo nagarete iru* [The Yangtze still flows]. Tokyo: Bungei shunjû sha, 1961.

"Japanese Demand Changes in Settlement Police as Terrorist Wave Continues Unabated," *CWR* 27 Sept. 1941, 108.

Jiang Shaozhen. "Du Yuesheng," in Li Xin and Sun Sibai, eds., *Minguo renwu zhuan* [Biographies of Republican personages]. Vol. 1. Beijing: Zhonghua shuju, 1978, 314–319.

Jiefang ribao, Shanghai, 3 June 1949, in Chinese Press Review, #904, 3 June 1949, 1.

Jing Shenghong. *Minguo ansha yaoan* [Major assassination cases of the Republican period]. Yangzhong: Jiangsu guji chubanshe, 1989.

Jingcha faling [Police laws]. N.p., n.d. (ca. 1944, probably published by the Wang Jingwei Ministry of Interior). Copy in the Shanghai Municipal Library.

Jonas, George. *Vengeance.* New York: Bantam Books, 1984.

Jones, F. C. *Japan's New Order in East Asia: Its Rise and Fall, 1937–45.* London: Oxford University Press, 1954.

Kamio Shigeru. "Wang Ching-wei vs. Chungking," *Contemporary Japan,* April 1940, 378–386.

Kedward, H. R. *Occupied France: Collaboration and Resistance, 1940–1944.* London: Basil Blackwell, 1985.

Kitaoka Shin'ichi. "China Experts in the Army," in Peter Duus, Ramon H. Myers, and Mark R. Peattie, eds., *The Japanese Informal Empire in China, 1895–1937.* Princeton: Princeton University Press, 1989, 330–368.

Koo, T. K. "Some Economic Documents Relating to the Genesis of the Japanese-Sponsored Regime in North China," *Far Eastern Quarterly,* 6, 1 (1946):65–77.

Kublin, Hyman. "The Evolution of Japanese Colonialism," *Comparative Studies in Society and History,* 2, 1 (1959):67–84.

Langer, William L., and S. Everett Gleason. *The Challenge to Isolation, 1937–1940.* New York: Harper & Brothers, 1952.

Li Enhan. *Riben jun zhanzheng baoxing zhi yanjiu* [A study of the Japanese army's wartime atrocities]. Taibei: Shangwu yinshu guan, 1994.

Lieu, D. K. "The Sino-Japanese Currency War," *Pacific Affairs*, 12, 4 (1939):413–426.

Liu Feng. "Zai wei jingchaju li de douzheng" [The struggle in the collaborationist police force], Wenshi ziliao gongzuo weiyuanhui, comps. *Wenshi ziliao xuanji Shanghai jiefang sanshi zhounian zhuanji* [Selections of historical materials special collection for the thirtieth anniversary of the liberation of Shanghai]. Shanghai: Shanghai renmin chubanshe, 1979, Vol. 1, 175–194.

Liu Gong. "Wo suo zhidao de Zhongtong" [The Central Committee Statistics Bureau that I knew], in Wenshi ziliao yanjiu weiyuanhui, eds., *Wenshi ziliao xuanji*, fascicle no. 36, 59–117. Beijing: Wenshi ziliao chubanshe, December 1962.

Liu Qikui. "Wang Kemin," in Huang Meizhen, ed., *Wang wei shi hanjian* [Ten Wang puppet traitors]. Shanghai: Shanghai renmin chubanshe, 1986, 334–363.

Lu, David J. *From the Marco Polo Bridge to Pearl Harbor: Japan's Entry into World War II*. Washington: Public Affairs Press, 1961.

Lutz, Jessie G. "Occupied China and Student Activism in the Christian Colleges." Paper presented at the commemoration of the fiftieth anniversary of the "July 7 Incident," City College of New York, July 1987.

Ma Guangren. "Ri wei zai Shanghai de xinwen huodong gaishu" [Brief account of the press activities of the Japanese and puppets in Shanghai], *Kangri zhanzheng yanjiu* [Studies of the War of Resistance against Japan], 1993, Vol. 1:172–183.

Madancy, Joyce Ann. "Propaganda versus Practice: Official Involvement in the Opium Trade in China, 1927–1945." M.A. thesis, Cornell University, 1983.

Mao Dun (Shen Yanbing). *Fushi* [Corrosion]. Chengdu: Sichuan renmin chubanshe, 1981.

Mao Xiaotian and Wang Mengyun. "Wang Wei 'tegong zongbu' qishiliu hao de jianli" [The creation of no. 76 "special mission headquarters" of Wang the Usurper], in Huang Meizhen and Zhang Yun, eds., *Wang Jingwei guomin zhengfu chengli* [The founding of Wang Jingwei's nationalist government]. Shanghai: Renmin chubanshe, 1984, 258–283.

Marsh, Susan H. "Chou Fo-hai: The Making of a Collaborator," in Akira Iriye, ed., *The Chinese and the Japanese: Essays in Political and Cultural Interactions*. Princeton: Princeton University Press, 1980, 304–327.

Marshall, Jonathan. "Opium and the Politics of Gangsterism in Nationalist China, 1927–1945," *Bulletin of the Committee of Concerned Asian Scholars*, 8, 3 (1977):19–48.

McWilliams, John C. "Covert Connections: The FBI, the OSS, and the CIA," *Historian*, 53, 4 (1991):657–678.

"Memorandum on the Blue Shirt Society." Special Branch Secret Memorandum, 9 Dec. 1940, in SMP, D-4685.

Michael, Franz. "The Significance of Puppet Governments," *Pacific Affairs*, 12, 4 (1939):400–412.

Mitchell, Richard H. *Janus-Faced Justice: Political Criminals in Imperial Japan*. Honolulu: University of Hawaii Press, 1992.

Miwa, Kimitada. "The Wang Ching-Wei Regime and Japanese Efforts to Terminate the China Conflict," in Joseph Roggendorf, ed., *Studies in Japanese Culture*. Tokyo: Sophia University, 1963, 123–142.

Morley, James William, and David A. Titus, ed. and transl. *Japan's Road to the Pacific War. The Final Confrontation: Japan's Negotiations with the United States, 1941*. New York: Columbia University Press, 1994.

Mote, Frederick W. *Japanese-Sponsored Governments in China 1937–1945: An Annotated Bibliography Compiled from Materials in the Chinese Collection of the Hoover Library*. Stanford: Stanford University Press, 1954.

Municipal Gazette of the Council for the Foreign Settlement of Shanghai. Shanghai: Municipal Council, 1941.

Nanjing shi dang'an guan, ed. *Shenxun Wang wei hanjian bilu* [Records of the interrogations of the Wang puppet traitors]. 2 vols. Jiangsu: Jiangsu guji chubanshe, 1992.

Nashimoto Yûhei. *Chûgoku no naka no Nihonjin* [The Japanese in China]. 2 vols. Tokyo: Heibonsha, 1958.

Nettelbeck, Colin. "Getting the Story Right: Narratives of the Second World War in Post-1968 France," in Gerhard Hirschfeld and Patrick Marsh, eds., *Collaboration in France: Politics and Culture during the Nazi Occupation, 1940–1944*. Oxford: Berg, 1989, 252–293.

"Nine Suspects Arrested for Tseng Killing," in *China Press*, 23 July 1938, filed in Shanghai Municipal Police (International Settlement) Files, D-8635, 22/7/38.

North China Daily News.

North China Herald.

Oakes, Vanya. *White Man's Folly*. Boston: Houghton Mifflin, 1943.

Office of Strategic Services Archives. U.S. National Archives, Military Reference Division.

"Opium Profits in North China," *Asia*, Oct. 1940, 551–556.

Pan Ling. *Old Shanghai: Gangsters in Paradise*. Hong Kong: Heinemann Asia, 1984.

Pan, Lynn [Pan Ling]. *Tracing It Home: A Chinese Family's Journey from Shanghai*. New York: Kodansha International, 1993.

Parssinen, Terry M., and Kathryn B. Meyer. "International Narcotics Trafficking in the Early Twentieth Century: Development of an Illicit Industry." Unpublished paper, n.d.

Peattie, Mark R. "Japanese Treaty Port Settlements in China, 1895–1937," in Peter Duus, Ramon H. Myers, and Mark R. Peattie, eds., *The Japanese Informal Empire in China, 1895–1937*. Princeton: Princeton University Press, 1989, 166–209.

"Political Terrorism Unabated Here; Court Judges Threatened with Harm," *CWR*, 21 Sept. 1940, 92–93.

Powell, John B. *My Twenty-Five Years in China*. New York: Macmillan, 1945.

Qiao Jiacai. *Dai Li jiangjun he tade tongzhi: Kangri qingbao zhan di yi, er ji* [General Dai Li and his comrades: Intelligence war in the War of Resistance, sets one and two]. Taibei: Zhongwai tushu chubanshe, 1981.

Qin Xiaoyi, ed. *Zhonghua minguo zhongyao shiliao chubian—Dui Ri zhanzheng shiqi* [Initial compilation of important historical documents of the Republic of China—The period of the war with Japan]. *Di er bian: Zuozhan jingguo* [Part two: Conducting the war]. Taibei: Zhongguo Guomindang dangshi weiyuanhui, 1981.

Zhonghua minguo zhongyao shiliao chubian—Dui Ri zhanzheng shiqi [Initial compilation of important historical documents of the Republic of China—The period of the war with Japan]. *Di liu bian: Kuilei zuzhi* [Part six: Puppet organizations]. Taibei: Zhongguo Guomindang dangshi weiyuanhui, 1981.

Records of the Department of State Relating to the Internal Affairs of China, 1930–1939. Government Documents Library, microfilm 31217.

Reed, Christoher Alexander. "Gutenberg in Shanghai: Mechanized Printing, Modern Publishing, and Their Impact on the City, 1876 to 1937." Ph.D. Thesis, University of California, Berkeley, 1996.

"Ri wei Huxi qu gongshu wei suo xia ge xiang, zhen zhang renmian shi yu Ri wei Shanghai tebie shi zhengfu laiwang wenjian" [Correspondence with the Japanese and puppet Shanghai special municipality government concerning personnel actions by village and town heads under the jurisdiction of the Japanese and puppet Huxi district office]. SAM, R18-1-266.

"Ri wei Shanghai tebie shi zhengfu guanyu biancha baojia hukou shi tong Ri wei Huxi qu gongshu wenjian laijian" [Documentary correspondence between the Japanese and Shanghai puppet special municipality government, and the Huxi district puppet government offices concerning the compilation and investigation of *baojia* and household registration]. SAM, R18-1-137.

"Ri wei suijing bu zhiding de 'Xiang qu fanggong ziwei tuanjie zuzhi tiaoli' deng wenjian" [Documents on the "Regulations for Village and District Anti-Communist Self-Defense Organizations" formulated by the Japanese and puppet Pacification Ministry]. SAM, R18-1-141.

Ristaino, Marcia R. "Russian Emigration in Shanghai, 1920–1945," in Karl Schlogel, ed., "Russian Emigration Worldwide." Beck, forthcoming.

"White Russian and Jewish Refugees in Shanghai, 1920–1944, as Recorded in the Shanghai Municipal Police Archives, National Archives, Washington, D.C.," *Republican China*, 16, (1990) 1:51–72.

Rousso, Henry. *The Vichy Syndrome: History and Memory in France since 1944.* Transl. Arthur Goldhammer. Cambridge, Mass.: Harvard University Press, 1991.

Roux, Alain. "The Guomindang and the Workers of Shanghai (1938–1948): The Rent in the Fabric." Paper presented at the conference on China's Mid-century Transitions, Harvard University, 8–11 Sept., 1994.

Rowe, William T. "The Qingbang and Collaboration under the Japanese, 1939–1945: Materials in the Wuhan Municipal Archives," *Modern China* 8, 4(1982):491–499.

Ruffé, R. D'Auxion de. *La bataille de Shanghai.* Paris: Editions Berger-Levrault, 1938.

Shanghai Evening Post and Mercury.

"Shanghai in Torment: August's Tragic Record." *Oriental Affairs*, 8, 3 (1937): 126–149.

"Shanghai Mayor Keeps His Promise to the Public," *Shanghai* (journal published by the Metropolitan Publishing Company), July 1941, 2–4.

Shanghai Municipal Archives.

Shanghai Municipal Council. *Report for the Year 1937 and Budget for the Year 1938*. Shanghai: North China Daily News & Herald, 1938.

Shanghai Municipal Police (International Settlement) Files. Microfilms from the U.S. National Archives.

Shanghai shenghuo.

Shanghai shi dang'an guan, comp. *Ri wei Shanghai shi zhengfu* [The Japanese puppet government of Shanghai]. Shanghai: Dang'an chubanshe, 1986.

Shanghai shi difangzhi bangongshi, ed. *Shanghai cidian* [Shanghai dictionary]. Shanghai: Shanghai shehui kexueyuan chubanshe, 1989.

"Shanghai Special Service Corps Arrest." Report by Detective Sergeant Pitt, in Shanghai Municipal Police (International Settlement) Files, D-8039a, 25/10/37.

Shanghai Times.

Shen bao.

Shen Zui. *Juntong neimu* [The inside story of the Military Statistics (Bureau)]. Beijing: Wenshi ziliao chubanshe, 1984.

"Wang Jingwei Henei yuci ji" [Record of Wang Jingwei's attack by an assassin in Hanoi], in *Zhengzhi ansha shilu* [Veritable records of political assassinations]. Hong Kong: Zhongyuan chubanshe, 1985, 77–84.

"Wo suo zhidao de Dai Li" [The Dai Li I knew], in Shen Zui and Wen Qiang, *Dai Li qi ren* [Dai Li the man]. Beijing: Wenshi ziliao chubanshe, 1980, 1–176.

Shi Yuanhua. "Chen Gongbo," in Huang Meizhen, ed., *Wang wei shi hanjian* [Ten Wang puppet traitors]. Shanghai: Shanghai renmin chubanshe, 1986, 129–195.

"Li Shiqun," in Huang Meizhen, ed., *Wang wei shi hanjian* [Ten Wang puppet traitors]. Shanghai: Shanghai renmin chubanshe, 1986, 429–475.

Shum Kui-kwong. *The Chinese Communists' Road to Power: The Anti-Japanese National Front, 1935–1945*. Hong Kong: Oxford University Press, 1988.

Silliman, Adam Borut. "Sino-Foreign Conflict and the Extra-Settlement Roads of Shanghai." Senior essay in History, Yale University, 17 April 1989.

Snow, Edgar. *The Battle for Asia*. Cleveland: World Publishing, 1942.

Stephan, John J. *The Russian Fascists: Tragedy and Farce in Exile, 1925–1945*. New York: Harper & Row, 1978.

Sun Guoqun. "Lun jiu Shanghai changji zhidu de fazhan he tedian" [On the development and characteristics of the prostitute system in old Shanghai]. Paper given at the International Symposium on Modern Shanghai, Shanghai Academy of Social Sciences, 7–14 September 1988.

Sun, Youli. *China and the Origins of the Pacific War, 1931–1941*. New York: St. Martin's Press, 1993.

Taiheiyô sensô e no michi [The Road to the Pacific War]. Taiheiyô sensô gen'in kenkyû-bu, eds. 8 vols. Tokyo: Nihon kokusai seiji gakkai, 1962–1963.

Tairiku shimpo.

T'ang, Leang-li, ed. *Fundamentals of National Salvation: A Symposium by Wang Ching-wei and Others.* Shanghai: China United Press, 1942.

Tang Zhenchang and Shen Hengchun, eds. *Shanghai shi* [A history of Shanghai]. Shanghai: Shanghai renmin chubanshe, 1989.

Tao, Chia-lin Pao. "The Role of Wang Ching-wei during the Sino-Japanese War." Ph.D. thesis, Indiana University, 1971.

Tao Juyin. *Gudao jianwen—Kangzhan shiqi de Shanghai* [Things seen and heard about the solitary island—Shanghai during the War of Resistance]. Shanghai: Shanghai renmin chubanshe, 1979.

　　Tianliang qian de gudao [The isolated island before daybreak]. Shanghai Zhonghua shuju, 1947.

Taylor, George E. *The Struggle for North China.* New York: Institute of Pacific Relations, 1940.

"Terrorism Again Hits Shanghai," *Shanghai* (journal published by the Metropolitan Publishing Company), July 1941, 5–11.

"Terrorist Killings Cause Japanese to Restrict Movements in Hongkew," *CWR,* 30 Aug. 1941, 393.

"The High Cost of Living and the Labour Situation," *Shanghai,* July 1941, 12–15.

"The Ivanow Murder and Japanese Intrigue in the Local Russian Community," *CWR,* 27 Sept. 1941, 97–99.

Thomasson, Robert de. "Prise de vues à Shanghai." *Les oeuvres libres,* 210 (Dec. 1938):277–347.

Tretiak, Daniel. "Political Assassinations in China, 1600–1968," in James F. Kirkham, Sheldon G. Levy, and William J. Crotty, eds., *Assassination and Political Violence: A Report to the National Commission on the Causes and Prevention of Violence.* New York: Praeger, 1970, 635–671.

Tsai, Hui-Yu Caroline. "One Kind of Control: The *Hokô* System in Taiwan under Japanese Rule, 1895–1945." Ph.D. thesis, Columbia University, 1990.

Tsao, Jr-lien. "On the Nature of the Chinese Capitalists during the Republican Period." Seminar paper, University of California, Berkeley, 1984.

"Two Sources of Anti-Japanism," in *The Osaka Mainichi and the Tokyo Nichi Nichi Supplement: The China Emergency,* 20 October 1937, 29, 32.

"Twelve Detained in Terrorist Probe May Be Handed Over," *China Press,* 30 July 1938, filed in Shanghai Municipal Police (International Settlement) Files, D-8635, 1/8/38.

"Twenty-four Terrorist Suspects Land in Police Net," in *China Press,* 24 July 1938, filed in Shanghai Municipal Police (International Settlement) Files, D-8635, 27/7/38.

U.S. Military Intelligence Reports, China, 1911–1941.

Usui Katsumi. *Nitchû sensô* [The Sino-Japanese War]. Tokyo: Chûô kôron sha, 1967.

Wakeman, Frederic, Jr. "Confucian Fascism." Paper given at the Modern China Seminar, Columbia University, April 1989.

　　Policing Shanghai 1927–1937. Berkeley: University of California Press, 1995.

Wakeman, Frederic, Jr., and Wen-hsin Yeh. "Introduction," in Frederic Wakeman Jr. and Wen-hsin Yeh, eds., *Shanghai Sojourners.* Berkeley: Institute of East Asian Studies, 1992, 1–14.

Wang, Ching-wei [Wang Jingwei]. *A la mémoire de M. Tsen-Tson-Ming.* Hanoi, 7 April 1939. Pamphlet in *Records of the Department of State Relating to the Internal Affairs of China, 1930–1939,* 893.00/14394.

Wang Fangnan. "Wo zai Juntong shisi nian de qinli he jianwen" [What I experienced and learned about during my fourteen years in the MSB], in Wenshi ziliao yanjiu weiyuanhui, eds., *Wenshi ziliao xuanji,* fascicle 107, 140–166. Beijing: Zhongguo wenshi chubanshe, 1987.

Wang Yangqing and Xu Yinghu. "Shanghai Qing Hong bang gaishu" [A general account of Shanghai's Qing and Hong Gangs], *Shehui kexue* (Shanghai) 1982.5, 63–65.

"Wave of Local Terror Rises as Gunmen Kill Chinese Banker Here," *CWR,* 23 Aug. 1941, 361, 373.

Weakland, John H. "Chinese Film Images of Invasion and Resistance," *China Quarterly,* July–Sept. 1971, 439–470.

Wenxian. Shanghai: Zhonghua daxue tushu youxian gongsi.

White, Lynn T., III. "Non-governmentalism in the Historical Development of Modern Shanghai," in Laurence J. C. Ma and Edward W. Hanten, eds., *Urban Development in Modern China.* Boulder: Westview, 1981, 19–57.

Who's Who in China: Biographies of Chinese Leaders. Shanghai: China Weekly Review. Fifth ed.

Williamsen, Marvin. "The Military Dimension, 1937–1941," in James C. Hsiung and Steven I. Levine, eds., *China's Bitter Victory: The War with Japan 1937–1945.* Armonk: M. E. Sharpe, 1992, 135–156.

Woodhead, H. G. W., ed. *The China Yearbook.* Tientsin and Shanghai: North-China Daily News and Herald, 1912–1939.

Wu, T'ien-wei. "Contending Political Forces during the War of Resistance," in James C. Hsiung and Steven I. Levine, eds., *China's Bitter Victory: The War with Japan, 1937–1945.* Armonk: M. E. Sharpe, 1992, 51–78.

Xin shenbao.

Xu Youwei. "Lixingshe yu Riben (1932–1938 nian)" [The Vigorous Revival Society and Japan, 1932–1938]. Paper presented at the 13th International Association of Historians of Asia Conference, Sophia University, Tokyo, 5–9 September 1994.

Xu Zhaoming. "Hanjian Zhou Fohai goujie Juntong ji qi xiachang" [Chinese traitor Zhou Fohai's unsavory alliance with Military Statistics, and his final outcome], in Wenshi ziliao yanjiu weiyuanhui, eds., *Wenshi ziliao xuanji,* fascicle no. 64, 202–216. Beijing: Zhonghua shuju, 1979.

Xu Zhucheng. *Du Yuesheng zhengzhuan* [A straightforward biography of Du Yuesheng]. Hangzhou: Zhejiang sheng xinhua shudian, 1982.

Xu Zongyao. "Zuzhi Juntong Beiping zhan heping qiyi de qianqian houhou" [Organizing Juntong's Beiping Station before and after peace broke out], in Wenshi ziliao yanjiu weiyuanhui, eds., *Wenshi ziliao xuanji,* fascicle no. 68, 126–151. Beijing: Zhonghua shuju, 1980.

Yang Yang. "Wu Sibao," in Huang Meizhen, ed., *Wang wei shi hanjian* [Ten Wang puppet traitors]. Shanghai: Shanghai renmin chubanshe, 1986, 476–506.

Yeh, Wen-hsin. "Dai Li and the Liu Geqing Affair: Heroism in the Chinese Secret

Service during the War of Resistance," *Journal of Asian Studies,* 48, 3 (1989):545-562.

"The Liu Geqing Affair: Heroism in the Chinese Secret Service during the War of Resistance." Paper presented to the Association for Asian Studies, 10 April 1987.

"You guan Ri shiqi Huxi qu Caojiadu zhen zuzhi ziweituan qingkuang baogao, guan zuo tuanyuan mingce" [Rosters of militiamen and officers, and reports about the condition of the self-defense corps organized in Caojiadu township of Huxi district during the Japanese period]. SAM, R18-1-282.

Yu Zidao. "Lun kangzhan chuqi zhengmian zhanchang zuozhan zhongxin zhi zhuanyi" [The change of battleground focus in the frontline battlefield in the early days of the War of Resistance], *Kangri zhanzheng yanjiu* [Studies of the War of Resistance against Japan], 3 (1992):1-21.

"Wang Jingwei guomin zhengfu de 'qing xiang' yundong" [The Wang Jingwei Nationalist Government's "clean up the villages" movement], in Fudan daxue lishi xi, ed., *Wang Jingwei hanjian zhengquan de xingwang* [The rise and fall of Wang Jingwei's traitor régime]. Shanghai: Fudan daxue chubanshe, 1987, 302-349.

Zhang Fangren. *Jinrong manji* [Random notes on finance]. Shanghai: N.p., 1942.

Zhang Jishun. "Shi kong yi wei: Zhanshi Shanghai de baojia zhidu" [A traditional institution in a modern context: The *baojia* system in wartime Shanghai]. Paper presented at the Seminar on Urban Culture and Social Modernization of Twentieth-Century China, Center for Chinese Studies, University of California, Berkeley, 2-3 December 1994.

Zhang Weihan. "Dai Li yu 'Juntong ju'" [Dai Li and the Military Statistics Bureau], in Wenshi ziliao yanjiu weiyuanhui, eds., *Zhejiang wenshi ziliao xuanji,* fascicle no. 23, pp. 79-151. *Neibu* publication. Zhejiang: Renmin chubanshe, 1982.

Zhang Yun. "Zhou Fohai," in Huang Meizhen, ed., *Wang wei shi hanjian* [Ten Wang puppet traitors]. Shanghai: Shanghai renmin chubanshe, 1986, 196-259.

Zhong Heming. *Riben qin Hua zhi jiandie shi* [History of espionage during the Japanese aggression against China]. Hankou: Huazhong tushu gongsi, 1938.

Zhonghua minguo weixin zhengfu zhenggang [Political program of the Chinese National Reform Government]. Nanjing: Zhonghua lianhe tongxun she, 1939.

Zhong Wu. "Jianshe Dongya xin zhixu de fangong" [Counterattacking the construction of an Asian new order], *Wenxian,* 10 Mar. 1939, A4-A6.

Zhongyang ribao [Central China Daily News].

Zhu Zijia (Jin Xiongbai). *Wang Zhengquan de kaichang yu shouchang* [The beginning and end of the drama of the Wang régime]. Vols. 1-4. Hong Kong: Chunqiu zazhi she, 1959-1961. Vols. 5 and 6. Hong Kong: Wuxingji shubaoshe, 1964, 1971.

Zhu Zuotong and Mei Yi, eds. *Shanghai yi ri* [One day in Shanghai]. Shanghai: Huamei chuban gongsi, 1938.

Index